ADOLPHE SAX
1814-1894

His Life and Legacy

ADOLPHE SAX 1814-1894

—*His Life and Legacy*

WALLY HORWOOD

EGON PUBLISHERS LTD
Meeting House Lane, Church Street
Baldock, Herts SG7 5BP

First published in paperback edition
by Bramley Books, 1980

Revised, casebound edition
published by Egon Publishers Ltd
Meeting House Lane, Church Street
Baldock, Herts SG7 5BP
1983

Copyright ©
W. W. Horwood

Printed in England by
Streetsprinters
Meeting House Lane, Church Street
Baldock, Herts SG7 5BP

ISBN 0 905858 18 2

All rights reserved. No part of this publication may be reproduced or transmitted in any form or by any means, including photocopying and recording without permission in writing from the Publisher.

Dedication

Correcting the work of a friend can be a dangerous business!

EDNA and **MAXWELL HOLGATE** not only combed every word in the proofs and, together with **CAREY BLYTON**, made many useful and helpful suggestions; they succeeded in cementing warm relationships begun long ago.

In extending to them my grateful thanks, I have to say that any shortcomings still remaining are entirely my own and are there in spite of them.

Acknowledgements

To Her Majesty the Queen for gracious permission to quote from Queen Victoria's private journal.

To the many correspondents and well-wishers, most of whom I have never met but who helped substantially to make this work a reality, my warm appreciation. Some will find their names mentioned in the text.

In addition, my particular thanks are due to Kenneth N. Deans of the University of Georgia, and Edward S. Walker, authority on ragtime in England, for several fruitful leads; Lyndesay G. Langwill, O.B.E., M.A., for delving willingly and often into his extensive library; Howard Somers for information on the American band scene; Jimmy Staples for details of dance-band saxophone sections, David Page for his photographic expertise; Pat Pisani for her painstaking labour in translating Kastner; Robert Mackworth-Young for searches into the archives of Windsor Castle; Dr. Hugh Macdonald of Oxford University for help with many points, especially in connection with Berlioz and the *Salle Herz* concert; and E. A. K Ridley of the Horniman Museum who not only combed Adam Carse's files for me but, in a lively correspondence, put the case for the anti-Sax lobby so effectively. The production was organised by Larry Ewin.

Much of the research for the book was done in the reading room of the Bermondsey District Library to whose staff I am indebted for their unfailing courtesy and persistent efforts in obtaining for my use many rare and out-of-print books.

Finally, two friends without whose efforts the book could not have been written: Mrs. Betty Rannie, B.A., former Deputy-Head of Swanley School, who gave up many days from a hectic life to search for information and to undertake copious translations; and Philip Bate, whose initial encouragement was the direct cause of the work being started, and whose sustained, practical and scholarly assistance has seen it to a conclusion.

Contents

Acknowledgements
FOREWORD BY PAUL HARVEY, LRAM, ARCM
Preface

I	Dinant and Brussels	17
II	Saxhorns and Saxophones	29
III	Paris	43
IV	The Distin Family	57
V	Reforms	69
VI	Conspiracies	79
VII	Triumphs and Disasters	87
VIII	Litigation	95
IX	Abortive Inventions	109
X	Counter-Actions	121
XI	Decline	139
XII	Influence on Clarinet Design	147
XIII	The Nebulous Saxhorn	153
XIV	The Saxophone Phenomenon	165
XV	The Classical Saxophone	181
	Postscript	191

Appendices

A	The Concert at the *Salle Herz* 3rd February, 1844	195
B	Advertisement in "Musical World" June, 1853	201
C	Saxophone patent, 21st March, 1846	203
	Bibliography	205
	Index	208

List of Illustrations

1. Adolphe Sax at 30 *from a lithograph by Baugniet 1844* — 15
2. Adolphe Sax *Bust in Dinant Museum* — 16
3. Charles-Joseph Sax *from a lithograph by Johann Schubert* — 21
4. Dinant in the Meuse Valley as it is today — 22
5. Collage of Sax's instruments — 25
6. Omnitonic horn invented by Charles Sax — 27
7. Birth Certificate of Antoine Joseph Sax — 28
8. Drawing for the Saxhorn patent of 1845 — 30
9. Brass instruments by Sax — 31
10. Ophicleide fitted with a bass clarinet mouthpiece — 35
11. Adolphe Sax — *portrait by Pollet* — 36
12. Cover of the first saxophone Method — 1846 — 41
13. Saxophone fingering chart — *G. Kastner 1846* — 42
14. "The illustrious Rossini takes M. Sax's trumpet to be a steam engine" — 45
15. "The musician for whom M. Sax has made his new trumpet" — 46
16. A brass band equipped with Sax's instruments in a Brussels bandstand — 53
17. The Distin Family Brass Quintet — 54
18. Cover of the Revue *La Musique des Familles* — 56
19. Saxotrombas — 61
20. Photograph of Adolphe Sax at 40 — 62
21. "M. Armand Marrast is forced to replace his little bell with one of Sax's instruments" — 67
22. "A use for the saxophone in time of war" — 68
23. Instruments made by Adolphe Sax — 78
24. The Adolphe Sax Musical Instrument Factory in the Rue Saint-Georges — 85
25. Bass clarinet by Desfontenelles of Lisieux (1807) — 86
26. Exhibition of Industrial Products — 1849 — 94
27. A concert in the Sax factory in honour of a visiting 'eastern potentate' — 97
28. A demonstration of Sax's instruments before an invited audience at the Rue Saint-Georges factory — 98
29. A corner of the Sax factory — 101
30. The Sax factory in full production — 102
31. The Sax factory — work in progress on the upper floor — 107

32.	The Sax bass clarinet	108
33.	Sax's gigantic showcase flanked by two more 'monstrosities'	111
34.	*"Excuse me; may one visit the interior of this establishment?"*	112
35.	Trombone with six ascending valves	117
36.	Trombone with seven valves and thirteen bells	118
37.	Saxhorn bourdon in EE-flat	120
38.	Trombone by Sax having six ascending valves and seven independent tubes and bells	123
39.	Sarrusophone *versus* Saxophone	124
40.	Prospectus and Price List issued by Adolphe Sax and Company	127
41.	Page from a Sax prospectus	128
42.	Adolphe-Edouard Sax (1859-1945)	131
43.	Saxophone — *The Illustrated London News, July 7, 1849*	132
44.	Saxophones from sopranino to bass — *Kneller Hall collection*	137
45.	E-flat alto saxophone, among the instruments which gained First Prize at the Paris Exhibition of 1867	138
46.	Alphonse Sax (1822-1874)	145
47.	Sax's kettledrums — 'sans kettles'	146
48.	A handbill of Sax's products, about 1850	151
49.	The Swindon Citadel brass band of The Salvation Army with its octet of saxophones	152
50.	The British Brass Band — a home for the modern saxhorn	159
51.	An illustrated price-list showing some of Sax's brass instruments	160
52.	The Brown Brothers Saxophone Sextet	164
53.	Isham Jones — an early saxophone "technician"	171
54.	A pioneer versatile saxophone 'section'	172
55.	An early British broadcasting dance band	175
56.	Rudy Wiedeoft (1893-1940) — a pioneer of the 1920's saxophone craze	176
57.	An early saxophone compared with a contemporary model	180
58.	A modern saxophone chamber group — *The London Saxophone Quartet*	185
59.	E-flat contrabass and E-flat sopranino saxophones	186
60.	Description of a saxophone mouthpiece, written and signed by Adolphe Sax	190
61.	A modern memorial to Adolphe Sax on the site of his birthplace at Dinant	193
62.	Motif by Daoust for the Committee of the Sax Festival, Dinant	194
63.	Drawing for the original saxophone patent, 20th March 1846	199
64.	Sax's original description of his saxophone attached to the Patent of 20th March 1846	200
65.	Final page of the saxophone patent of 20th March 1846	202

FOREWORD

by

PAUL HARVEY
LRAM ARCM

*Professor of Clarinet
Royal Military School of Music, Kneller Hall*

Leader: London Saxophone Quartet

Library shelves are full of biographical studies of composers, conductors and executant musicians, but how difficult it is to find anything about the men without whose artifacts music could not exist: the designers and makers of the instruments.

I frequently receive requests from students engaged in projects and dissertations on the saxophone for information on its invention and development. Here, at last, is an authoritative source to which I can refer them.

It would be true to say that Adolphe Sax had more influence on more different forms of music making than any other instrument designer. The fact that one of the instruments to which he gave his name has come into such prominence as a leading voice in the development of jazz should not make us forget that it was Sax who gave the symphony orchestra a viable bass clarinet, and brass and military bands the ubiquitous family of saxhorns!

Yet even a person with no interest in jazz, classical saxophone, orchestras or bands (I suppose such people must exist) could still be fascinated by Adolphe Sax as a character. Everybody loves an eccentric, and when he is also a genius in his chosen field, an obsessional fanatic, extravagant in his loves and hates, hot tempered, impetuous and generally larger than life, who can resist him?

Wally Horwood has been under the spell of Adolphe Sax for many years; most of them spent in painstaking research for this book. As a saxophonist, a brass band enthusiast, an experienced journalist and a scholarly collector of historical information, I can think of nobody better qualified to write the definitive biography of this fascinating character of the nineteenth century.

PAUL HARVEY

Preface

The name of Adolphe Sax finds a place in many reference books next to his chiefly remembered works, the saxhorn and the saxophone. Anyone wishing to find out more than the scanty information usually given soon encounters difficulties since even the more well-known sources of information, mostly in French, are not easily accessible to the general reader. To remedy this, the initial aim of this work was a modest one; merely to present in an easily readable form such facts as could be found among writings of Sax's contemporaries.

As work progressed, two main features emerged; one encouraging, the other disconcerting. With the help of friends and correspondents in many parts of the world, fresh details came to light and some hitherto obscure points became clear. The account thus became more complete and authoratitive than at first was thought possible. At the same time, the identification of "facts" became a problem. Almost all of the sources consulted were, in a highly controversial situation, strongly biased in favour of the subject.

It has been suggested that the writings of such as Berlioz, Comettant, Fétis and Kastner, where they touch on Sax, ought to be discounted as utterly unreliable since their object was more to write propaganda than to record history. Certainly Sax was by no means the genius they would have us believe but, in searching for the truth beneath their enthusiasm, there is no virtue in over-reaction. It will be seen that Sax was often arrogant and self-opinionated, yet to deny him any gracious virtues whatsoever is to go to the other extreme. The fact that, as an unknown, he was able to win the confidence and friendship of so many of high standing and, even more significantly, keep most of those friendships throughout his active life, must say something for his ability and integrity.

Sax's adversaries who, after all, had good reason to oppose him, did not record their case with anything approaching the enthusiasm of his supporters. In seeking justice for the opposition, it is perhaps fortunate that Sax's friends so often leave themselves open to challenge. In some cases, they are left to state their views before the flaws in their arguments are pointed out. Where there are two or more available sides to an argument, these are presented; where tentative conclusions may be drawn, such are suggested. All too often, however, it is a case of setting the scene and allowing the perceptive reader to interpret as he will.

This is essentially a story of a man, his failures and his achievements. The writing has in mind the general musically-inclined reader who is probably not particularly knowledgeable on the subject of acoustics and the theory of musical wind-instruments. As Sax was a technician engaged in a technical calling, it is inevitable that certain explanations of his work must be attempted in order that the reader might at least get a glimpse of the issues involved. In keeping such explanations brief, there is the risk of offending the more knowledgeable in these matters with over-simplifications. However, to have dealt with them more fully would have meant digressing from our main purpose and duplicating material contained in so many scholarly works some of which are listed in the bibliography.

Apart from any enlightenment which may be gleaned from these pages, it is hoped that a measure of entertainment will not be lacking. The piquant humour — albeit unintentional at the time — of certain situations ought not be overlooked.

The controversy which surrounded this man in his lifetime is by no means dead, the last word on the subject is far from having been said. Nevertheless, if this first attempt at a complete biography and assessment in English prepares the ground, it will have fulfilled its purpose.

Boundstone, Farnham, Surrey, 1979.

Wally Horwood

Adolphe Sax at 30, from a lithograph by Baugniet (1844)

Adolphe Sax
Bust in the Dinant Museum

I
Dinant and Brussels

The plaudits of the crowd are for the musical performer. His instrument, without which he would be dumb, is rarely given a thought. Its maker must be content, in comparative anonymity, with a pride of craftsmanship and the profits of his trade. For every Paganini remembered, a hundred fine fiddle-makers lie forgotten. A music mechanic whose name becomes familiar to the world at large is a rare phenomenon. Perhaps only two have achieved this distinction: Stradivari and Sax.

The juxtaposition of these names may raise cries of "Sacrilege!" in some quarters. Stradivari, the supreme master luthier, fashioned instruments which, after nearly three hundred years, are unsurpassed for beauty of tone and construction. The possession of a "Strad" marks a violinist of renown. But Sax! Wasn't he the fellow who perpetrated that ghastly saxophone? What is left of him apart from a few dusty museum pieces?

Fortunately, this unenlightened reaction is less prevalent today. The once rigid schisms in music are rapidly being bridged. The excesses of style which earned the saxophone a bad reputation in the so-called "jazz-age" are now a distant memory. The instrument may now be evaluated at its not inconsiderable true worth. For longevity, wind instruments cannot be judged in the same way as stringed, the best of which actually improve with age over a long period before succumbing to inevitable deterioration.

The 19th. century saw a spectacular leap forward in the emancipation of wind instruments from their simple, incomplete and generally unsatisfactory state, so that, even when an instrument has been carefully nurtured to survive a century, technical progress will have made it obsolete for modern purposes.

It is not in tangible heirlooms that we must look for any claim Sax may have to immortality; rather in the effect his existence had both on the musical life of his day and in the years since his death. This effect is rather more considerable than is at first suspected. To say that the saxophone is his greatest achievement is to mention but a part of the story. His overall work in the field of wind instrument manufacture not only had a profound effect on his contemporaries and immediate successors, tenuous but distinct threads connect him with aspects of musical life today.

Sax was more than a prolific inventor. His capacity for inventiveness was compulsive. Even in the darkest periods of his life, vilified by enemies, badgered by creditors, slighted, insulted, and with a painful death in prospect, his hands never ceased to realise the ideas fermenting in his brain. It so happened that parentage and upbringing set him on the course of musical instrument making. Had fate thought otherwise, there is no doubt that this inventive flair would have found outlet whatever his calling.

Dinant, the old Belgian town in the Meuse Valley, with its brooding citadel perched on the Bayard Rock, has, in its turbulent history, acquired fame for its gingerbread biscuits, its ancient craft of copper-beating, and two illustrious musical instrument makers. For father Sax, although overshadowed in popular recognition by his eldest son, has himself an honoured place in his profession. It was he who taught his son the mysteries and skills of an art he had discovered for himself without any formal tuition. It is fair to say that the life of Charles Joseph Sax was a foreshadowing of the life of his son, without which he could not have made the impression he subsequently did.

Charles was born in Dinant on February 1st, 1793. He studied architecture at an early age and was able, it is said, to draw plans of houses with professional skill at the age of 13. At 15 he become an apprenticed cabinet-maker in Brussels demonstrating a skill with his hands which caused a marquetry table encrusted with an elaborate bronze ornamentation to be considered a masterpiece. About this time he played the serpent with a local music society. The wages of an apprentice were sparse; serpents were expensive. He was annoyed at having to use a borrowed instrument. Studying its construction, the curved wooded sections, leather binding and simple keywork, he felt he could make a fair replica. The result was highly promising; the exercise was to be remembered with profit in quite a short time.

With the coming of the machine age, Charles Sax forsook his quiet occupation for a job in a large factory making spinning machines. As an engineer he was no less adept, quickly rising to a position in charge of the workshop. At 20 he married a local girl, Maria Masson. Their first child, a boy, was born on November 6th, 1814. The Certificate of Birth drawn up three days later gives the occupation of the father as "Joiner and Cabinet Maker".[1]

Had not the tide of battle at Waterloo suddenly swung in favour of the Allies, it is doubtful whether the career of the instrument maker would ever have begun. The fall of Napoleon and the First Empire led to the closure of the factory and the dismissal of the workers.[2] It was then the serpent was remembered.

With nothing to lose, Charles Sax went to Brussels and took a modest house in the Rue de L'Evêque. With no money for tools, he made his own and began to make serpents and flutes. They sold quite well, the quality was good, making enough to sustain him and his growing family. In the five years from 1815 to 1820, progress was truly astounding. Turning the combined skills of draughtsman, craftsman and engineer to good account, the range of manufacture was extended to include clarinets, bassoons and instruments in brass. King William I appointed him "Instrument Maker to the Court of the Netherlands"; a contract for the supply of instruments to Belgian military bands was forthcoming, together with financial assistance to make its fulfilment possible. This period was crowned when he was only 27 by the award of the 1820 Industrial Exhibition medal for a display of instruments said to be comparable with the best of Germany and France.

Not only could a comprehensive list of brass and woodwind instruments be offered, Sax found time to make violins and violas, to patent a new piano conception, a harp with a keyboard and a guitar with a harp-like sonority. An impressive diversity of skills to which must be added a deep and painstaking research into problems connected with the French horn.

Before the perfection of the valve had given all brass instruments an even, chromatic compass, horn players had solved their problems by a simple expedient. By inserting the hand into the bell of the horn at varying depths, the pitch of a note could be altered by a tone or a semitone. A prodigious technique had been developed on these lines, satisfactory enough while the music remained in one key. For a change of key, a composer had to allow several bars of rest in the score to permit a horn player to detach a piece of tubing, known as a "crook", and insert another appropriate to the new key. With the increase of chromaticism in music, the practice was irksome to composers and players alike.

Horn makers were very much concerned with attempts to construct a quick-change mechanism. In 1824, Charles Sax produced his own version of an "omnitonic horn" which, although in appearance evocative, as Morley-Pegge puts it, of a forkful of spaghetti,[3] was both practical and manageable. By an ingenious sliding-rod device, he was able to allow only that portion of extra tubing necessary for the required key to be utilised. It is for the *cor omnitonique* that Charles Sax is most remembered. He worked to perfect the system until 1846, by which time the obvious superiority of valve mechanism, either to produce a fully chromatic instrument or merely as a means of rapid recrooking, made further work unnecessary.

The nationalist revolution of 1830 and the subsequent Dutch invasion of Belgium were troublesome times for the populace. Amid the turmoil in Brussels, Sax had for a time to close his small workshop. He turned the enforced respite from the physical making of instruments to good advantage by delving deeper into theory. Working in isolation, he had to discover for himself the reasons why different instruments had different characteristic tones, that these tones were affected only by the proportions of the tube's bore (cylindrical, conical, or a combination of both) and the method of vibrating the air-column, such as the oboe's double reed, the clarinet's single reed, the trumpet's cup mouthpiece or the flute's open hole. He perceived the necessity of placing tone-holes, normally covered by the fingers, in scientifically calculated positions rather than arbitrarily to accommodate the span of the hand. His research in this field was among the first carried out, where trial-and-error had for so long been the rule.

In all this work he was watched and assisted by his eldest son, growing up and taking an ever-increasing interest in the business. One would give much to know what passed between father and son at that time. The relationship seems to have been a good one, founded on mutual respect. It was thus the young lad received a thorough grounding in the craft which was to carry the name of Sax to posterity.

Although christened Antoine Joseph, the boy seems always to have been called Adolphe. In later life he always signed as such and even used the adopted name on patents and official documents. Of his mother, little is known. She was fully occupied in bearing and caring for eleven children, five girls and six boys, most of whom did not survive into maturity. Her only recorded saying is: "The child is doomed to suffer; he won't live!"

This was after young Sax had been hauled by a passer-by, nearly drowned, from a swiftly flowing river by which he had been playing with friends. Coming on top of all the narrow escapes from death he had suffered in his short life, the distraught mother's reaction is understandable. The first part of the prophecy was to prove all too true.

Before he was two, he fell headlong down three flights of stairs and cracked his head on a stone floor. When only three he almost expired through drinking a mixture of vitriol and water in mistake for milk, being narrowly saved by the application of liberal doses of olive oil. Three other poisoning mishaps followed involving white lead, copper oxide and arsenic as well as the swallowing of a pin. A gunpowder explosion gave him severe burns and threw him a considerable distance; he was again burned when a frying pan was knocked over A lifelong scar on his head was caused by a falling roof-stone. Once he went to bed in a room where some newly varnished objects were drying, being found in time to prevent asphyxiation from the fumes. No wonder the people of the locality called him, "Young Sax, the Ghost!"

These childhood accidents point, perhaps, to a trait in the boy's make-up which was to show itself in another guise later on. To say that he was accident-prone is to shift responsibility on to Fate for what was, in many instances, the consequence of his own actions. As a child he was clearly unable to perceive potential danger in a situation; as a man he was equally oblivious as to the probable reaction of others to his initiatives. This tragic blind spot was to cast a shadow over all his future attainments and indeed cause a lifetime of suffering.

With the future mercifully shielded, the handsome young Adolphe was showing distinct promise both as a craftsman and as a musician. In spite of his near-fatal misadventures he never seems to have been hurt by the misuse of his father's tools. This must point to careful paternal instruction in their correct use. At an early age he was able to make toys for himself and, as is so natural in a child, to try to copy exactly his father's actions. Well before his teens he was able to drill the pieces of a clarinet to perfection, to perform all the intricate tasks connected with the making of keywork, and to make bells and other parts of brass instruments with the skill of an adult.

As a wise father, Charles Sax encouraged rather than pushed his son into the trade. At fourteen, after a good formal education which all the children enjoyed, Adolphe became a music student. Not at the Royal Conservatoire as so many contemporary biographers state, since this institution was not founded until 1832, but at its forerunner, the Royal School of Singing.[4] Here, apart from instruction in the vocal art, he studied the flute with Professor Labou. It was later he took up the clarinet with Valentine Bender, the famous Belgian Guides bandmaster, and found his real forte as an executant. Progress was rapid and Bender was pleased with the potential virtuosity shown by his pupil. Joseph Küffner, eminent German bandmaster and composer, happened to hear Sax play when visiting Brussels in 1834. Impressed, he dedicated to him a work for two clarinets.

There is little doubt that Sax could have made a successful career as a clarinet virtuoso probably, by so doing, achieving a greater degree of happiness in life than eventually became his lot. The pull of the family workshop was too strong. No one more than an advanced player could appreciate the many flaws inherent in the clarinet of the day. So natural, with all the necessary tools and equipment at his disposal and a fast developing skill in their use, that he should wish to experiment to find ways of overcoming the problems.

At sixteen his first exhibits were displayed at the Brussels Industrial Exhibition of 1830; two flutes and a clarinet wrought in ivory which were the subject of favourable comment. The first pieces to incorporate innovations of his own were shown at the 1835 Exhibition. A 24-keyed clarinet into which Sax had poured much thought and experiment received an honourable mention. François Joseph Fétis, a leading musicologist, teacher and champion of Sax, criticises this clarinet as having fine external features without overcoming any of the acoustical problems.[5] For the next five years, Sax worked at the clarinet until, by 1840, he had added an impressive list of modifications. His instrument became a model for its day and for many decades after, as well as providing others with a basis for further experiment.

As the fourth decade of the century ran its course, the predominance of the younger Sax in the family business became steadily more apparent. Since his was no formal apprenticeship, there is no clear dividing line between the time when Adolphe worked at his father's direction and when he would use his own initiative. Both were keen innovators; work of an experimental nature was always to be found in the workshop. It may be that Charles Sax, with the need to produce instruments for sale to make a living, left much of the actual experimenting to his son, lending his experienced counsel to the other's practical work. At any rate, projects which were to put the name of Sax on everybody's lips were begun at this time. Among these were the construction of valved bugle-horns, and an instrument which combined a single-reed mouthpiece (similar to the clarinet) with a conical metal tube. These were to become known respectively as saxhorns and saxophones.

One major undertaking to reach fruition in a completed state was the bass clarinet. Largely abortive attempts to construct an instrument pitched an octave below the ordinary clarinet had been made by Heinrich Grenser in 1793, Desfontenelles in 1807 and Gottlieb Streitwolf in 1828. It is not likely that Sax knew of, or at least was inspired by, any of them. He must, however, have known of the practical instrument which had come into being in 1832 through the combined talents of clarinettist Isaac Franco Dacosta and maker Auguste Buffet. This was widely praised at the time and it was said that Meyerbeer wrote the famous solo in *Les Huguenots* especially for it.

The original specification of Sax's bass clarinet is dated June 19th 1838 although this must have been the culmination of many years' work. In its conception, Charles Sax deserves credit for his early work on boring techniques and his study of proportions. The bore of the Sax instrument was certainly of generous proportions compared with its predecessors; this resulted in the characteristic exotic quality of tone.

One physical problem inherent in keyed bass instruments has taxed makers for many years: how to get tone-holes in their scientifically-measured places in the tube, yet at the same time close enough together that the fingers could cover them. Various expedients were tried; undulating shapes as with the serpent, and thick-walled tubes into which slanting holes were bored, always with something less than success. Sax discarded these in favour of a straight tube with holes correctly positioned, brought under the fingers by means of covered cups. He added a second speaker-key to facilitate the sounding of the top register. According to Berlioz, it had 22 keys, perfect intonation and great intensity of tone.[7]

A novel feature was the bell. The normal instrument descending to E, pointed straight at the floor. To prevent the sound being lost, Berlioz describes a "concave metallic reflector" which, placed beneath the bell, deflected the sound forward. Alternatively, a bell curving upwards could be fitted. This took the compass down to C. Later, for military band use, a more manageable shape was available, made in brass and called *clarinette base recourbée à pavillon de cuivre*.

Charles-Joseph Sax (1790-1865)
From a lithograph by Johann Schubert

Dinant, in the Meuse Valley, as it is today.
A town famous for its copper-beating, gingerbread biscuits and the Sax family.

On passing through Brussels in 1839, the celebrated conductor, François Antoine Habeneck, had the opportunity of hearing Sax perform on his own bass clarinet. The combination of the virtuoso player with an instrument of revolutionary design made a great impression. Habeneck declared, "Compared with this instrument, the old clarinet is a monstrosity". Returning to Paris he insisted that a Sax bass clarinet replace the existing one in his Opera orchestra.

Fétis, too, after having warmly praised the Dacosta-Buffet model in the *Revue et Gazette Musicale* of 13th March 1834, wrote again in that journal on 10th January 1841 of the superiority of the Sax construction. His opinion was that "M. Sax's bass clarinet only keeps the name of its predecessors".

As a player, Sax was no less enthusiastic than as a maker. He was a member of several musical societies including *La Grande Harmonie Royale* and the Philharmonic Society. There he began to feature his new instrument, often in specially written pieces. Already the jealousy of others which was to plague his life was becoming apparent. When the *Grande Harmonie* wished to adopt the Sax clarinet, M. Bachman, the musician who played part, refused to use it saying that, if it were adopted, he would resign and cede his place to Sax. To which the inventor rather sarcastically replied: "I will be sorry, Sir, if the public finds itself without your fine talent but I find myself unable to accede to your demands." His next action was typical of the man. He challenged Bachman to a duel — fortunately a musical one — demonstrating convincingly amid the resulting publicity, the superiority of his invention. Sax was forthwith appointed the new bass clarinettist to both musical societies.

This incident gives an insight into Sax's character. So dedicated was he to his craft, so convinced of his own outstanding powers, that he could accept no criticism or even tolerate ignorance of his work. At the slightest hint of either he was ready to challenge, ready to attack any detractor, eager to convince the doubter by demonstration.

In 1839, when still only 25, he read in a newspaper that Dacosta, who was solo clarinet at the Paris Royal Academy of Music, proposed to exhibit and play in various countries a bass clarinet which he had perfected. This caused the young man acute agitation. Convinced his own instrument to be vastly superior, he must have chafed at being confined to Brussels, a comparative backwater in the musical sense, where his genius could not adequately be recognised. He packed his bass clarinet and some other instruments, and set off — some say on foot — for Paris.

Finding Dacosta, Sax was able to examine the rival instrument. If he pointed out that this was but a little improvement on the old model he must have used unaccustomed tact. He was able to persuade Dacosta to listen to his own rendering of the *Huguenots* solo and get him to acknowledge the Sax bass clarinet as infinitely superior. If there was any reluctance to concede the point, at least Mme. Dacosta was in no doubt. "When M. Sax plays," she told her husband, "*your* instrument sounds like a kazoo".[8] Afterwards Dacosta was gracious enough to say that "the young virtuoso triumphed over the most difficult modulations and difficulties in a way not possible on the old instrument".

Sax was nothing if not enterprising. Utilising to the full his time in the capital, he sought out people prominent in the musical hierarchy. Something of a reputation had preceded him, thanks to Habeneck and others. This, with his easy charm, good looks and sincerity, opened doors to the famous. Composers in particular were happy to see him. Pleasant relationships were begun with Meyerbeer, Berlioz and Halévy who listened with professional interest to Sax's demonstrations and discourses. In an impressive display on his bass clarinet, Sax played a compass of four octaves[9] before many prominent musicians, including Meyerbeer and professors from the Conservatoire. Jean Georges Kastner, who was to become a lifelong supporter of Sax, suggested that the inventor be put in charge of a special class at the Conservatoire for teaching the new instrument. The idea, however, was not taken up.

Forced eventually to return home, he, as so many have done before and since, carried Paris in his heart. Excited by what he had seen at the Exhibition, by the encouragement given by the famous musicians, life in Brussels must have seemed dull by comparison. It would never be the same again.

Deep tragedy hit the family. Charles Sax, who had devoted the best of his resources to the rearing of his children, saw the deaths of eight of them at this time. Only Adolphe, his young brother Alphonse and a sister remained. To dull the pain of such bereavement, father and son must have immersed themselves into their work. For the son, the position was becoming unbearable. The unsettling effect of the Paris trip did not wear off and there were tempting offers to set up as a manufacturer in London and St. Petersburg. Regard for his parents kept him at home until his back received a last straw.

With customary care and thoroughness, Sax prepared a display of instruments for the Brussels Exhibition of 1841. This included items in wood and brass, among them clarinets of advanced design and his bass clarinet. This would possibly have been the first public showing of the saxophone but for a misadventure to be considered later. The examining committee was delighted, recommending Sax for the highest award, the Premier Gold Medal. However, the Central Jury demurred. He was, they pronounced, still a young man: if they were to give him the first prize now, there would be nothing better to offer next year.

This fatuous ruling disgusted Sax. "If I am too young for the gold medal", he declared, "I am too old for the silver". From that moment he decided there would be no "next year". Paris loomed large in his thoughts; he began to make preparations to leave. It is possible that news of his decision reached the French capital for, not long afterwards, he received a visit from a most distinguished Frenchman. This removed any shadow of doubt he might have had.

Lieutenant-General Comte de Rumigny personified the best in French military tradition. He was gazetted sub-Lieutenant from Fontainebleau in 1805 and, in nine glorious years, had risen to the rank of colonel. The *Légion d'Honneur* was awarded him after his bravery in the field had become a byword. Witnessing an heroic dash through a hail of bullets at Waterloo, Marshal Ney was heard to exclaim, "That young colonel considers himself immortal." For his zeal he found himself demoted at the Restoration but his attachment to the house of Orléans brought him high status when Louis-Philippe was elected king in 1830.

Combining the qualities of patriot, musician and man of culture, de Rumigny perceived the role music should play in the morale of an army. French military music was at a low ebb and held in poor repute by musicians and the public. The general was disturbed by the motley collection of high-priced, inefficient instruments which constituted French military bands.

In Prussia, Wilhelm Wieprecht was carrying out the reformation of military bands which already put those of France to shame. De Rumigny chafed at the knowledge that "a simple German bugle could set at defiance the French trumpets by making a smart reply with sounds nearly right to sounds which are totally wrong".[10]

Being told of a remarkable young inventor in Brussels, the general made it his business to visit the workshop, to see and hear the many fine instruments and to hear of plans for the future. Here indeed was the man to put French military music on a par with other nations. The effect of the congratulations and encouragement from the King's favourite *aide-de-camp* must have been for Sax a heady tonic.

Other sounds of encouragement were coming from Paris. Halévy employed an eminent violinist to carry a letter to Sax in Brussels. He wrote:

> I am taking advantage of M. Vieuxtemp's stay in Paris and his immediate return to Brussels to ask you for news of the instruments which you demonstrated to me and which you are now perfecting. Your efforts are worthy of the interest of all composers. You will increase the number and power of orchestral effects, thanks to your new and excellent combinations of sounds we have already had the chance of trying at the Conservatory. Make haste to complete your new family of instruments and come to the rescue of poor composers who are seeking new sounds and of the public which is demanding them.[11]

Charles Sax advanced all the arguments he could to dissuade Adolphe from taking the step. He realised how much he would miss his son on a personal and professional level. From what we know of the older man, he would not have attempted to block genuine advancement. He knew, at least by reputation, of the close clique of Parisian instrument makers, their bitter

Collage of Sax's instruments
Almanac de l'Illustration 16th July 1864

resentment of any intruder. He could have reminded Sax of the treatment meted out to such outstanding musical inventors as Theobald Boehm and Ivan Müller; how Sebastian Erard had his workshop and equipment seized and had to get a licence from Louis XVI himself before he could continue to make his pianos and harps.

It was of no use; Adolphe seemed convinced as to where his spiritual home lay. With only 30 francs in his pocket — a fact carefully concealed from his father — but with high hopes and supreme self-confidence, he left for Paris, fame and fortune.[12]

Notes on Chapter 1

1. The Certificate of Birth reads (in translation):
   On the ninth day of the month of November 1814 at 10 o'clock in the morning.
   Registration of the Birth of Antoine Joseph Sax on the sixth instant at eleven o'clock in the evening, son of Charles Joseph, joiner and cabinet maker and of Maria Joseph Masson, living wife, living in Dinant. Sex of child has been established as masculine.
   First Witness: Joseph Guilbert, aged 21, living in Dinant.
   Second Witness: Jean Adam Elbe, aged 55, living in Dinant.
   On the application made to us by Charles Joseph Sax, father of the child, and, after reading, signed:
           Guilbert   C. J. Sax   Elbe
   Attested according to the law by me, Nicolas Joseph Bouget, Burgomaster of the District of Dinant, carrying out the functions of a Public Officer of the Civil State.
                                                       (signed) N. J. Bouget.
2. Brenta (p.55) states that the spinning-machine factory was at Ghent, some eighty miles distant from Dinant. As the family was living in Dinant towards the end of 1814 and C. J. Sax became unemployed shortly after the Battle of Waterloo (18th June 1815) it would appear that his career as a mechanic was a short one.
3. R. Morley-Pegge: *The French Horn*, p.58.
4. École Royale de Chant, founded 1823. See Brenta p.58 (footnote).
5. Fétis, p.414.
6. Lavoix, H: *Histoire de l'instrumentation*, p.124 "This was a bassoon-shaped instrument, pitched in C derived from the *basse guerrière* of Dumas. The famous solo in *Les Huguenots* is stated to have been played on it".
7. *Journal des Débats*, 12th June, 1842.
8. Brenta, p.59. "Kazoo" (Fr. Mirliton) — a toy instrument: the player hums into a tube to vibrate a disc of gauze or tissue paper, which produces a reedy tone.
9. Kastner: *Traité Général*, Supp. p.25.
10. Kastner: *Manuel Général*, p.230.
11. Kastner, p.237, dates Halévy's letter to Sax in Brussels as 14th August, 1842. Sax, however, had arrived in Paris and visited Berlioz prior to June 12th, the date on which Berlioz's celebrated article appeared in the *Journal des Débats* which made the public aware of Sax. (See Page 38).
12. Fétis, p.415.

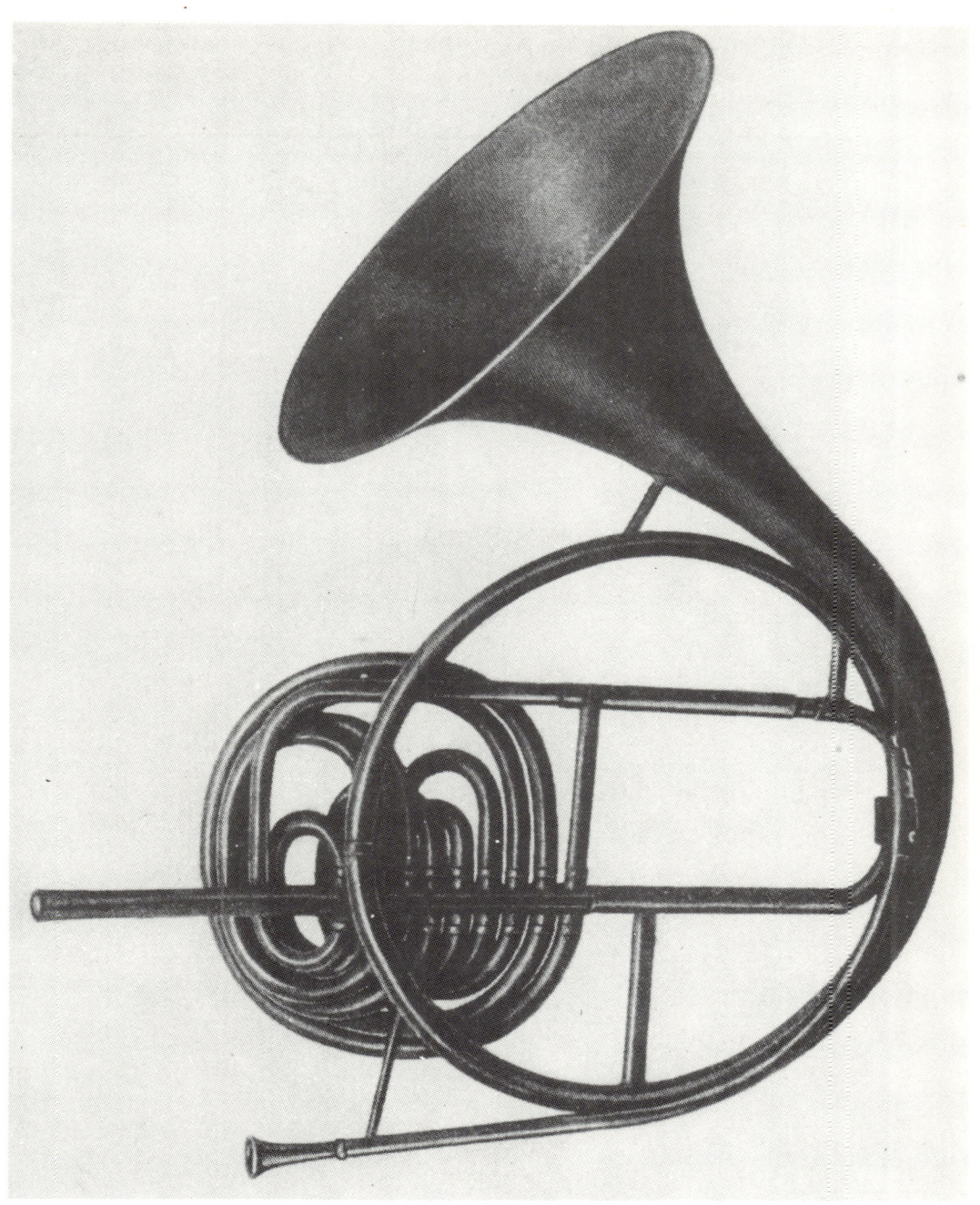

Omnitonic horn invented by Charles Sax

Du Seize jour du mois de novembre mil huit cent quatorze, à 8h

Acte de Naissance de Antoine Joseph Sax.

Le Six du courant, à onze heures du soir, fils de Charles Joseph Mornaisin, à Dinant et de Marie Joseph Masson, Jouant Demeurant à Dinant Maquelin

Premier témoin Joseph Guilbert, âgé de Vingt six ans, domicilié à Dinant

Second témoin Jean Adam Auguste Mans, âgé de Cinquante Cinq ans, domicilié à Dinant

Sur la réquisition à nous faite par Charles Joseph Sax, père de l'enfant

et ont, après lecture faite Signé

Constaté suivant la loi par moi Nicolas Joseph Bouges, Bourgmestre de la commune de Dinant, faisant les fonctions d'officier public de l'état civil.

Birth Certificate of Antoine Joseph Sax, 6th November, 1814

II
Saxhorns and Saxophones

There is no doubt that Sax's change of venue was a vital turning point in his life. It may, therefore, be advantageous to use this natural break in the narrative to consider two projects. Both were concerned with "families" of instruments, both bore the name of their innovator, both were conceived in Brussels but brought to maturity in Paris.

As an instrument maker of his time, Sax was different from most of his contemporaries in the scope of his operations. Pierre points out that it was unusual for a maker to construct both woodwind and brass instruments since the tooling and process of manufacture is completely different in each case.[1] Charles Sax had no inhibitions about applying his talents to any instrument which took his fancy. Adolphe did not, in general, go quite so far; he was involved with a comprehensive range of wind instruments then in use, both wood and brass.

This was probably due to a conception, discovered by the father for himself, that the material from which a wind instrument is made is, so to speak, immaterial. The only criterion is its durability in use and its malleability in manufacture. Thus he tended towards metal even in the construction of "woodwind" instruments, particularly in the larger sizes. In addition, he was very much concerned with "brass" in the orchestral sense — trumpets, cornets, French horns, trombones, tubas — with a keen mind set to overcome the peculiar problems attaching to this instrumental class.

For centuries, brass instruments had been restricted in the number of notes available to their simple harmonic series. Their tubes yield a fundamental note; increased pressure with some change of the "lip" sounds an octave higher, more pressure brings a further fifth, and so on — the notes getting closer together as the range gets higher. Trumpeters in the days of Bach and Handel performed remarkable feats of stratospheric playing on natural trumpets. At best this technique, the prerogative of a few virtuosi, could only allow more flexible playing in the taxing high register. Horn players, as we have noted, overcame the difficulty to some extent by the system of hand-stopping. The slide trombone was, of course, fully chromatic but when the slide principle was transferred to the trumpet the short distances between its shifts demanded fine execution and a keen ear. Consequently, the slide-trumpet too became a virtuoso instrument. With conical bores the slide was obviously impossible.

Early efforts to chromaticise by an alternative method looked to the shortening-hole system characteristic of woodwind instruments. This was first applied to the bugle, whose widely tapering tube was pierced with appropriately-sized holes which were opened and closed by means of keys. The key-bugle had a vogue of about twenty-five years: it was never entirely satisfactory due to the inferior tone produced when anything less than the whole tube was in use. First-class players did, however, achieve remarkable results.

The path by which brass instruments ultimately achieved an even, chromatic compass by means of the valve can only briefly be touched on here. Charles Clagget, a London Irishman, demonstrated in 1788 the effect of welding together two horns or trumpets in different keys with a common mouthpiece. A valve-switch enabled the harmonic series of each to be utilised at will.

The first valve to work on the principle of diverting the air-column through additional tubing, thus lowering the pitch, was the work of either Heinrich Stölzel or Friedrich Blühmel in Berlin around 1814. The former is often given the credit but there is reason to believe that he may have passed off Blühmel's work as his own. Whatever the truth, the invention seems to

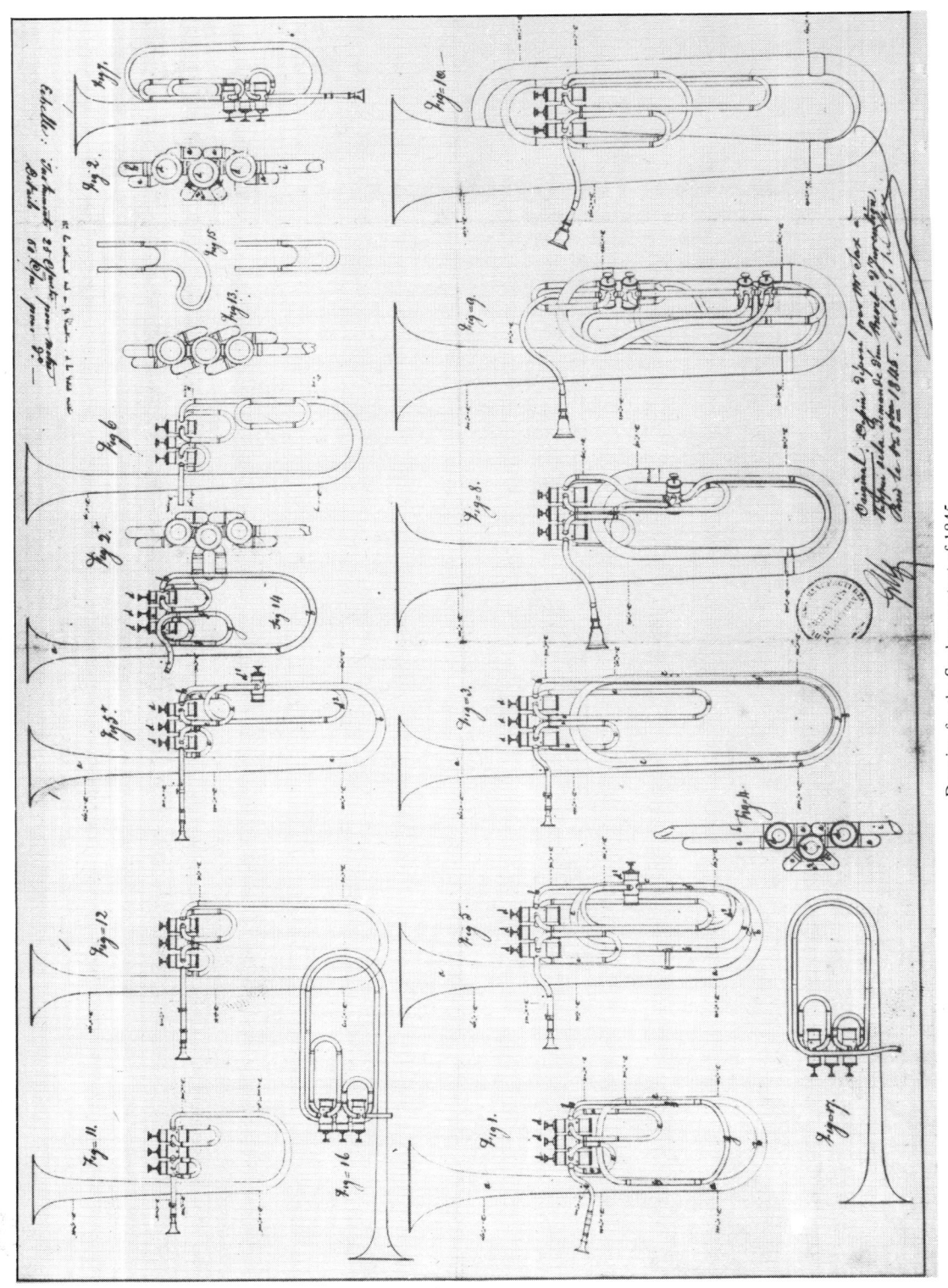

Drawing for the Saxhorn patent of 1845

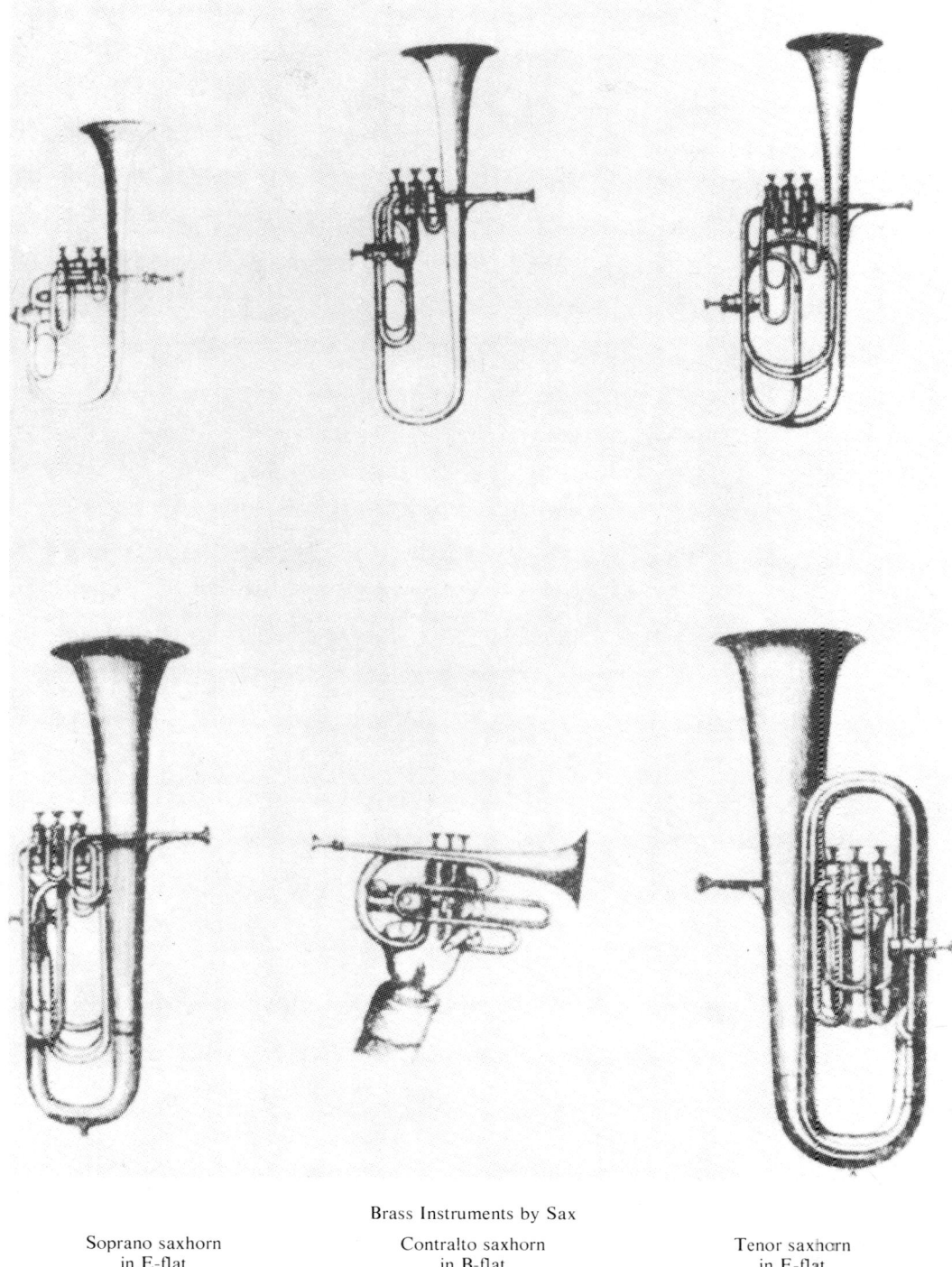

Brass Instruments by Sax

Soprano saxhorn in E-flat
Bass saxhorn in B-flat
Contralto saxhorn in B-flat
Cornet with compensators
Tenor saxhorn in E-flat
Contrabass saxhorn in E-flat

Kastner: Manuel general de musique militaire — 1848

have been of a piston movement.

In 1824, John Shaw, a Derbyshire farmer, patented his "transverse spring slides", an ingenious but complicated mechanism prone to leaks. The idea was improved upon in 1830 by Leopold Uhlmann of Vienna with a double piston movement which was popular for many years. The *Berliner-Pumpen* valve, a stumpy, squat improvement on the Stölzel, was brought out in 1835 by W. F. Wieprecht and J. G. Moritz. Many others were involved in attempts to improve the piston valve; it reached the form as we know it today in the hands of the Paris maker, Etienne François Périnet.

An alternative to the piston is the rotary valve, a more delicate, complex mechanism but none the less efficient. Although not popular in Britain, except among horn players, it is widely used on the Continent. Blühmel may have been responsible for its invention as early as 1827 although there is some uncertainty as to whether his really was a rotary valve. Otherwise, next in line for credit is Josef Riedl of Vienna. His *Rad-Maschine* of 1832 has remained unaltered in essence to this day.

It will be noticed that, contrary to widespread belief, Sax played no pioneer part in the development of the valve; it is significant that, soon after the 1841 Exhibition, either the father or the son visited the maker Moritz in Berlin, and purchased from him some cornets and a bass tuba fitted with *Berliner-Pumpen* valves.[2] Sax was a skilled maker of this intricate component; his main contribution to valve improvement was the elimination of the nine sharp angles which occured in the windways in and out of the three valves to the detriment of tone and intonation. He took out a patent for his straight tubes on 17th August 1843.

A small, partly conical, horn known as the *cornet-de-poste* had been fitted with valves between 1826 and 1828. This became the immensely successful *cornet-à-pistons*, known in England as the cornopean, which quickly ousted the key-bugle from military and civilian bands, and from light orchestras. Sax, in Brussels, made fine cornets after the French pattern, incorporating free, open-bottom valves, rather clumsy in appearance, but effective in operation. While Charles Sax was still working on his omnitonic horn, Adolphe was fitting, with distinction, valves to the French horn. Jean Mohr, a worthy pupil of Gallay who did so much to keep alive the old method of hand-stopping, used one of Sax's horns with which he was well pleased. At this time, horn players often regarded valves as a quick and easy substitute for crooks; Sax's horn outfits were made to include sets of three and seven crooks. Horns and cornets were fitted with *Berliner-Pumpen*-type valves. Sax also made rotary valves which Berlioz later extolled as being superior to the piston.

Bugle horns, brass instruments with well tapered bores, had been fitted with valves before 1830, mainly in Germany. An instrument akin to the B-flat baritone had been used in public about 1828; the flügel horn, of the same pitch as the cornet but with a more generous bore, was widely used in Austria and Germany. So, too, was the tenor (or alto) horn pitched midway between the flügel horn and the baritone. These were all well represented in Wieprecht's Prussian army bands by 1842.

Danays, a French maker, obtained a patent in 1838 for a set of valved bugles known as *clavicors;* tenors in F and E-flat, and baritones in D-flat, C and B-flat. Made by A. G. Guichard, these were intended to replace the alto ophicleide in military bands. A similar set of instruments were being made about 1844-5; the Néo Alto, a tenor instrument in F or E-flat, together with three- or four-valved bombardons in B-flat bass and E-flat contrabass, comprised a kindred family.

Fully aware of the possibilities of the valved bugle, Sax, in Brussels, had conceived the idea of a matched family covering all pitches. He may well have taken a specimen experimental horn on his exploratory visit to Paris, although the complete family could have progressed no further than the drawing board.

Seeing that he was by no means the first in this field and that even his valve systems, however finely executed, were blatant copies, what gave Sax such an edge over his rivals in the manufacture of this type of instrument? It does seem that the quality of his workmanship was altogether admirable, especially when compared with the poor specimens over which de

Rumigny was so indignant. Further, the proportions of his horns, fitted as they were with wide-coned, deep-cupped mouthpieces, produced a richly contrasting tone to the orchestral trumpets, trombones and French horns. A flair for publicity and friends in high places was certainly no disadvantage.

Almost immediately after his arrival in Paris, Sax set to work to realise his plans for a new family of valved bugles. It was not until 1844 that he had made enough progress to warrant a public presentation. The set of instruments drawn for the 1854 patent consisted of five pieces: E-flat soprano, B-flat contralto, E-flat alto or tenor, B-flat baritone or bass with three valves, and a bass in B-flat with four valves. The last two were of the same pitch, the four valved bass having a wider bore. Valves were fitted as close to the mouthpiece end as possible to reduce the amount of cylindrical tubing to a minimum.

The first to come from the workbench were coiled trumpet style with forward pointing bells. They had no tuning slides and were fitted with *Berliner-Pumpen*-type valves. Before 1848, Sax had adopted a uniform "tuba" shape, even the smallest horn having an upright bell. Rotary valves were sometimes used, as later were the slender Périnet-style pistons.

Additions to the original set were a contrabass in F which could be crooked into E-flat and with three or four valves, and another contralto in A with a crook attachment into A-flat. Two or three years later appeared a B-flat contrabass and a sopranino in B-flat, an octave above the contralto. 1855 saw a sub-contrabass in EE-flat, an octave below the contrabass. This, in common with the sopranino, was of little practical value and had but a brief existence. Early instruments, even the smallest, had four valves allowing the compass, at least in theory, to be extended to the fundamental. Later, and more practically, four valves were restricted to the wide-bore bass members.

So far we have studiously avoided the use of the term "saxhorn". Despite any claims made by or on behalf of Sax he must have known as we can now see clearly that his fine instruments could in no way be said to have been "invented". In fact there is no evidence to suggest that Sax personally ever made such a claim. He was content with *bugles-à-cylindres* or *bugles-à-pistons*; the nomenclature used at the first public appearance was the innocuous "improved bugle".

Sax seems to have suffered from over-enthusiastic friends who, with the best of intentions, pushed his claims often beyond the bounds of veracity. It was John Distin, an instrumentalist we will shortly meet, who claimed that it was his family who first coined the name "saxhorn" Georges Kastner, Sax's friend and biographer, in his *Manuel général de musique militaire* of 1848 makes no claim that Sax invented the valved bugle horn. He does insist, however, that the new product was so superior to existing faulty instruments of a similar type that a special name was justified. In the same way, he asserts, as great improvements to instruments are referred to by such names as the Meifred horn, the Boehm flute, the Klośe clarinet, so it is proper to use the term Sax horn.[3]

Reasonable as this sounds today, we must consider that Sax's friends widely acclaimed his instrumental family as something completely new in musical instrument construction. He himself may probably have thought it ungrateful to contradict what was plainly intended for his good. He certainly never denied the claims and must therefore be considered an accessory. Perhaps later he regretted it. His name now firmly affixed to the instruments, together with the use he made of the 1845 patent, brought nothing but trouble in ensuing years.

Between 1825 and 1845, valved instruments of all shapes and sizes were made more-or-less to order by various "inventors" as required by bands and orchestras. Apart from the fine workmanship and designs of his individual instruments, Sax's contribution to this branch of instrumentation was the production of a matched, homogeneous set in a wide range of pitches.

The second of Sax's instrumental families conceived in Brussels was the saxophone. Here we need have no inhibitions about using the name at the outset. This really was an invention in the best sense of the word; no arguments by his detractors then or since have been able to nullify the claim.

Reduced to basic essentials, a saxophone is a conical tube of fairly generous proportions, pierced at appropriate intervals on the shortening-hole system and allied to a mouthpiece with a single beating reed similar to that of the clarinet. An instrument answering to this description, apart from the scale of the bore, existed some fifteen years before, made by William Meikle, a Scottish bandmaster. Meikle's alto fagotto,[4] made of wood and looking very much like a tenor bassoon, was sufficiently confused with that instrument as to be known as the "tenoroon". Instead of the bassoon-type double reed, however, it has a small single-reed mouthpiece. Its slender proportions with small tone-holes gave it a refined and mellow tone. The alto-fagotto had a surprisingly short and nebulous existence. It is doubtful that Sax knew anything of it, at least at the time he began to work on the saxophone. Since he was able to bring out a practical construction which has not changed its essentials to this day, the shadowy forerunner in no way affects the validity of his invention.

The fact that metal was used for the saxophone right from the start is of no consequence. As we have noted from Charles Sax's researches, any non-porous material will produce the same tonal results provided the proportions of the bore and the method of vibrating the air-column are constant. Because this fact has not always been appreciated, even by the knowledgeable, a lot of nonsense has been written about the saxophone. Consisting as it does of a brass body fitted with a "woodwind" mouthpiece, it has often been assumed that it combines the qualities of orchestral brass and woodwind, or perhaps some intermediate quality between the two.

Brass was chosen simply because the making of a tube with the amount of taper required would have been difficult in wood, practically impossible for the larger instruments. Today, the traditional wooden flute is strongly challenged by flutes in metal without any of them sounding other than flutes. Metal clarinets have been made which retain completely the clarinet's peculiar *timbre*. For further proof one has only to look back some years to a brand of alto saxophone made from a high-grade plastic material. One of these was used by the writer for a time and they enjoyed a short vogue with a few notable players. Whatever the subsequent drawbacks of this material in use, it could not be faulted on the score that it made the instrument sound like anything other than an alto saxophone.

Individual players can, of course, prefer one material to another. This is a matter of fine personal choice and the difference is not normally perceptible to the ordinary listener. The saxophone does indeed blend happily with all sections of the orchestra or wind band, not because it is a brass, reeded instrument but because it is a saxophone. The French horn has similar qualities.

The reason why Sax invented the saxophone has been an intriguing question for years. Before asking why, it would be reasonable to enquire how and when. Sax left no personal account to suggest the path by which he arrived at the new instrument; it will be interesting to examine one or two suggested theories.

Fétis, writing in 1864, bemoans the clarinet's imperfections and suggests that these will not be overcome until a conical bore is adopted.[6] Lavoix states quite definitely that the invention of the saxophone sprang directly from a desire to make an octave-speaking clarinet.[7] For the same scientific reasons that a brass instrument sounded by the lips in a cup mouthpiece will produce higher harmonics with the use of increased pressure, so will a shortening-hole type of instrument sound further registers above its fundamental. With the flute, a cylindrical "open" pipe, increased pressure will obtain a second register one octave above the lowest. Similarly with the oboe and bassoon, conical pipes where the second octave is activated by the opening of a small vent hole covered by a "speaker" key. This process is known as "overblowing". The clarinet differs from the instruments mentioned by reason of it being a cylindrical tube which overblows not at the octave but at the twelfth.

This at once gives to the clarinet its rich *timbre* and its great range but, at the same time, presents the maker with some difficult problems in bridging the gap between the registers. As we have seen, Sax worked hard and long at improving the clarinet. Still he could not have been completely satisfied with the results and it is feasible that, in experimenting to see how far he could go with a tapered tube, he accidently discovered the saxophone.

Feasible but improbable. For one thing, Sax's knowledge of acoustics would have told him in advance that, in achieving an octave-sounding instrument with a conical bore, the clarinet's

Ophicleide fitted with a bass-clarinet mouthpiece conjectured to be an experiment carried out by Sax which led to the invention of the saxophone

Adolphe Sax
portrait by Pollet

peculiar tonal qualities would be destroyed. Secondly, had he approached the question from this angle, he would have made his first conical tube to the approximate length of the clarinet resulting in effect, in a soprano saxophone. We know, from Kastner, Berlioz and others that the first saxophone was of the bass register.

Kastner gives an account of the saxophone's invention thus:

One day, when M.A. Sax was going through his empty workshops he began to look at pieces of wood and sheets of brass as if he were seeing them for the first time. Lost in thought, he let his mind wander to the discovery of an important conception. . .He knew that wood gave a softer sound. . that brass gave a much more vigorous, noisier sound than that of wood. He knew that, by reason of these characteristics of differences in sound. Wood instruments in orchestras, and particularly in military bands, are powerless in competing against a choir of brass instruments, and that, in symphony orchestras, string instruments do not match woodwind instruments in sonority.

He thus felt there was room for improvement. Already, improvements to soprano and bass clarinets had fulfilled his expectations, but, with regard to brass, wasn't the problem insoluble?

Adolphe Sax meditated for a few moments. Then, by sudden inspiration, resolutely started work. The first attempt failed; and the second. After an interval of one or two days he tried again but was unsuccessful. Still Sax was not disheartened and proceeded with a third test. The result he obtained surpassed even his own forecast. He had just created an instrument which possessed a completely new sound, one that the human ear had never heard — so powerful, ample, expressive and fine.

By its peculiar sound, the instrument was going to offer the best accord that could be imagined between the loud and weak sounds of the orchestra. . .bringing together power and softness, it could not be crushed by the one and would not crush the other. In a word, a perfect instrument.[8]

There is an air of myth and romance about these words. The writer falls into the trap of linking constructional material with intensity of tone and, with proper respect to the saxophone's undoubted merits, the extravagance of the last sentence is laughable. Yet the account is worthy of serious consideration even if only to find if any underlying truth is hidden.

Kastner makes no mention of an octave-sounding clarinet. He gives the impression that Sax posed himself the question as to the effect of allying a clarinet mouthpiece with a conical tube of suitable proportions before attempting to find an answer by practical means. Having arrived at the practical stage he would surely wish to hear the anticipated sound as soon as possible and with least trouble. After all, the result may have been so disappointing as to warrant no further effort. In this way he may very well have seen a ready-made conical tube and a clarinet mouthpiece for the first time in a new light.

Some years ago, Philip Bate, authority and author of several eminent works on musical wind-instruments, carried out experiments which yielded promising results. When material for this book was being gathered, the writer approached Mr. Bate who agreed to repeat the operation. We were fortunate in having the two essential ingredients to hand; an ophicleide (which may be simply described as a bass key-bugle) and a bass clarinet mouthpiece. It took merely a minute or two to attach the mouthpiece, by means of adhesive tape, to the mouthpipe of the ophicleide. Admittedly, because of the age of the instrument, only a limited range of notes was possible, but the quality of those produced was completely and unquestionably saxophone-like.

An even more convincing demonstration took place at the Royal College of Music, London, when, during the World Saxophone Congress of 1976 the present author was addressing the assembled delegates concerning the origins of the saxophone. Paul Sargeant, accomplished clarinettist and performer on obsolete wind instruments, demonstrated a very serviceable ophicleide by first using the normal cup mouthpiece to show the euphonium-like qualities of the instrument. Then, in view of the audience, a bass clarinet mouthpiece was substituted. The subsequent quality of tone must have put the question of the saxophone's derivation beyond all reasonable doubt to any that heard it.

An exercise such as this is not, of course, conclusive. Whatever is said or done today can be nothing more than speculation. Nevertheless this particular theory has its merits. We know that Charles Sax made excellent ophicleides; Adolphe was a noted exponent of the bass clarinet. It would have taken no longer for him to have made the same test; with a brand-new ophicleide the results must have been even more impressive.

The ophicleide, being an instrument of bass register, tallies with the fact that the first saxophone was of similar pitch. The proportions of the ophicleide's bore are not far removed from those of a saxophone of a like size. It is interesting to note that many of the cartoons which later appear in connection with Sax's activities depict ophicleide-like contraptions, although these instruments never appear to have been made in Sax's Paris establishment. This, however, is not offered as serious evidence; cartoonists are notoriously inaccurate with form and detail when depicting instruments of music.

A fifteen-year patent, No. 3226, for a family of saxophones was taken out on 21st March 1846. This was merely the culmination of many years of activity; the instrument existed long before then. The first clue we have to its existence is found in a story told by Kastner. This concerns the Brussels Industrial Exhibition of 1841. Sax had prepared a collection of nine instruments for his entry. Apparently, prior to the opening, these were carelessly left in a dark corner. While the maker was absent, one of the exhibits, wrapped in a linen cloth, received a violent kick which sent it flying across the room. The damage was such that it had to be withdrawn.

Was this an accident or malice? Kastner has no doubts that it was "puerile baseness" showing that already, while still comparatively unknown, Sax had drawn upon himself the virulent hate of someone. Further asserted is the fact that the damaged piece was none other than the first example of the saxophone.

Opinions differ as to the justification of this assumption. Kochnitzky finds Kastner's account far from clear and does not entirely accept that the point is proved. Conversely, Brenta is prepared to go along with Kastner for the reason that the book contains a dedication to Sax from his friend, tending to prove that the inventor approved of what had been written.[9]

This premise, which ought to be indisputable, is nevertheless open to question. We have to remember that Kastner was writing at a time when Sax had suffered many years of trials and troubles at the hands of his enemies. It could be that the supporters of Sax had by then developed a persecution complex which places upon every untoward happening, even in retrospect, an aura of malice.

It has been observed that Sax was not disposed to challenge or correct any statement made in his favour. If the truth of this particular episode is accepted because the subject did not disapprove of it, so must the vague and romantic account of Sax's prime idea of building a new instrument. If one is suspect, so must be the other. Incidently, while on the subject of reliability, it is interesting to note that Fétis and Kastner, both intimates of Sax, state incorrectly the month of his birth: October and December respectively.[10]

Although it is unlikely that Sax had with him a saxophone on his early trip to Paris in 1839, it is just possible that the idea had germinated in his mind and some experimental work had been carried out. The "new family of instruments" referred to in Halévy's letter to Sax in Brussels probably meant saxhorns, although there is the possibility that the writer had been intrigued by a conveyed description of a new instrumental conception. Allowing for the fact that Sax's life must have been very full just before and for some time after his settlement in Paris, there does seem to have been a considerable lapse of time between the event of the damaged instrument and its first public appearance on 3rd February 1844. Even then, the instrument used was in a barely playable state.

With all this conjecture, it is still possible that Kastner is correct. What is indisputable is a famous article by Hector Berlioz printed in *Journal des Débats* for 12th June 1842. This is in all probability the first ever mention of the saxophone in print. In what Kochnitzky so aptly terms "the birth certificate of the saxophone", Berlioz writes:

Le Saxophon (sic), *named after its inventor, is a brass instrument with nineteen keys, whose shape is rather similar to the ophicleide. Its mouthpiece, unlike that of most brass instruments, is* similar to the mouthpiece of the bass clarinet. Thus the Saxophone becomes the head of a new group, that of the brass instruments with reed. It has a compass of three octaves beginning from the lower B flat under the staff (bass clef); its fingering is akin to the flute or the second part of the clarinet. Its sound is of such rare quality that, to my knowledge, there is not a bass instrument in use nowadays that could be compared to the Saxophone. It is full soft, vibrating, extremely powerful, and easy to lower in intensity. As far as I am concerned, I find it very superior to the lower tones of the ophicleide, in accuracy as well as in solidity of the sound. But the character of such sound is absolutely new, and does not resemble any of the timbres heard up till now in our orchestras, with the sole exception of the bass-clarinet's lower E and F. The notes of the higher compass vibrate so intensively that they may be applied with success to melodic expression. Naturally, this instrument will never be suitable for rapid passages, for complicated arpeggios; but the bass instruments are not destined to execute light evolutions. Instead of complaining, we must rejoice that it is impossible to misuse the Saxophone and thus to destroy its majestic nature by forcing it to render mere musical futilities.*

If this full and enlightening description is to be taken literally, it points to an instrument resembling in pitch the modern bass saxophone, this being the only size capable of sounding a B-flat below the bass stave (discounting the contrabass which came much later).

Nowadays, all saxophones, whatever their pitch, are treated as transposing instruments reading from the treble stave, with a compass extending downwards to at least (written) B-flat. Illustrations of early saxophones in Kastner's *Manuel Général* show the lowest note to be B-natural only. If the first saxophone was an instrument built in C and Berlioz is correct, it must have been fitted with an extension to B-flat, the last semitone being omitted from later models only to be restored some years after Sax's death. On the other hand, it could have been built in B-flat with no extension downwards past its tonic note, as with the flute.

The stated range of three octaves is extraordinarily ambitious, especially for a bass instrument. The highest half octave is obtained by inducing the tube to yield higher harmonics by means of irregular fingering combinations, known as "fork" or "cross fingering", assisted by a developed degree of lip control. Although this register is nowadays being more and more utilized by advanced players, average saxophonists for many decades never attempted it. Sax himself later deleted the highest seven semitones from the officially claimed compass on account of their poor quality.

Despite Berlioz's lavish praise, Sax apparently took to heart the one implied criticism concerning the saxophone's inability to render rapid passages. Whilst this might well have been true for this primitive bass saxophone it need not apply to saxophones of a higher pitch.

A drawing attached to the 1846 patent, signed "Adolphe Sax", and dated 20th March 1846 depicts eight sizes of saxophones and an enlarged picture of a mouthpiece. No. 1 is described as "Tenor in E-flat" and looks surprisingly like a modern baritone saxophone. Saxophone No. 2 is a larger instrument in C or B-flat corresponding, in all probability, to the very first instrument made. Berlioz compares the saxophone to the ophicleide and, if any further proof is needed for this theory of derivation, it can be found in this drawing. This bass saxophone is obviously modelled directly on the ophicleide, with bell upermost.[11]

Nos. 3 and 4, respectively. "Contrabass in G or A-flat" and "Bourdon in C or B-flat" are also of ophicleide shape; Nos. 5, 6, 7 and 8 correspond to the B-flat tenor, E-flat alto, B-flat soprano (straight body but with a curved mouthpipe and E-flat sopranino. At the time of the patent, only nos. 1 and 2 had actually been made, the rest appear in the outline form only and it is doubtful that the two largest instruments were made at any time.

By 1847, Kastner was listing the family of saxophones as high soprano in F or E-flat, alto in E-flat, alto-tenor in B-flat, tenor— baritone in E-flat, bass in C or B-flat and contrabass in F or E-flat. Berlioz's list of 1856 does not mention the contrabass or the high soprano in F; otherwise the nomenclature conforms to modern usage: sopranino, soprano, alto, tenor, baritone and bass. These were pitched for orchestral use in F and C alternately, and for military purposes, in E-flat and B-flat.

The construction of the F — C range seems to belie assertions that Sax's idea for saxophones was due solely to an effort to find a link between the wood and brass of the military band. Rather it would seem that he was fully aware of the new tone-colour he had created and would have liked his instrument to be adopted into all kinds of musical ensembles. Could his life have been unnaturally prolonged, it is interesting to speculate how he would have reacted to its later staggering popularity.

'A perfect instrument. . .impossible to misuse. . .by forcing it to render mere musical futilities". Such words must have rung hollowly in the ears of many a staid musician when one particular type of aggregation took to the saxophone so enthusiastically in the 1920's.

Notes on Chapter II.
1. Pierre, C: *Les Facteurs*. p.348
2. Pontecoulant: *Organographie*, p.225.
3. Kastner, *Manuel général*, pp.246/7
4. F.G. Rendall in *The Saxophone Before Sax* suggests that Meikle's alto fagotto might be a later development of a "mysterious instrument" called the Caledonica mentioned in Dalyell's *Musical Memoirs of Scotland* (Edinburgh, 1849) but otherwise unknown. *(The Musical Times*, 1st. Dec. 1932. pp. 1007— 1079)
5. Fritz Rose, writing in *Signale*, August 15th, 1928 (reported in *The Musical Times*, November 1st. 1928) claimed to trace the saxophone back to the 17th. century, citing an instrument built by Dom Domencio del Mela (b.1683) as "the prototype of the modern saxophone". This was presumptuous. Examination of the instrument, No. 160 in the Museum of the Florence Conservatorium, shows it to be a bass clarinet.
6. Fétis: p.414
7. Lavoix, H: *Histoire de l'instrumentation, p. 127.*
8. Kastner: *Manuel général,* pp. 234/5.
9. Kochnitzky, p.10; Brenta, p.60 (footnote).
10. Fétis: p. 413; Kastner, p.230
11. See Appendix C.

Sax's close friend, Georges Kastner, published his
Method for the saxophone in the year of its patent.

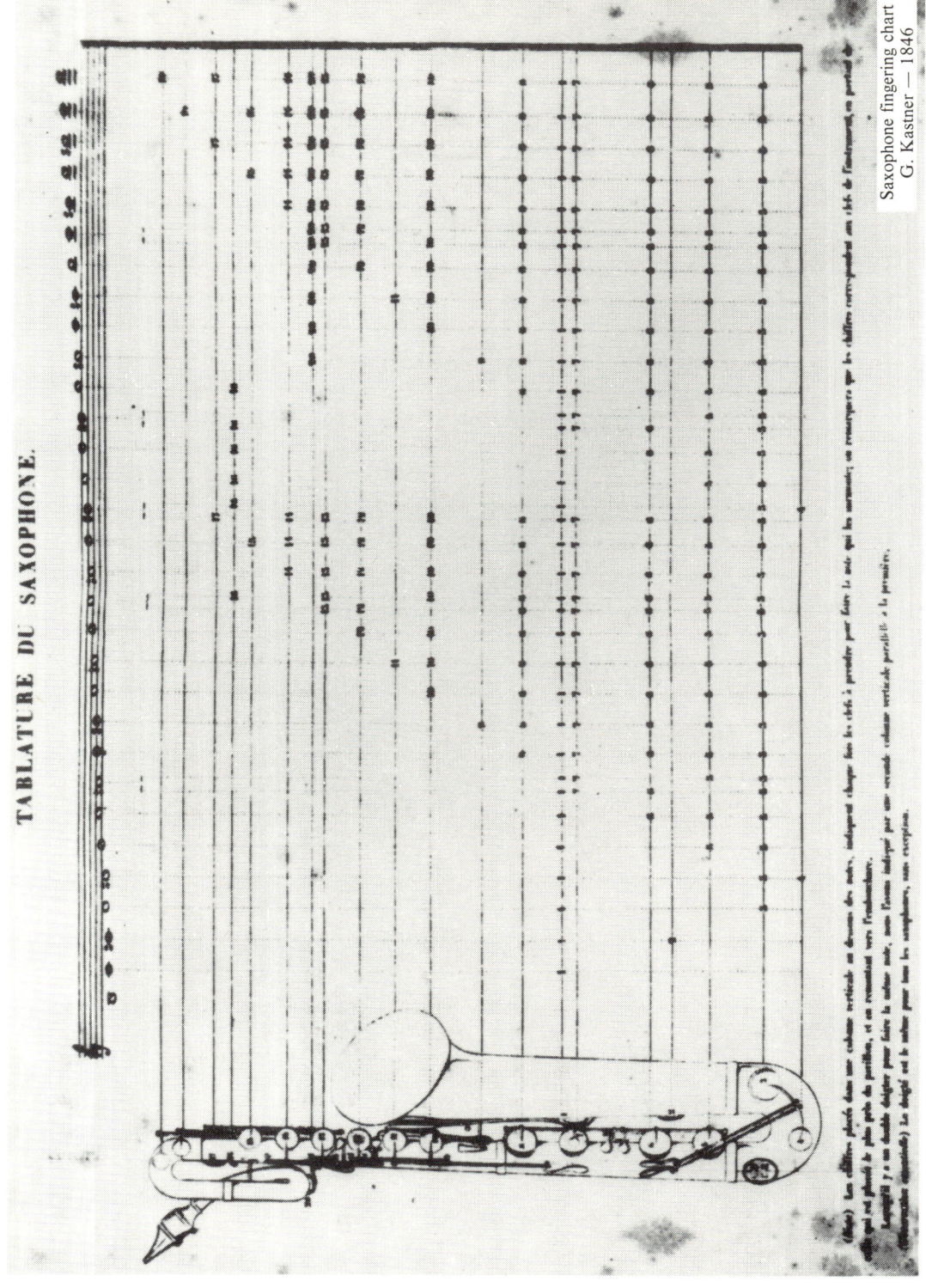

III
Paris

On his arrival in Paris in the Spring of 1841, Sax by his demeanour, could have had no inkling of the hornet's nest he was about to disturb. In spite of the fact that he had practically no material resources, he appears to have come to his chosen city without the slightest trace of humility, as if expecting, almost as a right, that the means by which he would make his name would be automatically put at his disposal. His greatest assets were, of course, the friends he had already made and as a first practical step towards getting established, it was towards these he naturally turned.

Hector Berlioz, at 38, was some eleven years older than Sax and shining brightly in the musical firmament. Larger than life in all that he did; his friendships, his enmities, his sayings and writings; nothing emphasised more his extravagant personality than his musical compositions. As a master of orchestration, he was most happy when writing for enormous forces. He and Sax had taken to each other from the start. They had much in common temperamentally. Both were romantic visionaries, liberal idealists with sweeping enthusiasms, quick to give and take offence, both with unbridled self confidence.

Berlioz was delighted to renew the aquaintance of three years before. Then he had been vastly impressed by the promise of the young inventor, the promise of new and dazzling tone colours, of technical innovations that would enable existing instruments to reflect more easily a composer's thoughts. Again Sax discoursed on his work, his ideas and aspirations. He demonstrated his instruments including his revised clarinet with a metal mouthpiece, his rich-toned bass clarinet and his experimental saxophone. The composer was deeply impressed. Their friendship was cemented for all time, a friendship which neither was ever to regret. As they parted, Berlioz made a cryptic remark: "Tomorrow, you will know just what I think of what you have just shown me."

As a writer of prose, Berlioz was no less adroit than with musical notation. For the past seven years he had written what had become a celebrated column in the influential, intellectual *Journal des Débats*. His views and opinions on the current musical scene reached a wide audience; the accolade of recognition was bestowed upon any young musician lucky enough to deserve a mention.

Perhaps Sax was aware of the point of Berlioz's words. The fulfilment of the promise must have elated the inventor beyond words. The next issue of *Débats*, on June 12th 1842, was headed "Adolphe Sax's Musical Instruments". After pointing to the progress made in the development of some instruments, particularly pianos and strings, he deplores the fact that the making of brass and woodwind had remained in a state of infancy.

"*But*", he goes on, "*today it has taken a road that cannot fail to lead it towards magnificent achievements. M. Adolphe Sax of Brussels, whose work we have examined, has without any doubt made a powerful contribution to the revolution which is about to take place. He is a man of far-seeing, clear-sighted intelligence, self-willed with a persevering spirit able to withstand all trials, enormously skilled, always ready to replace even specialist workmen who were unable to comprehend or carry out his plans. At the same time, he is a calculator, an expert in acoustics and when necessary, a smelter, a turner and embosser*".

The article goes on to describe in technical detail some of Sax's works, and then concludes "*Composers will be indebted to M. Sax when his new instruments are in general use*". If he perseveres, he will get the support of all friends of music".

Literally overnight, the name of an obscure Belgian instrument maker became known to anyone and everyone even remotely connected with the musical life of Paris. A public concert was arranged at the Conservatoire attended by most of the distinguished professors of that establishment. Auber, Halévy, Habeneck and Monnais were there, as, of course, was Berlioz.

The self possessed, handsome Sax stood before this august assembly, playing on and talking about his various instruments. Few, if any, other manufacturers could have put on such a show; his father's wisdom in ensuring his son had a playing proficiency equal to his craftsman's skill was apparent. Resounding applause was as much for the performance as for the novelties of construction. Friends and well-wishers gathered round. Lasting friendships were formed with Meyerbeer, Kastner, Fétis, Spontini Donizetti; the aristocratic, music-loving de Rumigny signified his pleasure and approval.

Yet, in the ensuing days, the hero of the occasion learned the brutal lesson that glory alone is not enough. Sax, who had taken temporary lodgings in the cheapest of apartments, simply had no source of income. His new found friends, influential as they were in musical circles, were not so affluent as to be of much practical help. For three days he went without food.[1] After such a triumph, this must have been a most depressing anti-climax. It was a situation Sax was to know many times in ensuing years.

All the same, behind the scenes strings were being pulled. At the point of lowest ebb, a visitor called at his rooms with an offer of 4,000 francs as a loan to enable an instrument factory to be set up. Sax gratefully accepted. When news of this act of faith got around, others, sensing a promising investment, followed suit. Eventually, a sum of about 12,000 francs was accumulated and the project began to become a possibility.

The money was little enough against the requirements of an instrument-maker's workshop. Since Sax was a worker in both wood and metal, many expensive specialist tools would be essential. Moulds, anvils, drills, mandrels, welding equipment, together with stocks of high quality brass sheeting and hardwood blocks — all must be acquired before a single instrument could be made. Then, to fashion the raw materials, skilled workmen must be engaged, trained and paid. At this time, unemployment was widespread. Recruitment of labour was nothing like the problem of training it to carry out intricate and accurate tasks.

Above all was the need for suitable premises. What can only be described as a dilapidated old shed, whose chief virtue was its cheapness, was located at No. 10 Rue Saint Georges. In this very down-to-earth quarter of Paris, the Adolphe Sax Musical Instrument Factory commenced in business.

We have noted already the jealousy with which established Parisian manufacturers guarded prerogatives. There were many long founded houses making musical wind instruments. Some made a speciality of a single instrument. Hardly any made both brass and woodwind. Many factories were just assembly points, or what today would be called production lines, for components made elsewhere. Bells would be made at one place, valves at another. Drilled wooden tubes, forged keywork, mouthpieces; every part had its own small specialist maker so that the manufacturer who eventually marketed the instrument did little more than fit the parts together and engrave his name on the bell.[2]

The system was inefficient inasmuch as there was no general standard of inspection and no instrument could be better than its worst component. But it did give employment to a maximum number of people and, in any case, it was the way the work had always been done.

Sax's ideas were the very antithesis of established practice. Laudable as were his aims in terms of efficiency, he made the first of many blunders in failing to anticipate the probable effects of his actions. He intended to produce each part of every instrument under his personal strict supervision so that any instrument bearing his name as an indication of its quality would have been wholly and completely made in the Sax workshop. Only in this way, he argued, could a consistently high standard be maintained.

"The illustrious Rossini takes M. Sax's trumpet to be a steam engine."

"The Musician for whom M. Sax has made his new trumpet"
Le Charivari, 21st October 1855

Even had he attempted this revolutionary procedure quietly and by stealth, opposition would surely have followed. As it was, Sax adopted a blatantly superior attitude right from the start, calculated, could he have but seen it, to extract the absolute maximum reaction from his competitors.

However much they were upset by this young prodigy from Brussels, existing makers could not help but be impressed by his initial impact. At first, they made apparently friendly overtures towards him. Their motives were most likely devious. They certainly were not pleased at anyone trying to intrude into their comfortable realm, but if this foreign upstart could command the respect of so many eminent musicians, they seemed to feel that it might be more profitable to associate with him. Sax either perceived their intentions or else was disdainful of their inefficient methods as against his own consummate skills. He would have nothing to do with them. He proceeded to set up his workshop careless of their vituperations and threats.

At a time when working hours were interminably long compared with today's standards, it is well to consider the stupendous efforts Sax must have made to achieve success. To make the business pay it would be essential to produce instruments for sale with the least possible delay. It is likely that some commissions were immediately forthcoming through the influence of his friends. His first tasks, then, would be to set the workshop to order and train his workmen. Steady routine production of this nature was vital in order to sustain the programme of experiments never far from his mind.

In an amazingly short time, the little factory was turning out a wide range of instruments, all under the vigilant eye of the proprietor. When his men had finally left for home at the end of a long day, their employer must often have worked well into the night testing theories, trying this and that in a quest for perfection. Valved bugles occupied much of the time and, of course, the instrument which was increasingly responding to development, the saxophone. On the 17th and 24th August 1843 he took out his first French patents, one for improvements to brass instruments, the other for woodwind, principally the clarinet.

Business prospered as the quality of workmanship became known. Orders poured in from musicians of all grades almost as fast as the rain from the leaky roof. The old shed soon became inadequate and had to be enlarged. In the autumn of 1842, Berlioz left for an extended tour of Germany. Impressed by the reconstructed military bands he heard, he, like de Rumigny, saw in Sax a means by which the glory of France would cease to be overshadowed by the military music of Prussia. A profuse letter writer, his correspondence published in *Débats* between August 1843 and January 1844 gives a clue to the activity and progress he had witnessed in the Rue Saint-Georges in a few short months.

From Stuttgart he cynically prophesies that *Paris will discover the cylinder valve trumpet ten years after everyone else has adopted it. The able instrument maker, Adolphe Sax, who has now settled in Paris, has conclusively demonstrated the superiority of his system (cylinder) over the piston method.*

At Dresden, Berlioz found much to admire in the military bands but suggested that regimental bandmasters *would do well to apply to our incomparable Adolphe Sax for a few clarinets.* Discussing, from Berlin, the merits of the tuba over the ophicleide, he is pleased to note that *Adolphe Sax now makes admirable tubas in Paris.*

The most enlightening comment of this period is contained in a letter dated October 8th 1843. This was addressed to the crippled composer and poetess, Louise Bertin and reveals that Berlioz kept well in touch with events in Paris even when far from home:

Adolphe Sax is now making rotary-valve trumpets, large and small in all possible keys, familiar and unfamiliar, instruments whose excellent tone quality and finished workmanship are indisputable. It is scarcely to be believed that this gifted young artist should be finding it difficult to maintain his position and make a career in Paris. The persecutions he suffers are worthy of the Middle Ages and recall the antics of the enemies of Benvenuto, the Florentine sculptor. They lure away his workmen, steal his designs, accuse him of insanity and bring legal proceedings against him. Such is the hatred inventors inspire in rivals who are incapable of inventing anything themselves. Fortunately he has been able to count on the protection and friendship of General de Rumigny and until now this has helped to endure the sordid struggle. But how much longer will it suffice? It ought to be the Minister of War's responsibility to see that a man of such rare and useful accomplishments is given the position his ability and exertions entitle him to. Our military bands are still without either rotary valve trumpets or bass tubas. If French military music is to achieve the standard of Prussian and Austrian, we will have to manufacture these instruments. A government order to Adolphe Sax for 300 trumpets and 100 bass tubas would be the salvation of him.[3]

Such was the situation which had developed in a few short months of Sax commencing business. There is no doubt that established manufacturers would have made life difficult for anyone attempting to enter their tight circle unbidden. In this particular case, and whatever they said in public, they must have been uneasy at the extent of the intruder's skill and his evident influence in high places. His arrogant disdain did nothing to ease their fears. They felt their very existence to be threatened; they hit back viciously in self preservation.

One of the first to feel the power of the established manufacturers was Gaetano Donizetti. Like most composers who had examined Sax's work, he was entranced and enthused. His opera, *Don Sebastian*, was in preparation and he wrote into the orchestration a special part with the Sax bass clarinet in mind. This was reckoning without the orchestral musicians. Many of the foremost instrumentalists had close ties with certain manufacturers receiving fees as consultants or advisers and, in some cases, as owners or partners. Consequently, both had an interest in blocking Sax; no player would agree to perform on a Sax instrument. They claimed that these were faulty.

Characteristically, Sax immediately challenged the loudest mouthed critic, Buteux, the principal clarinet of the Opera orchestra. He defied this gentleman to play certain music on his clarinet which Sax would perform with ease on his. The challenge was not taken up. Instead, it brought from the orchestra the threat that, if the inventor attempted, as he had suggested, to take a place in the orchestra and play the part himself, the musicians would walk out *en masse*.

The desperate Donizetti, for all his regard for Sax, could not see the production of his opera placed in jeopardy. He was compelled to acquiesce. The opera was duly given in November 1843 without Sax's bass clarinet. Although an apparent defeat, Sax got a great deal of favourable publicity from the incident. The matter was taken up indignantly by Parisian composers and widely reported in the press. Sax himself wrote a letter for the *Gazette des Théâtres* on November 3rd 1843:

M. Buteux, who is the first clarinettist of the opera, announces in the letter which you have just published that he has tried out my bass clarinet at two rehearsals and, because this instrument did not respond in a manner which he expected, he found himself obliged to make use of another. I have only a few words to reply to M. Buteux. If he finds my instrument bad, that is his right. But I recall to him that he has not always held this opinion, because at my house in the presence of more than fifty people, he himself, in making the comparison of the instrument which he is playing today with mine, on several occasions, found that the last one, i.e., mine was very much superior to the former.

M. Buteux says that he has twice tried my instrument in rehearsals. This is wrong. I do not know what he had in mind in making such an error. Because it is easy to deny today what happened on a private occasion, I offer M. Buteux the chance of having the question decided by that great judge, the public. After this, everything will be said and done.

I therefore propose to M. Buteux, the first clarinettist of the Opéra to choose whatever piece of music he likes and to play it on his instrument. I will play the same thing on mine and we will play this to the public.

If the comparison which can be made between his instrument and mine is not to my advantage, I will declare myself defeated. I further offer to play on my bass clarinet a piece which I defy M. Buteux, the first clarinettist of the Royal Academy of Music, to play on his own.[4]

Although such opposition retarded the acceptance of Sax's instrument in Paris, its superiority could not be for long suppressed. It was later taken up by E. Duprez and used with great effect in *Les Huguenots* and *Le Prophète* of Meyerbeer.

It was likely that the large order for instruments as recommended by Berlioz would have been more of an embarrassment than salvation to Sax at this time. Due to the activities of his enemies, the maker was having great difficulty in keeping production going. He would painstakingly train workmen to his own high standard, only to have them enticed away by bribes and offers of better pay. There was nothing in the nature of formal notice to leave. Rather, the most difficult moments were carefully chosen so that the proprietor, on returning from a business call in another part of the city, would find his house and workshops completely abandoned and left to the mercy of the intruder.

On many occasions, the premises were broken into, expensive tools stolen. furniture wrecked and, worst of all, plans and models, the product of countless hours of patient research, damaged or taken away.

Despite all of this, the man resignedly set out to make good the losses and, by perseverance and hard work, keep and enhance his reputation. Seeing that physical loss was no deterrent, his enemies switched, with better effect, their tactics to commercial matters. On the one hand they saw to it that he was, in certain quarters, refused the normal terms of credit for necessary raw materials; on the other, they harrassed him for breach of contract immediately he was not able to honour a delivery date. Thus many orders had to be turned away, there being no hope of fulfilling them within the time stipulated.

When Berlioz wrote about Sax's persecution, this had at least stopped short of attempted assassination. Now it would appear that there were some who were prepared to go this step further. Attacks on the person of the inventor were mounted, diabolical conceptions like the incendiary device designed to roast him alive in bed, salvation being due to too short a fuse causing a premature outburst. On another occasion, an ambush was carefully laid which seems to have been for no other purpose than murder. He escaped from a tight spot by keeping a cool head and showing a disconcertingly brave front to his attackers.

Another attempt in 1845 had a most tragic outcome and involved one of Sax's loyal and trusted employees who had occasion to come back to the inventor's residence after midnight. This call was quite out of the ordinary and was to lead the unsuspecting caller to his death. As he stood at the door awaiting a reply to his knock, a figure emerged from the shadows, stabbed him through the heart and disappeared into the night.

At the inquest it was shown that robbery was not the motive for the killing, neither was anything in the nature of a personal feud to be implied. In fact, the man had led an upright and inoffensive life to exclude motive of revenge or spite. The significant thing to emerge was that Sax was not at home when his employee called; he had been detained on business and arrived home not long after the crime had been commited. The two men corresponded closely in build; there seemed little doubt that Sax's life had been spared at the expense of his innocent servant.[5]

The murder had a sobering effect on the opposition. After it, Sax went about in less fear of his life although the war raged with undiminished fury with the various Courts as battlegrounds.

A clerk and a book-keeper on Sax's staff were induced to pass out vital information regarding the exact state of his finances. At the most inauspicious moment, existing creditors began to press hard for settlement so that ruin suddenly faced him.

Amid a desperate situation, another sledgehammer blow fell. Sax was swindled out of 4,000 francs in a way, if one considers the naive way in which Comettant[6] relates the episode, which seems to reflect badly on the sense, both business and common, of the victim.

It would appear that a well-dressed gentleman called at the workshop. His prepossessing manner and pleasant talk engaged Sax. The man said how much he admired the inventor's work and offered a loan secured on the factory's effects and equipment. This was thankfully agreed and a debenture pledging property to the value of 4,000 francs was signed on the spot. The visitor invited Sax to accompany him to the bank to get the money. On the way, taking advantage of cover afforded by congested traffic, he slipped away taking with him the valuable document. Not only did Sax not get the money; he was placed in a position of having to find 4,000 francs in order to redeem the debenture. A court order distraining his goods and property was imminently awaited.

The effect of these evil acts on the business-naive instrument maker was catastrophic, Rather than face the dishonour of bankruptcy he contemplated suicide. Many friends stood by him but their help in terms of ready cash did not amount to much. Salvation was forthcoming from his most formidable supporter. General de Rumigny had taken to calling at Sax's workshop from time to time, attending the little concerts which were put on to stimulate interest. The General's first good impressions were upheld. Realising himself to be a musical amateur, he was prudent enough to seek the opinions of notable musicians. Reinforced by the praise heaped upon Sax's products by composers and conductors, the General was determined that the little manufacturer should not be driven out of business by the machinations of unscrupulous rivals. He put the difficulties before Queen Marie-Amélie, wife of Louis-Phillipe, who found the money to pay off Sax's creditors. The solicitude and comfort afforded by these great people must have meant as much to Sax as the financial help. The crisis was contained; the workshop was soon again working to capacity and prospects looked brighter. A petition bearing the signatures of sixty high-ranking Belgians then living in Paris, together with those of many foremost French musicians, was sent to the King of the Belgians. This begged the King to install his distinguished countryman as a Knight of the Order of Leopold.

The antipathy of executive musicians was not entire. A few, including some outstanding players, were friendly to Sax and interested in his work. It was these who would gather at the Rue Saint-Georges workshop to perform music in company with the inventor. An ever growing collection of musical instruments was displayed; Sax would discourse upon them together with his own manufactures and the small group would demonstrate the effect. The lectures were not confined to merely pointing out the advantages or disadvantages of this over that. They covered the theory of sound as applied to wind instruments bringing in the experience and discoveries of father and son over the years.

In consequence, the audience extended beyond the musician. Scientists, writers, government officials up to ministers and diplomats found something of interest. To have such an assembly hanging on his words must have been compensation enough to Sax for all his troubles. It seemed to be the salt of life to him; a fortune was nothing by comparison. The lecture-concerts were of a practical value to the inventor since they received detailed and eulogistic coverage in the press.

At the Paris Industrial Exibition of 1844, despite the high opinion of the jury, Sax received only the silver medal. His display included valved bugles, described as "Sax Horns" (the term "Sax Bugles" having been discarded, so Brenta tells us, because of the association with the currently inefficient bugle). In addition, this Exhibition saw the first public showing of the saxophone.

For the purpose of demonstration, Sax played to the jury on an instrument they thought to be a bass clarinet but which, in reality, was a tenor saxophone. Members of the panel, which included Daniel Auber, the eminent composer, were enraptured by the novel construction. But, according to Comettant, it was Habeneck, the early supporter of Sax, who on this occasion struck a note of discord. He hinted that the invention was made to appear better than it really was because of the excellence of the player, declaring, "He will play just as well on a broomstick".

Sax was clearly offended. He placed his prowess as an inventor far above that of instrumentalist. "If you praise me as a player rather than an inventor", he said with dignity, "and as here only invention is important, then I shall withdraw. I came only because I could find nobody able or willing to play the instrument". Habeneck apparently had the grace to admit that this was so.

The citation accompanying the silver medal, and addressed to *Sax et Cie, Paris,* states:
These artists are the inventors of a bass clarinet which they have called "saxophone"; it is

outstanding in its clearness and beauty of sound. This instrument could have a permanent place in our orchestras, giving new effects.

The saxophone was played consecutively with Raoux's valveless horn, in the making of which, the method of beating the brass lightly with a hammer was highly praised. Comettant suggests that the order for first and second prizes was inadvertently reversed but there was no reason to doubt that the jury's intentions were properly realised. Mariel Auguste Raoux represented a family which had been making French horns of unsurpassed design and quality for nearly two hundred years. He won another gold medal in 1849 and was the first brass instrument maker to be made a Chevalier of the Legion of Honour. A vehement opponent of Sax, he become so disgusted with the unsuccessful outcome of ruinous litigation that, in 1857, he sold out the ancient family business.

Perhaps there is an element of retributive justice in the dissolution of the House of Raoux. When Sax was in the process of forming a registered company whose shares were on offer to the public, rival manufacturers, with whom Raoux was associated, got to work on undermining the morale of shareholders. Comettant tells how individual shareholders would be invited to dinner, plied with good food and wine, during which the conversation would turn apparently by chance to the subject of the new Sax company. Derisory remarks concerning "stupid people who exchanged good money for bad trumpets" would be made; clever inuendos like, "In the hands of the clever Sax, brass doesn't turn to gold, but gold to brass", and "What good are the shares? After finishing an instrument the result is nothing but wind".

From the disquiet thus engendered, an emergency meeting of shareholders was held at the *Café du Passage de l'Opéra* at which the cry went round, "Who wants shares in the Sax company at half price?". This was duly reported in the press with the result that the value of the shares fell well below their original value. Had it not been for 20,000 francs advanced by his friend, the painter Gudin, Sax would have been faced with a huge deficit for advertising and preliminary expenses in connection with the share issue.

An important visitor to the workshop concerts at this time was Rossini. At 52, the Italian master had virtually retired as a composer, content to rest his reputation on a host of masterpieces written in earlier years. His use of rich sonorous effects in the orchestra had given rise to adverse comment from, of all people, Berlioz, who complained about his noisiness. It was many years later that Rossini was able to return the charge. His *Petite Messe Solenelle* was scored for only three instruments; two pianos and a harmonium. When urged to orchestrate it, he eventually agreed feeling that, if he did not do the job himself, posterity might give it over to Sax and his saxophones or Berlioz with a monstrous modern orchestra.

Rossini was an intimate friend of the composer Michele Carafa who suffered in his time humiliation at the hands of both Sax and Berlioz. Despite this, and his objection to the possible use of the saxophone in his Mass, he was greatly entranced with the instrument saying, when he visited the Rue Saint-Georges, that it was the most beautiful sound he had ever heard. On returning home, he communicated with Sax through his friend the clarinettist Liverani, and was the means of having Sax's instruments adopted by the Bologna Conservatory. His *La Corona d'Italia*, composed for military band in 1868 and offered to King Victor Emanuel II, included specific parts for Sax's instruments, which were lavishly praised. Saxophones were ordered from Paris for its first performance. At the composer's funeral, a band composed entirely of Sax's instruments, played Gevaert's arrangement of Beethoven's Funeral March as the priest gave the final absolution.

Honour for giving the saxophone its first public showing in a major work goes to Sax's friend and supporter, Jean Georges Kastner. His opera, *Le Dernier Roi de Juda*, was given at the Paris Conservatoire in concert form on 1st December 1844 with a saxophone included in the score. There is no suggestion that he had any difficulty in recruiting players, showing that the opposition to the maker was by no means universal.

However, this was not the first time the new instrument had been heard in public. Much earlier in the same year, Berlioz realised an idea of putting on a concert during which some of Sax's instruments would be introduced. In fact, this would be taking an item from the Rue

Saint-Georges informal concerts and placing it in a larger setting. A curious thing about Berlioz, an arch-champion of Sax and always loud in praise of his work; the actual use of Sax's instruments in his works is minimal. There was a small part for saxhorns in the original version of "The Trojans"; nothing for saxophones anywhere. That he once intended to use them in an opera is evident from his autograph score of "The Damnation of Faust" (1846). There are two staves left blank at the beginning of the last movement, the "Ciel Scene", intended for E-flat and B-flat saxophones, presumably alto and tenor. Why these were not finally included is a mystery. In listing a theoretically ideal orchestra of 467, Berlioz provides for five saxophones but no saxhorns.

The concert given at the *Salle Herz* on February 3rd[7] 1844 provides one of those hilarious episodes with which, at times, Sax was unwittingly involved. A basically serious man, he was not without a certain sense of humour. Rank-and-file musicians the world over are noted for the banter and leg-pulling which goes on in the company. Their happenings on that night must have given rise to a good deal of chaff at Sax's expense for some time after.

For the purpose of demonstrating the instruments, Berlioz arranged a simple choral piece of his own which he had composed some fifteen years previously. It was scored for six instruments; three brass and three reed. The former group was played by Dauverne, one of two brother trumpeters in the Opera orchestra; Dufresne, a popular cornet soloist at the musical concerts and Jean Baptiste Arban. The last named was a particularly close associate of Sax, then, as a young man, on the threshold of a brilliant career which was to make his a legendary name in the annals of cornet playing. The reed instruments were played by Messrs. Leperd and Duprez with Sax himself rendering the bass line on the saxophone. [8]

Rehearsals, under the direction of Berlioz, took place at Sax's establishment. On the day of the concert, the saxophone was far from being ready and Sax had to work well into the evening getting it into a reasonably playable state. Certain keys were secured with string and liberal doses of sealing wax were applied to maintain air-tightness. It was after nine o'clock in the evening when all the performers were assembled and the audience was beginning to grow restive, that Sax arrived clutching his saxophone. Musicians and listeners settled expectantly.

The sextet's performance opened with a loud *tutti* chord. Then, in the words of Comettant:
. . . each player in turn played a beautifully executed passage, showing off the advantages of the instrument he was playing. The last and most important passage was given to the saxophone. There was a note held in the middle of the final passage. Sax played this note in the drawn-out fashion, making it rise and fall and giving it every possible nuance. He had forgotten the fingering of the note following and it was to gain time that he prolonged the note. At last, his memory returned but he was now out of breath. The passage came to an end amid loud applause from the hall who saw in this extended and beautifully modulated sound the proof of good taste and happy inspiration on the part of the player.

In fact, every second of that held note must have been a nightmare to the breathless Sax. Comettant's assertion that he had forgotten the fingering of his saxophone does seem, on the face of it, most unlikely. The inventor was an outstanding performer on the clarinet and the fingering of keyed instruments would be intuitive for him, even allowing for some deficiencies in the makeshift instrument he was playing. It seems more likely that the temporary attachments and seals made with the string and sealing wax were not equal to the strain of actual usage; he may well have held the note while struggling with his spare hand to rectify the fault.

It may be further conjectured that Sax would be much averse to letting the fact that his new instrument leaked becoming generally known. Of the two evils, the stigma of him, an accomplished instrumentalist, forgetting fingering was the lesser. The concert had been well attended by many who did not wish the inventor well. To have stopped playing, explained the difficulty and craved the audience's kind indulgence in circumstances which today would probably bring a burst of sympathetic applause, would then have played right into the hands of his enemies. They would have been quick to exploit the supposed failure and inefficiency of his work. As it was, a cool head and capacious lungs turned potential disaster into triumph.

A brass band equipped with Sax's instruments in a Brussels bandstand

The Distin Family Brass Quintet played Sax's first saxhorns
George, Henry, John, Theodore, William

Symbolic, perhaps, of the way in which the saxophone has struggled against circumstances for decades until only now is it beginning to get a just recognition and evaluation from all branches of the musical fraternity.

Notes on Chapter III
1. *Fétis*, p.415
2. *ibid.*
3. Extracts from Berlioz's correspondence from *The Memoirs of Berlioz*, trans. David Cairns, pp. 336, 372, 380, 409, 495.
4. Comettant, p.25.
5. Brenta, p.66.
6. Comettant, pp.63-66.
7. *ibid.,* p.52.
8. See Appendix A.

Cover of the Revue, "La Musique des Familles"
21st September 1889

IV
The Distin Family

Early in 1844, a meeting took place in Paris which was to have lasting repercussions; not only on those directly involved, but on the musical scene much further afield, particularly in Great Britain. The fortuitous encounter of Sax with the Distin family[1] is tinted according to the differing viewpoints. Each of the two main parties felt the other to be in his debt. The fact remains that both did rather well out of the association.

The story really begins in 1814 when 16-year-old John Distin, joined the Grenadier Guards as a key-bugler. He had already made a name in the South Devon Militia playing the slide-trumpet; two years previously he had played solo trumpet in Handel's *Dettingen Te Deum* at the Exeter Festival.

With the Guards he was a distinguished soloist, using John Halliday's keyed-bugle-horn. At Distin's suggestion, the inventor added a sixth key; later the instrumentalist initiated the addition of two shake keys to facilitate playing in the Italian *coloratura* style.

After Waterloo, the Grenadiers went to France as part of the Army of Occupation. Distin's playing was particularly noticed by the Grand Duke Constantine of Russia who requested a copy of what was to him a new instrument, to take home. There being no time to send to England, a French maker, Jean Halary-Asté, was commissioned to make a replica. His work was apparently to the satisfaction of all; not least his own. Some years afterwards, he brought out his own brand of keyed brass instruments of which the ophicleide became the most celebrated.

On leaving the Guards, John Distin became a member of King George IV's Household Band. The King was personally interested in his musicians and on one occasion is known to have enquired after Distin when the trumpeter had to miss a performance because of lip trouble. Later on, Distin took charge of the band in the service of the Marquis of Breadalbane. As a slide-trumpeter, John Distin was judged second only to the great Thomas Harper. He was in demand at important music festivals and was first trumpet in the orchestra at the coronation of Queen Victoria while Harper was placed in the gallery to play fanfares.

When Distin was 39, married to a lady who played the piano and bore him four sons, he again came to public notice. His greatest asset was his fame as a brass player; it was natural that his children would want, and be encouraged, to copy their famous father. Two of the boys, when aged about nine or ten, had attracted attention with their horn playing. In 1837, when the boys' ages ranged between 12 and 19, they appeared in Scotland as a brass quintet. The instrumentation was a slide-trumpet, a trombone and three hand-horns, accompanied by Mrs. Distin at the piano with their 5-year-old sister as a singer.

Taking into account the universal appeal of youthful performers and their undoubted proficiency commensurate with their years, their success was assured. They toured Scotland, England and Ireland as a miniature brass band to the acclaim of press and public alike. Their repertoire of popular-music arrangements included a selection from Bellini's *Norma*. In London, they received engagements for series of daily concerts in leading concert rooms and an appearance at the Drury Lane Theatre. By 1844, after seven years of touring the British Isles, John Distin felt it was time to try his family's fortunes abroad. The early part of the year found them in Paris and about to make the acquaintance of Adolphe Sax.

At this point, accounts handed down to us become biased according to the viewpoint. Not that there was any acrimony. On the contrary, Sax and the Distins seem to have got on very well. The trouble was that Sax's supporters felt that they had to exploit any situation to his advantage even if absolute veracity had sometimes to be sacrificed. Their attitude was bound to arouse resentment on the other side so that we must look on both versions with a degree of reserve.

According to Comettant,[2] the Distins had fared badly on their Continental concert tour. Audiences had been vociferous in their disapproval; cat-calls and laughter greeted them wherever they went, so that the family was having difficulties in getting further engagements. At an audition for the Vivienne concerts they apparently failed completely, the failure being due to their inferior instruments: a slide trumpet played by John Distin, with the four sons on a cornet, a slide trombone in D-flat, a key-bugle and a French horn.

On February 3rd the quintet were present at the *Salle Herz* where for the first time they heard the saxhorn. Next morning they could not wait to present themselves at the Rue Saint-Georges workshop and the fateful meeting took place.

Comettant continues: *They had not the skill necessary to make the combination a good ensemble. Sax began by reforming their inferior instruments. He replaced them by five new instruments. Then, one by one, he made them play and showed them the nuances in a few bars from* Robert le Diable *arranged for five instruments. Having given them their first lesson he made them play together.* So great was the improvement by this homogeneous group of instruments that John Distin cried, "We are saved" and embraced Sax "in a transport of joy".

From that day their success was assured. Berlioz had them for a concert at the *Opéra Comique* where they played a full selection from Meyerbeer's *Robert le Diable* on their saxhorns. So well was this received that immediate engagements for the famous Conservatoire concerts followed during which they received medals. At the Paris Exhibition of the year they delighted King Louise-Phillippe who spoke to them in English and paid them handsomely when they played before the Royal Family at the Tuileries. From fiasco to fame . . . all due to Sax's instruments. Such was the view of the Saxophiles.

Events as seen from the Distin side have a rather different complexion. According to Henry Distin,[3] one of the sons, writing from Philadelphia in his 77th year,[4] he first heard the saxhorn at a "grand concert given by a famous singer" when the family quintet were also on the bill. As a brass instrumentalist, Henry immediately saw the possibilities of the instrument and, on being told that it had been made by "a little manufacturer", paid an early visit to the workshop next morning. Here he found Sax, sleeves rolled up, supervising busily his workmen. He discovered that Sax had then only made three saxhorns which he describes as an E-flat soprano, a B-flat contralto and an E-flat alto. A loan of these was arranged and the Distin family spent the afternoon in their hotel room trying them out The verdict was unanimously enthusiastic.

Sax was sent for. He listened to their playing and eagerly agreed to make certain alterations at the Distins' suggestions. He further agreed to immediately make five new instruments for the quintet who continued to give concerts in and around Paris until the order was complete. Then, after much hard practice, they brought out the instruments in public at the *Opéra Comique* concert as "Adolphe Sax's grand new invention, Sax horns". From here the account of the success of the family and the instruments roughly coincides with that of Sax's supporters.

It will be noticed that there is no hint of the party's alleged disasters in Belgium and France; the whole tone conveys the impression that Sax was delighted — even flattered — by the Distin's interest. He appears eager and almost servile in his efforts to please. John Distin declared that, not only was his quintet the first to introduce saxhorns in Paris, it did much to complete the family of saxhorns by assisting in the perfection of the tenor and bass instruments. He also claimed that "without egotism, we were the making of M. Sax's name as a manufacturer". Even the name "saxhorn" was given at the Distins' insistence whereas Sax had previously called his instruments *bugles-à-cylindres*.

The exact truth, of course, may never be known. We can but pick out the possibilities bearing in mind not only the partisan colouring but the obvious memory failure of Henry Distin fifty-two years after the event. The latter point is emphasised by examination of a large lithograph by Baugniet which shows the Distins with *four* saxhorns, an E-flat soprano played by father John, Henry holding a B-flat contralto, Theodore with an E-flat tenor and George who has a B-flat baritone. The first three seem to be the ones Sax had already made before meeting the Distins. The last was made while the family waited. The fifth instrument, in the hands of William, although probably made by Sax, is in fact a German or Austrian flugel horn.

The two sides are clearly at variance as to where the Distins first heard the Saxhorn played. If, as Comettant suggests, it was at the *Salle Herz* concert on February 3rd they would have known the maker to be present on the platform playing his prototype saxophone. It is clear that the Distin family were not present as performers in the Berlioz programme. Henry Distin says that they were engaged to play at a concert where they first heard the saxhorn and that he gained the name and address of the maker from his French companion. He does not even hint that Sax was there in person.

Then there is the question of the lesson in saxhorn technique. Had the Distins and Sax both been on the same bill it would appear to be superfluous to want to hear them again the next day. The idea of the Distins taking these strange instruments and, after the briefest of explanations, transforming themselves into a sparkling ensemble smacks too much of romantic fiction. That they should practice assiduously in their hotel room for several hours before asking Sax to hear them is much more convincing.

We cannot be sure of the exact date on which Baugniet's lithograph was drawn (it was published in London in July 1845). It may have been done for publicity purposes about the time of the *Opéra Comique* concert in April. If so, it is not unreasonable to infer that the instruments illustrated are actually the three prototypes, and the further instrument was all that Sax was able to make in the time available. The presence of a "non-saxhorn" would imply that Sax did not have time to construct a fifth instrument of the family pattern. This apparently renders inaccurate the statement that Sax made five saxhorns expecially for the Distins in time for the *Opéra Comique* concert although he could, of course, have done so by a later date.[5]

John Distin's claim that "saxhorn" was a name contrived by his family is contradicted in Henry Distin's Philadelphia letter where he specifically states that the name appeared on the printed programme at the concert where he first heard the instrument.

It is doubtful that the Distins were as much of a failure prior to their introduction to the saxhorn as was made out. Although not uncommon for an artist to be a success in one country and a failure in another it hardly seems likely that a simple party of brass instrumentalists should be acclaimed in England and derided just across the Channel. Further, after seven years of professional playing, it surely must be supposed that they had had the wit to provide themselves with efficient instruments. If Sax was prepared to allow the family to take away on loan the only three exisiting specimens of his new instrument he must have known of them previously and been satisfied with their integrity and ability. In 1846, Meyerbeer was so moved by their performance that he wrote to them praising "the noble style of their delivery and their ensemble" together with "the great mastership of their production." Such musicianship could hardly have been taught to them by Sax, least of all in one lesson.

The Distins' oft-repeated statement that their "silver saxhorns" had been presented to them personally by the King of the French is open to doubt. If pure invention is to be ruled out it may be that the mere handling of the instruments by the interested Louis-Philippe on the occasion that the five played to the Royal Family was gilded into a "presentation".

Sax had a nose for publicity. There is no doubt that he quickly perceived the wisdom of co-operating with the Distins. In those days of slow communications, what better advertising was there than this famous group who drew the crowds and who would, by so doing, publicise the saxhorn and its maker wherever they went? Sax organised a number of auditions for this very purpose and later engaged the family particularly to go to Germany in order to make his instruments known there. It is not known how much the Distins paid Sax for his work. If he gave them the instruments gratis he could have written off the cost as advertising without a qualm. For so it turned out; the Distins with their saxhorns went from triumph to triumph.

After playing in and around Paris for several months, the family, towards the end of 1844, returned to England. They were fêted by press and public wherever they went.

Commemoration china jugs were made, incorporating bass-reliefs of the family with their instruments. On December 3rd 1844 they played at a Jullien Promenade Concert at Covent Garden. Following the concert, an exchange of letters took place in the columns of the "Musical World" which it is as well to quote in full as they throw light on some interesting details not noted in any other source.

A "Foreign Visitor Resident in London" wrote:[6]

"When the Distin family a short time since were engaged to play at the concerts of M. Jullien, they announced their performance for the first time on instruments which had been presented to them by his Majesty King Louis-Philippe. It appears to me that as a mere matter of justice, the Messrs. Distin should have the public know that the instruments called Saxhorns *on which they were about to play, were the invention of M. Sax, by whose influence they (the Messrs. Distin) were enabled to perform before the King of the French, who presented them with five hundred francs for their pains. One of these instruments (Saxhorns) was offered in person by M. Sax to his Royal Highness Prince Albert who honoured M. Sax by accepting it. These things should be made known, in justice to an artist of very great talent, and most unpretending manners".*

John Distin, writing from No. 6 Foley Place, Great Portland Street, was quick to reply:[7]

"When we were engaged by M. Jullien to perform at Covent Garden we particularly requested M. Sax's name to be mentioned and to call the instruments "Saxhorns". *(the name which we gave them, as M. Sax thought of calling them cylinder Bugles). But the party who had the arrangement of these concerts said* the name of Saxhorns should be omitted, *as they had already (previous to our visit to London) been played by some parties at the Adelaide Gallery, and proved a failure. It will be seen that it was* not *by our wish that the name of Sax was left out of* **these bills, we never on any occasion omitted his name in our concert bills. As regards the Saxhorn** *presented by M. Sax to His Royal Highness Prince Albert, which the "Foreign Artist Resident in London" describes as "one of the* same *instruments", he is in error; as we have* seen *and* tried *it at Windsor Castle. It has* not *the same mechanism but is a very old German or Italian invention, called the "Double Cylinder" but*[8] *manufactured by M. Sax. We were the first who successfully introduced these instruments to the public in Paris — we played at all the principal concerts throughout the season. During this time we assisted and perfected the tenor and bass instruments, making the set complete; and performed at the great concert of M. Berlioz at the* Opéra Comique *and received the* only *encore during the concert. As a* proof *of our success we were presented with a silver medal by the "Conservatoire Royal de Musique" and "Society of Fine Arts"; and; without egotism, we were* the making of M. Sax's *name as a manufacturer. We performed before His Majesty King Louis Philippe through the interest of General de Rumigny. His Majesty conversed with us for some time and said, "I am delighted with your performance; I never expected to hear such beautiful sounds from such instruments. I return you my best thanks for the pleasure you have afforded me.* Are the instruments of English manufacture? We answered, "No, your Majesty; they are the invention of M. Sax" *— at the same time turning around and introducing M. Sax to His Majesty instead of M. Sax introducing us to him as the "Foreign* **Visitor Resident in London" asserts. The King certainly did, as is stated, send us a present of 500** *francs, and to M. Sax a considerable sum, as we understood, to reimburse him for the instruments. It is our intention to do every justice to M. Sax".*

Sax had preceded the Distins to London where, with musicians Laurent (who was leader), Arban and Dubois, he played on October 14th 1844 at the Royal Adelaide Gallery in the Strand. After a few performances, the "Sax Horn band", as it was billed, became disillusioned with the quality of the concerts and returned to Paris. The identity of the "Foreign Visitor" remains an intriguing mystery. Again some reserve is desirable in reading John Distin's reply. Since it was de Rumigny, *aide-de-camp* to Louis-Philippe, who arranged for the party to play before the King, it seems unlikely that His Majesty would not already have been told about the instruments and who was their inventor. Distin seems to be suggesting that the King actually paid Sax for the instruments the inventor had made for the Distin family. A further mystery is the peculiar instrument presented to Prince Albert which, according to the letter, seems to have been a kind of Flugel horn fitted with double-tube Vienna valves similar to the instrument

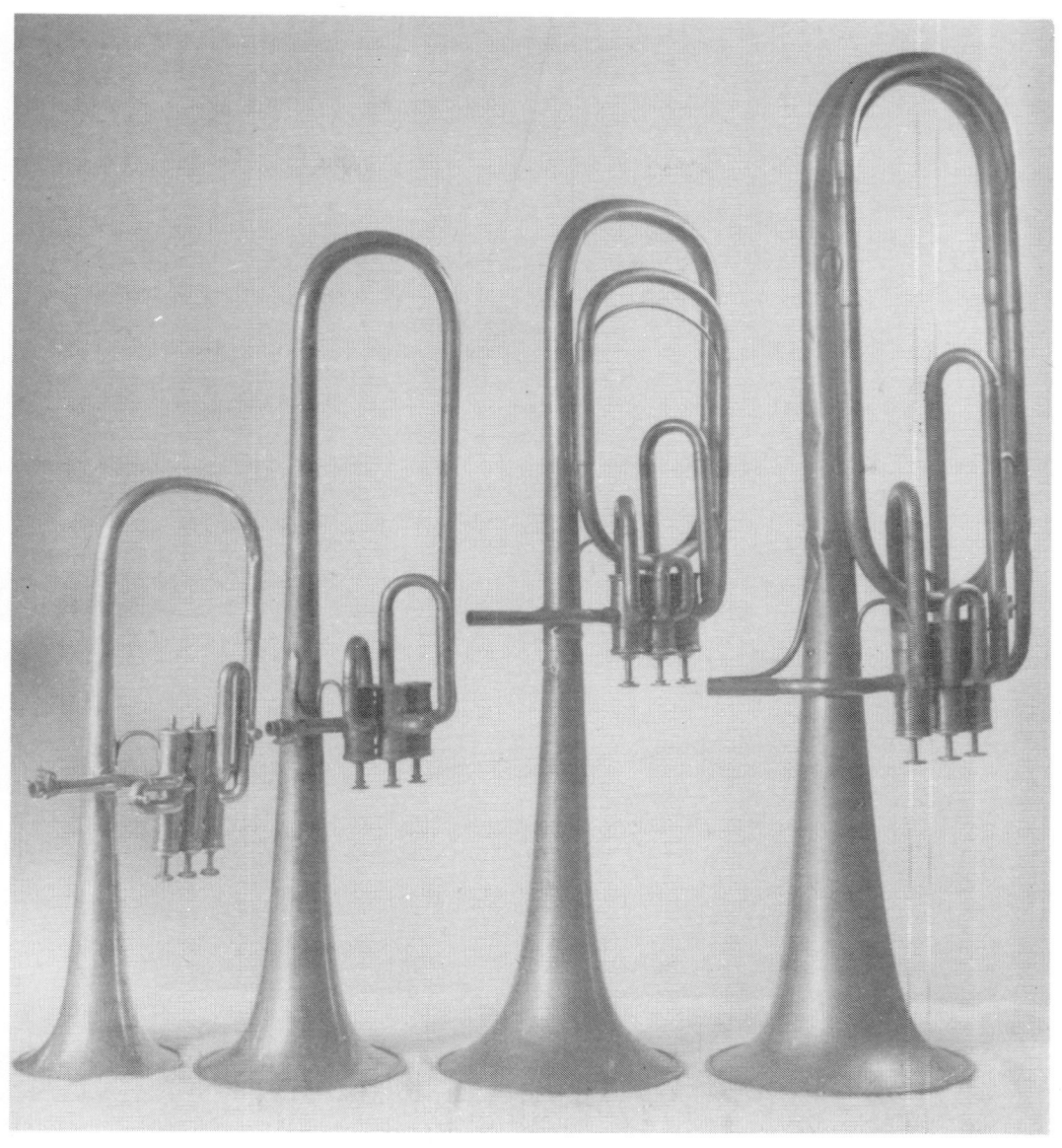

Saxotrombas — another of Sax's hotly contested inventions.
These had a more gently tapering bore than the saxhorn with a tone described as 'less strident than the trumpet, gentler than the bugle'.
All are fitted with valves of patterns pirated by Sax. The three largest have squat Berliner-pumpen valves whilst the smallest has the slender Périnet type.

Photograph of Adolphe Sax at 40

played by William Distin. It seems strange that Sax did not offer an original construction to so high a personage but there is no record that John Distin's assertion was ever so challenged, either by the "Foreign Visitor" or anyone else.

That the Distin's recital at Windsor Castle was enjoyed by the Royal Family is evident from an entry in Queen Victoria's Journal dated December 14th 1844 and quoted here by the gracious permission of Her Majesty the Queen:

"... *Mama &c, to dinner, after which there was some very good music & the Distin family, a father, & his 4 sons, played most beautifully and really touchingly on a species of trumpet or horn, called the Saxe Horn".*

There is, however, no mention of the musicians playing on an instrument presented previously to Prince Albert and a current search reveals no trace of such an item in the Royal Collection.

On his first visit to Paris, Henry Distin had sought out not only Sax, but other leading manufacturers with the idea of eventually becoming a manufacturer himself. Under the title of Distin & Sons, the family commenced selling musical instruments from their London residence in 1845. The next year, with Henry giving it special attention, the business was transferred to No. 31 Cranbourne Street, Leicester Square, where it acted as agent for Sax's instruments. According to Algernon Rose,[9] after paying initial expenses there was nothing left with which to buy stock. To remedy the situation, Henry Distin took advantage of an unexpected enquiry. Whilst whitewashing the empty store, a man called wishing to buy a cornet. The proprietor explained that his stock was as yet unpacked but promised to produce a fine instrument if the customer would wait for twenty minutes. This being agreed, Henry took a cab to Messrs. Behread, Blumberg & Company, a wholesale import house in the city, and obtained on approval a cornet worth twenty-five shillings.

Returning to the shop he proceeded to regale his customer with florid variations on *Carnival of Venice*. Delighted, the man happily parted with ten guineas for the instrument and thereby laid the foundation of Henry Distin's fortune. Although in modern terms the incident savours of sharp practice, the sheer audacity of it so deserved to succeed that one is tempted to fall back in justification on the precept of *caveat emptor.*

Early in 1846 the family quintet commenced a series of tours which took them from Windsor Castle to many parts of Europe including Prussia, and to the United States of America. For the next nine years, thousands of people in diverse places were introduced to the saxhorn. The party's instrumentation of four saxhorns and a flugel horn remained unchanged until 1848 when George, who played the bass part, died. The tragic loss of a brother and a key instrumentalist did not for long deter the family from carrying on. William abandoned the flugel horn and took over the bass, thus achieving a true saxhorn quartet.

By the middle of the 1850's, after nearly twenty years of constant touring, the Distin family brass party began to show signs of disintegrating. The individual members must have got along together very well for all this time. Although none of them appears to have accumulated much capital over the years, economic necessity must have been less pressing as individual aspirations began to be assertive.

Old John Distin never forsook his first love. In 1857, a crowd of 20,000 packed the Crystal Palace for his "farewell concert" although he was still appearing as trumpet soloist a year later. Theodore became an opera singer and a composer of songs. He was to be seen at Covent Garden in 1860, dying at the age of 70 in April 1893. William, who died in 1884, also found fame as a singer, his fine bass voice earning him a presentation to the Prince Consort when singing on one occasion in the Chapel Royal.

Henry Distin took an increasing interest in the business of wind-instrument making and selling, and it is with him we are now most concerned. He built up a flourishing business over the years, particularly in connection with the Sax agency. His most famous transaction took place in 1853 when he arranged for an English brass band to be fully equipped with saxhorns.

That magnificent and truly British institution, the brass band, has roots which reach back to the mediaeval minstrels, town waits, the church bands which followed Cromwell's disapproval of organs, village bands of casual instrumentation and, of course, the military. It was in the squalor of the Industrial Revolution that this music was nurtured. It will be seen that Adolphe Sax, albeit indirectly, played a major part in its eventual fruition.

In spite of the long hours of hard labour demanded by the *laissez-faire* economic theories of the day, a few enlightened employers were aware of the inhumanity inflicted on the individual by this policy. Certain of them were attracted to music as a way of bringing some light into grey lives. Quite early in the century, John Streitt of Belper took his employees to concerts and paid for their musical tuition. The Yorkshire and Durham miners were given a small band-room and helped to form a band. In 1825, bands were formed in many northern villages and town bands provided welcome recreation and pleasure for the hard working classes.

These bands had no standard instrumentation; they were made up of such motley pieces as the individual members could or were disposed to play upon. Because many of the performances took place in the open air, wind instruments tended to predominate.

Two things above others combined to give working-men's bands impetus at the time. The first was the coming of the railways and the end of the almost complete isolation of one community from another. The cost of travel was reduced; cheap excursions could be arranged for special events. For the first time physical barriers for ordinary people were breached; in the case of amateur musicians, the standards of their neighbours could be heard, to be attained or surpassed.

The second stimulant was the invention and introduction into Britain of the *cornet-à-pistons*. Known here as the cornopean, it was quickly taken up by wind bands as being in every way superior to the key-bugle. A man with little education or leisure to practice found he could manage a line of melody or harmony in a fraction of the time it would take him to learn a part on a stringed or woodwind instrument. As valves became more dependable, makers vied with each other to apply them to every conceivable length and shape of tube. This is what amateur bands had been waiting for. Hands gnarled and sometimes deformed by long hours of toil in the factory, field or mine could manage the three large pistons where they would have been too clumsy amid the delicacy of woodwind keywork. Moreover, since the technique of all sizes of bugle-horn is basically the same, players could change from one pitch to another with nothing more to learn than an adjustment of embouchure.

The tendency to drop woodwind in favour of brass gathered momentum. In Monmouthshire, the band attached to the Blaina Ironworks became all-brass in 1832. Other bands followed. By the early 1850's, two bands whose names are still famous today, Besses o' the Barn and Black Dyke Mills, were exclusively brass. Sax's walking advertisement, the Distin family, brought the saxhorn to the eager notice of the band fraternity; saxhorns found their way in small numbers into the still haphazard instrumentation, next to hand horns, ophicleides and sundry coils of brass.

The spirit of competition has always been high in amateur bands. Early contests took on the spirit of sporting events. Strong partisan feelings were never repressed especially when the verdict of the judges was adverse. Nevertheless, pitting skills against others undoubtedly led to a gradual improvement in standards. When Stalybridge Old Band attended the first recorded contest in 1818, it mustered a trumpet, two French horns, a bugle horn, a serpent, two bassoons, a bass horn, four flutes, four clarinets, cymbals, drum and triangle. Three years later, a contest held to celebrate the coronation of King George IV was won by Clegg's Reed Band, later to become Besses o' the Barn. They played "God Save the King" with three clarinets, piccolo, key-bugle, trumpet, two French horns, trombone, two bass horns and a drum. By the time eight bands entered the first Belle Vue, Manchester, contest of 1853, most of the woodwind had been discarded.

Money for instruments and equipment was an ever-present source of difficulty. Apart from the few copper coins which was all that bandsmen and their supporters could afford, bands were financed from casual collections at performances and the generosity of a few altruistic employers and well-wishers. In 1851, Endersby Jackson, the first great conductor and organiser of brass bands, attempted to initiate a contest at Burton Constable. Local bands were enthusiastic and set to with a will to prepare themselves. It says much for their undaunted spirit that they were not put off by poor and inefficient instruments.

The prospect of re-equipping a full band with new instruments was indeed a daunting one. Yet rumours began to circulate in connection with the Mossley Temperance Band who were said to be in contact with Henry Distin of London with a view to importing twelve valved bugle-horns from the Paris factory of Adolphe Sax. These were to incorporate all the latest improvements adopted by M. Sax up to time of manufacture.

In this case, rumour was justified. The Mossley Band received their saxhorns in time to play a piece of their own choice and to sweep the board at the first Belle Vue contest of 1853. All the instruments had upright bells and most of them were pitched in A-flat. The fact that this curious pitch would cause difficulties when the authorities decreed B-flat and E-flat to be standard contest pitches was not foreseen on that triumphant day.

Mossley's sensational win at Belle Vue underlined the superior results obtainable by amateur bands when using sets of matched and homogeneous instruments. The demand for saxhorns was stimulated. The name stuck and some bands, proud of their new acquisitions, incorporated "Saxhorn" into their titles. Sax and his saxhorn, through the good offices of Distin, laid the function of a virile brass band movement, properly organised with a standard instrumentation.

Although this sales deal had been mutually advantageous to the maker and the importer, a rift had begun to develop in the relations between Distin and Sax. The first sign appeared in 1851, the year Sax received the Council Medal for his display of 85 instruments at the Great Exhibition in London. Carse suggests that this distinction started the estrangement although it is hard to see why unless Sax had been by-passing his agent in taking orders.

It would seem that Sax, conscious of the moral debt to him by the Distins (as he saw it) thought that Distin should put the major part of his business energy in pushing the sales of Sax's instruments in the British Isles. Distin could not have seen the position in that way. Being in business to make profit and a living, any legitimate trade was grist to his mill. In 1850 he had commenced manufacturing on his own account at No. 9 Great Newport Street. The following year he was advertising himself as "Instrument Maker to Her Majesty's Army and Navy".

One of his first products was a set of "Euphonic Horns" on which the family performed. They claimed these as "newly-invented" although they were no more than another variation of the valved bugle-horn. It is astonishing the number of "inventions" claimed for this instrument. Around 1870, Distin "invented" the "Ballad Horn", a circular instrument akin to the baritone saxhorn but pitched in C. Its purpose was to enable amateurs to play directly from the voice part of songs with pianoforte accompaniment without transposition. "There is no doubt it will be a great favourite in drawing rooms" ran the advertising "blurb".

Anyone who could make brass instruments could jump on the bugle-horn bandwagon. It was only necessary to twist the tubing into a slightly different form, with or without a variation to the bore, think of an exotic name and claim a new invention. When Distin started to make valved bugle-horns and, worse still, import them from Sax's rivals, the fury across the Channel knew no bounds. Comettant raved at "these perfidious Englishmen"; berated them for being so ungrateful to the man who had rescued them from degradation as to deal with Sax's imitators. The outcome was that, in 1853, Distin lost his agency for Sax's instruments, which was given to Rudall, Rose and Carte.[11]

Henry Distin did not appear to be disconcerted by this action. The business in Great Newport Street did well. This became the head office when Cranbourne Street was abandoned in 1859. The firm expanded into adjacent premises; No. 10 in 1861 and No. 11 in 1866, assuming the title, Henry Distin and Company in 1862. In 1868, Distin sold out to Boosey and Company for £9,700, most of which he lost soon after in unsuccessful concert promotions. The business continued under the old style until 1874.

Some of the confusion which arises from the terms "saxhorn" and "tuba" was accentuated by Distin. In his advertising he seems, quite arbitrarily, to have labelled all brass instruments with upward-pointing bells as "tubas", those with forward bells as "saxhorns".[12] This is quite incorrect as Sax made his instruments in both shapes.

As an old man writing to Endersby Jackson from the U.S.A. where he had emigrated, Henry Distin still speaks highly of Adolphe Sax's "artistic innovation of open valved free air passages, as introduced by him in his famous Sax horns".[13]

In the final reckoning, the Distins and Sax were completely complementary. The beneficial effect of their association was mutual. Their combined influence on the British Brass Band Movement is a lasting memorial to them all. Because of their better business sense, the Distins had more comfortable lives. They are now almost forgotten. The name of Sax, who finished a troubled life in obscure destitution, lives on.

Notes on Chapter IV.
1. Carse, A: *Adolphe Sax and the Distin Family* — 'Music Review' Nov. 1945. pp. 194-201.
2. Comettant: *Manuel général* pp.53-4.
3. *'The British Bandsman',* March 1889, pp.132-134; April 1889, pp.154-5.
4. Endersby Jackson: *Origin and Promotion of Brass Band Contests,* 'Musical Opinion', July 1896, pp.673-5.
5. An E-flat tenor saxhorn with rotary valves made by Sax for Theodore Distin and now in the Adam Carse collection at the Horniman Museum, London, is stated by Carse in the catalogue as not being of the first set made by Sax for the Distin family in 1844.
6. *'Musical World'* 23rd January 1845, p.41.
7. *ibid*, 13th February 1845 (letter dated 4th February 1845).
8. The word 'but' had originally been misprinted as 'not'. John Distin was obliged to write a further letter ('Musical World' 20th February 1845, p.90) to correct the reversal of meaning. He added: "I wish to give M. Sax credit for all he deserves".
9. Rose, A: *'Talks with Bandsmen'* pp.210-211.
10. In 1862, John Farmer published a piano solo entitled, *"The Distin-guished Galop".* Caricatured on the cover are members of the family in various postures, some of them undignified, with their saxhorns.
11. See Apendix B.
12. Such an advertisement appeared on the back of a song-sheet, *"Never Say Die",* Words by J. E. Carpenter, music by Theodore Distin.
13. Henry Distin emigrated to America during the 1870's, manufacturing brass instruments in NewYork, before transferring his business activities to Philadelphia in 1882. He continued to be an instrumental performer, appearing in his 70th year with Patrick Gilmore's band. On an E-flat bass tuba, he rendered variations on 'The Last Rose of Summer' and, as an encore, 'The Huntsman's Chorus' from Weber's *Der Freischutz* ". . . without touching the pistons. . . . with his fingers". After the concert he presented Gilmore with a silver-plated "pocket" cornet. — 'The British Bandsman' April 1889, p. 155.

"M. Armand Marrast (President of the French Chamber of Deputies) is forced to replace his little bell with one of Sax's instruments"
Le Charivari, 22nd October 1848

"A use for the saxophone in time of war"
Le Charivari, 15th November 1854

V
Reforms

Unscrupulous opposition from rival manufacturers, exercised through executant musicians, continued to block the general acceptance of Sax's instruments in orchestras. Meyerbeer, like Donizetti, was forced to abandon an idea of including some of them in a new composition. Despite any desires they may have had to help the inventor, composers, conductors and promoters were powerless against any threatened walk-out by players. The situation did not, of course, pertain in the Army where soldier-musicians were in no position to betray any personal prejudices. It was natural that Sax should look for an outlet for his products towards what was, after all, the largest single consumer.

Berlioz was keen on the idea; his enthusiasms were echoed widely by other writers and in the press. Their view was that instruments of Sax's manufacture were more sonorous, were capable of greater volume and were always correctly in tune as compared with existing instruments. High ranking officers, Marshal Sebastiani and Lieutenant-General Moline de St. Yon, had been present at some of the workshop concerts. They were of the opinion that ten of Sax's instruments were more effective than twenty of anyone else's.

A similar viewpoint was apparently voiced in royal circles also. De Rumigny certainly had a long-standing dissatisfaction with the state of French military music especially as the Germans were by now so good at it. The King and some members of The Royal Family, too, were concerned that France should have a standard of martial music in keeping with her dignity and traditions. Urgent talks were held to see how best this could be achieved; almost inevitably, the name of the Belgian instrument maker who was having such a difficult time at the hands of his enemies was brought forward. De Rumigny's views carried much weight and it looked as if a way might now be found to help both the manufacturer and France at the same time.

Of all the royal entourage, none had a readier wit, none was more widely versed in the arts than the Duke of Montpensier. At the King's suggestion, this great personage visited the Rue Saint-Georges. Sax, who was never one to be overawed by rank, wealth or position, treated the Duke to his usual enthusiastic discourse, backed up by practical demonstrations on his instruments.

The Duke's extensive musical knowledge and his quick grasp of the problems of wind-instrument construction was impressive. The outcome of the meeting was a cycle of events which, when set in motion, infuriated Sax's enemies beyond endurance, brought practically the whole of the French musical-instrument industry near to ruin, lined the pockets of the legal profession and gave Sax himself a lifetime of worry and trouble.

On October 13th 1845 a fifteen-year patent was granted to cover a family of instruments now unashamedly known as saxhorns. Parallel with this was specified another instrumental family with the name of saxotrombas. These differed from the conical saxhorns in that their tubes were a combination of the cylindrical and the conical, with the cylindrical portion predominating. The latter section was somewhat larger in diameter than that of the trumpet or trombone to which instruments there was an affinity of tone. The various pitches of the saxotromba corresponded with those of the saxhorn.

After discussing band instrumentation with the Duke of Montpensier, and probably at his suggestion, Sax wrote three highly-significant letters; to Marshal Sault, Minister of War, to General de Rumigny and to the King himself. In these he set out in authoritative and unequivocal terms his views on the current state of military music.

His main contentions were that large bodies of clarinets, topped by piccolos, produced a shrill, squeaky treble; at the other end, ophicleides blared a gruff, inaccurate bass. He was especially scathing about horns, oboes and bassoons, declaring these to be unsuitable for open-air use and inadequate to sustain inner harmonies. The remedy, he insisted, lay in supplanting these with instrumental family groups of his own invention. Having improved on the type of instrument and on the prevailing abysmal quality of manufacture, Sax put in a plea for the soldier-musician and his poor conditions of service. His letter ran:

It rests with me to raise a delicate point. I wish to speak of the lowly status occupied by members of the bands. They are obliged to undertake special studies which would give them a certain standing among the middle class, but in the Army they are compared to simple soldiers. Does this not show the cause of their disgust and why they seek to free themselves from this situation in order that their talents might be recognised?[1]

To recruit a better type of bandsman, he submitted, a man should be able to look forward to a fair career and have a reasonable chance of promotion according to his efficiency and length of service. Bandmasters should be able to obtain commissioned rank.

The memoranda had an immediate effect. General Moline de Saint-Yon was Director of Personnel at the War Office; he arranged an audience for Sax with the War Minister. It was decided that Marshal the Duke de Dalmatie would arrange for two bands, one conventional, the other of Sax instrumentation, to be heard side by side at the Ministry. The contest took on a "David and Goliath" complex. Thirty-two bandsmen represented the established order; all that Sax could muster was nine, the rest having been enticed away. Yet so well did the small group demonstrate the superiority of their instruments that a second contest was arranged so that others could hear the effect. This time, Sault, de Rumigny, de Saint Yon, Sébastiani and other high army chiefs were joined by the Royal Dukes de Nemours and D'Aumale, and the Prince de Joinville.

Sax could do no better numerically than before. Again his instrumental superiority was proved beyond doubt. The royal party, after congratulating the inventor warmly, wanted to press on immediately with the reorganisation of bands along the lines suggested. Military chiefs, however, although personally convinced, wished to have their judgement backed on a wider base. They were particularly anxious not to be accused of partiality. It was therefore resolved that a Special Commission be convened, composed of distinguished talents, theoretical and practical, proved by accepted works. It would impartially examine the whole spectrum of military music and, having deliberated at length, make such recommendations as its wisdom dictated.

The commission, nominated by the Minister of War, met for the first time on February 25th 1845 under the presidency of General de Rumigny. To represent purely musical interests were Gasparo Spontini, Daniel Auber — head of the Conservatoire, Jacques Halévy, Adolphe Adam, George Onslow and Michele Carafa. These, together with the Count de St.-Andréa, were all members of the Institute of France. The army was represented by Count Gudin, Colonel of the 2nd Lancers and a gifted amateur violinist, Colonel Riban of the 74th Line Infantry, Colonel Savart of the Engineers and the Baron de Séguier. The last two named were acoustics experts. Georges Kastner was the secretary. Sax himself was invited to serve but wisely declined, having a vested interest in the findings of the Commission.

The first act of the body was to note the reason for its existence and to list the chief reasons for the inferior position of French military music. Supernumary, or civilian, bandsmen had been suppressed in 1834 as a threat to discipline. This move had robbed bands of their best soloists and players, many of whom were of foreign origin. In addition to their performing skill, supernumaries often acted as teachers to the younger bandsmen; since they had charge of only two or three players at a time, good results had usually ensued. Service conditions were poor for enlisted bandsmen. There was no encouragement for a promising player to apply himself to years of study to gain a proficiency which in civilian life would ensure a good living but which in the army would limit him to the rank of a common soldier without hope of promotion. No wonder only inferior musicians remained in the ranks.

Next, the Commission examined the quality of the instruments currently in use and the rules governing their application to the make-up of bands. A curious situation prevailed whereby regimental colonels had a full and entire discretion as to the constitution of their bands. The only compulsory stipulation was that bands must have some official bugles on which signal calls were made; the rest of the complement — up to 32 for the cavalry, 45 for the infantry — could be made up entirely at the whim of the officer commanding. He could, if so inclined, have all ophicleides, or all horns; strident bands with lots of cornets, bands weak and ineffectual in the open air with too many oboes and bassoons. Furthermore, the numbers provided for were maxima; there was nothing to compel a colonel to maintain a band to anything like full strength.

Invitations were sent to all principal manufacturers to submit specimen instruments for the Commission's consideration. The response was disappointing. A flugel-horn was rejected because of its faulty mechanism; a new invention under the name "emboliclave"[2] was offered as a substitute for the ophicleide but was turned down as being too fragile and complicated for military use. An E-flat contrabass was recognised as being identical with the Austrian bombardon. Other manufacturers refused to co-operate with the Commission or even to accept its constitution. They proposed an alternative list of names which, they felt, would be less biased in favour of Sax than were the existing members.

When this was refused, their fury erupted into vituperative and slander of a most violent kind, levelled at Sax, at the Minister of War, at the Commission collectively and severally and at Louise-Philippe himself. The adoption of Sax's instruments, they contended, would lead to dire consequences. A large number of military bandsman would always be found in hospital; ten thousand masters, craftsmen, workers skilled and unskilled, together with their wives and families be reduced to poverty, ten thousand bandsmen would be forced to start their musical education again, publishers of band music would be ruined by having stocks of useless music on their hands.

Only one manufacturer fully accepted the terms of the invitation; not surprisingly, Adolphe Sax. He submitted a comprehensive range of instruments of his own make and design, and was ready to answer technical and general questions put to him by the acoustics experts and the musicians. Although the Commission was at pains to keep all manufacturers informed of its deliberations, renewing its invitation to present their instruments, Sax virtually had the field to himself. The only opposition he encountered from within the commission came from Michele Carafa, director of the *Gymnase de Musique Militaire* since 1839. Berlioz, who had coveted his job, had at differing times described Carafa as "immovable as a blockhead" and "a musical odd-job man whose only recommendation is that he is not French". Carafa can hardly have forgiven Berlioz for his scathing review of the former's opera *La Grande Duchesse* which had had a run of two performances in 1835.[3] Of course, Berlioz's championship of Sax was blatant.

On the 7th and 11th March, Sax was given leave to read a report to the Commission. He reiterated proposals for drastic re-organisation in band instrumental families. Carafa argued a more conservative approach. Given proper balance and proportion, he insisted, a band of conventional components would prove satisfactory. Both arguments appeared to have some merit in theory; the Commission concluded that the issue could be decided only by a practical demonstration. To this end the *Gymnase* director and the inventor were invited to organise model bands based on their respective representations. These would be heard in the open-air before as large an audience as possible so that the views of the public might be considered.

The Champ-de-Mars is today a pleasant public park where one may sit and watch the world coming to visit Eiffel's geometric masterpiece. Looking towards the distant Military Academy framed by the striding legs of the Tower, a vision might be conjured of a colourful event staged there on April 22nd 1845. In those days, the ground was of much larger proportions. It had been the scene of many a troop review by kings and commanders through the centuries, often as a prelude to a bloody battle. On that day it was itself to be a battleground between contestants, each in deadly earnest.

Carafa and Sax were each required to muster bands of 45 players. Their respective lists given to the Commission before the contest demonstrates the differing conceptions:

Carafa	Sax
1 piccolo	1 piccolo
1 E-flat clarinet	1 E-flat clarinet
2 Solo B-flat clarinets	6 B-flat clarinets
7 First B-flat clarinets	2 saxophones
7 Second B-flat clarinets	2 E-flat soprano saxhorns
4 Oboes	4 B-flat contralto saxhorns
4 bassoons	4 E-flat tenor saxhorns
2 hand horns	2 B-flat baritone saxhorns
2 valved horns	2 B-flat bass saxhorns
	4 E-flat contrabass saxhorns
2 cornets	2 cornets
3 trumpets	6 trumpets
2 trombones	2 valved trombones
4 ophicleides	2 slide trombones
4 percussion	5 percussion
45	45

Berlioz was not slow in firing the first salvo. On April 1st 1845, three weeks before the contest, his article in *Débats* had the title, "The Reorganisation of Military Bands". This followed closely the line of Sax's original letter to the Commission, using Sax's arguments and recommendations as his own, thus giving them the weight of his very considerable standing. He deplored the use of instruments weak in the open-air — oboes, bassoons and horns — and wished these to be replaced by "long-ranging" instruments — saxhorns. Describing these in detail, he goes on to praise the way in which Sax has improved the German tuba and has something sarcastic to say about the inventor's opponents:

It is not a question of the interests of manufacturers but of the interests of art and the army. One can understand the owners of factories where instruments are made being upset but this should not and cannot have more influence on the decision of the Commission than the undoubted joy of the brass manufacturers who, if the reorganisation is made, will be assured of a sudden increase in profits. If we are to be influenced by such considerations we shall, following the chain of interested parties, come to the miners who mine the ore.[4]

Berlioz had no qualms as to the outcome of the approaching contest, stating that if anyone could demonstrate a better band than that Sax had proposed, may he be the winner.

Interest in the encounter between the bands was enormous, whipped up by press and poster. From early morning a crowd began to gather on the Champ-de-Mars, growing steadily until a force of resplendent foot soldiers and mounted hussars cleared the ground. By the late morning, the assembly had grown to 20,000 and the army detachments were barely enough to cope with it. The day had taken on a festive air, aided by the bright sunshine and clear blue skies. Every soldier who was not on duty elsewhere was present. The crowd hushed as the two rival bands marched on and stood in a single straight line in front of the Commission whose officers were in full dress uniform and dominated by the tall plumed hat of de Rumigny. The sun glinted gaily on helmets, buttons and sword-hilts as, promptly at noon, a signal for the proceedings to begin was given.

By way of warming up for the main event, a march-past of regimental bands had been arranged. Amid cheers of an expectant multitude, on came the band of the 11th Light Brigade. Their effort was judged "quite good" although they had illegal supernumaries playing piccolo, first trumpet and first trombone. Then appeared the 7th Line Band of 49 players including two saxhorns and getting an ovation for their remarkable quick march; followed by the 1st Line where an absence of trumpets earned them only fair rating. Lastly, the 62nd Line whose ensemble was considered "weak". These bands, although differing in instrumental detail, were representative of existing types, each having large clarinet and ophicleide sections.

An interval, after which an expectant hush heralded the star attraction. The two bands were drawn up some 150 yards apart. After a preliminary chord of E-flat minor, the bands of Carafa and Sax were each to play arrangements of an *Andante* by Adolphe Adam and a Quick March from *Le Diable à Quatre* by the same composer. This was to be the first hearing of music for a new ballet shortly to be produced at the Royal Academy of Music. Band parts had been distributed in good time for rehearsals. In the draw for order of play, Carafa was to play first. He had attempted to augment his combination to 49 and was required to dispense with two bugles and two flutes before commencing to play. Nevertheless, he did have the services of many professors and the best pupils from the *Gymnase*.

As Carafa's band opened the programme, consternation was rife in the other camp. Several of their players had failed to arrive, the opposition having used its familiar weapons of bribery and coercion to prevent them. Sax had dashed off in attempt to remedy the shortage.

With an agonisingly short amount of time to spare, the ranks of soldiers parted to admit a carriage. Inside was Sax and another musician with various instruments, some of which were in a barely complete state. They hurried towards the line of battle, the inventor clutching two cases. The band which eventually took the field shows signs of a hurried and makeshift rearrangement. There were no trumpets and no saxophones, the contrabass saxhorns and percussion were short by one player each. Two ophicleides, which Sax would hardly have accepted in other than dire circumstances, and a bass clarinet were added. Sax had two instruments strapped to his person, filling in the most vital passages as best he could.

As Carafa finished amid encouraging applause, the Sax contingent, still seven players short, took its place to play the same piece. This was the signal for a vociferous disturbance to be mounted among certain sections of the crowd. Some even managed to get between the soldiers, to hurl stones; insulting epithets filled the air, chief of which was "Go home, foreigner".

Distracting as this was, it could not obscure the fact that this band, particularly with its saxhorns sustaining rich inner harmonies, and its sonorous bass, made a much more pleasing sound than the previous band. In fact, the effect was electrifying, bringing thunderous appreciation from the vast assembly.

Each band in turn then played the march; then, as if to effect a temporary truce, the bands combined to play the march again in a welter of magnificent sound. Final items were of the competitors' own choice. Carafa rendered Auber's overture, *La Muette de Portici;* Sax's musicians, with the scent of victory in the air, gave out with a merry fantasia arranged by their musical director, M. Fessy. Applause was tumultuous leaving no doubt that, whatever the verdict of the Commisson, the people had already declared Sax to be the easy winner.

The Commission had indeed been impressed by what it had heard but wisely decided to give the matter mature consideration before saying too much. It limited itself to commending Carafa for his band's variety of tone-colour, Sax on his homogeneous sonority and rich bass, and regretting that resources did not permit bands of the size and instrumentation of the united forces.

Excitement was not yet done. There remained the question of all-brass bands as required by some regiments. To open the second half of the contest, music was heard from a conventional brass band, 27 musicians from that of the 74th Line. Carafa followed with a reorganised ensemble of 25 including ophicleides and some valved bugles. Sax's band was made up entirely of saxhorns, cornets and trombones of his own manufacture combined in a way not very dissimilar to what was eventually to become the standard instrumentation of the British Brass Band:

    2 E-flat soprano saxhorns
    2 cornets
    4 B-flat contralto saxhorns
    4 E-flat tenor saxhorns
    2 valved trombones
    2 slide trombones
    4 B-flat baritone and bass saxhorns
    3 E-flat contrabass saxhorns

23

Again the fine bass and satisfying blend of Sax's conception was evident. His band was cheered to the echo. There was general and enthusiastic agreement among all but the bigotted, civilian and soldier, musician and layman, that the victory of Sax's instrumentation over Carafa's was overwhelming. As they streamed away, buzzing excitedly after a good day's free entertainment, the press was getting ready its first editions. The name of Sax was on everyone's lips for days to come. The satirical *Le Charivari,* pattern for the famous London "Punch", described the clash in military jargon, likening the victory of *"Les Saxons"* over *"Les Carafons"* as equalling the best of Napoleon. Although its humour and excruciating puns may strike heavy-handed today, it would have afforded Sax and his helpers a good deal of delight. After all, against the most vindictive opposition they had won the verdict from the largest possible jury. All the inventor had now to do was to await the official decree and reap his reward.

Although the victory of the "Saxons" was overwhelming, anyone expecting a sudden dramatic pronouncement in favour of the winner was to be disappointed. The contest on the Champ-de-Mars was merely an experiment, the result of which would be noted and duly considered in the context of the Commission's overall terms of reference. In some respects, Sax's opponents were right. It was not just a question of suppressing some instruments and promoting others. Anything in the nature of a major reformation would have wide repercussions which must be borne in mind. Having undertaken the task at the expenditure of so much time and trouble, the Commission was not to be stampeded into any premature revelation of its findings.

All the same, within their conclave, members were elated by what they had heard. The Italian master, Spontini, was moved to say that, bearing in mind his many years experience in this type of music in Prussia and other parts of Germany and Northern Europe, French military music was to become the best on the Continent. He ascribed the confidence of his prophecy to the adoption and introduction of Sax's instruments which, he added archly, other armies did not possess. As a start towards achieving an ideal band instrumentation, each member was asked to submit a list which he, irrespective of cost or other non-musical consideration, thought best.

After comparing and discussing the various tabulations, the Commission was able eventually to get unanimous agreement on one. Its composition clearly reflects the impression made by the combined bands at the recent encounter:

     1 piccolo
     2 E-flat clarinets
     8 oboes (1st and 2nd)
    16 B-flat clarinets (1st and 2nd)
     2 F alto clarinets
     2 bass clarinets
     2 saxophones
     4 bassoons
     4 valved trumpets (Sax pattern)
     2 E-flat soprano saxhorns

4	B-flat contralto saxhorns
4	E-flat alto (tenor) saxhorns
4	B-flat bass saxhorns
4	E-flat contrabass saxhorns
2	hand horns
2	valved horns
3	slide trombones (alto, tenor and bass)
3	valved trombones (alto, tenor and bass)
5	percussion
74	

Although all agreed on the theoretical excellence of such a band, practical considerations pointed to the fact that military finances would not stretch to supporting bands of this size. A lot of re-thinking brought a resolution to modify the plan but not more than was absolutely necessary. Without committing itself to numbers, it was proposed that any band would have to include a piccolo, E-flat clarinets, B-flat clarinets, bass clarinets, saxophones, oboes, bassoons, valved trumpets, horns, saxhorns of all sizes, saxotrombas, slide and valved trombones and ophicleides.

This mixture of old and new instruments was arrived at only after the Commission had given each piece a thorough and detailed examination. It was agreed that Sax's clarinets were to be preferred to all others; oboes and bassoons were retained because they offered a variety of tone provided the actual instruments had good carrying power. No reason was offered for the somewhat surprising retention of ophicleides. The solid basis of the band was to be Sax's new instruments. These had, according to the Secretary's notes, always emerged winners in any test, had sonority, power, magnificence, capacity, precision and equality as well as simplicity of mechanism and ease of blowing and fingering.

The Commission recognised the saxophone to be of incomparable charm, with a wide dynamic range and equally resourceful in either solos or ensemble. Although the saxotromba had not been included in Sax's band, the Commission had examined the instrumental family and were impressed. Its power of tone, less strident than the trumpet, gentler than the bugle, assured it of a place in the new combination.

Above all it was the family of saxhorns on which greatest hopes were fastened. All agreed that any proposed band without them would be unthinkable. With saxhorns present in adequate numbers, not only would the previously insipid inner parts be heard, other instruments now considered weak in the open-air could now be used for their tone-colouring properties.

Sax's valves also came in for commendation. The maker himself had patiently, if pointedly, demonstrated to the Commission the shortcomings of certain valves, using a conventional flugel horn for illustration. He indicated how each valve had two acute corners in its tubing, so that, for a note requiring the depression of all three valves, the air-stream had to negotiate no less than six hairpin bends to the detriment of good tone. He further contended that the mechanism was fragile, prone to wear, and easily affected by rain and dust. A mere broken spring required the skilled services of a manufacturer, or a watchmaker, or an engineer to repair it. On the other hand, his valve system had none of these faults, the tube running in a straight line through the cylinders. Although Sax's valves were, in fact, pirate versions of patterns already existing, there is no doubt that those he manufactured were robust and highly efficient for their time.

Between existing band strengths of 45 players and the considered ideal of 74, the Commission eventually compromised with 55. This, although not comparing with the size of foreign bands, was artistically acceptable and economically practicable, especially as the extra players would be students. Cavalry bands were set at 36 players as were those of the Light Infantry. Each company would be provided with a consort of saxhorns.

The final disposition was then as follows:

	Infantry	Cavalry	Light Infantry	Each Company
Piccolo in C	1			
Clarinets in E-flat	1			
Clarinets in B-flat (omnitonic)	14			
Bass clarinets in B-flat. Brass bell. Sax system	2			
Saxophones	2			
Oboes (German model)	2			
Bassoons (with brass bells)	2			
Cornets — 3 valves	2	2		
Trumpets — 3 valves (Sax system)	2	4	6	1
Trumpets — French		2		
Horns — 3 valves	4			
Saxhorns — soprano in E-flat	1	2	6	1
Saxhorns — contralto in B-flat	2	7(a)	12	2
Saxhorns — contralto in A-flat		2		
Saxhorns — alto (tenor) in E-flat	2	2	6	1
Saxhorns — baritones in B-flat		3		
Saxhorns — bass in B-flat (4 valves)	3	3	6(c)	1
Saxhorns — contrabass in E-flat	4	3		
Saxotrombas		2		
Trombones — 3 valves (Sax system)	1	1		
Trombones — slide	2	3		
Ophicleides	2			
Percussion	5	(b)		
	54	36	36	6

(a) Solo; 3 First; 3 Second.
(b) A kettledrummer who would play a side drum when troops were on foot is optional.
(c) Kastner states ambiguously, "Bass in E-flat"

It was proposed to keep natural trumpets and bugles only for signal purposes; in bands, they were to be replaced by Sax-valved instruments. Thus a small valved piece could be conveniently transported and a quartet or more of parts would be easily available even in the smallest unit.

These excellent schemes were evolved against a background of mundane reality in the shape of cost. In order that there should be no excessive increase in military staff and, at the same time, help improve the standard of musicianship in the ranks, selected supernumaries were again to be allowed. Other improvements covered promotion opportunities for bandsmen to non-commissioned ranks, bandmasters to be commissioned after examination, the publication of a band journal, the supply of a metronome to each regiment, prescription of the E-flat-B-flat pitch, wooden cases for fragile instruments, an instrument repairer to each band and the immediate organisation of three model bands.

Annual budgets currently in force were 9,000 francs for infantry bands, 2,500 for the cavalry. This had to cover all instrument replacements and the considerable charges for repairs due to inevitable rough usage. The Commission was not optimistic at getting anything more for the infantry and felt the existing amount would just about suffice. However, the cavalry simply had to have its allowance doubled. Further, an initial allowance of 2,000 francs for the infantry and 3,000 francs for the cavalry would be requested. Together with the proceeds from the sale of the old instruments, this would serve to re-equip the bands.

The Commission's report was finally ready for submission to the Minister of War who readily expressed his congratulations on the Commission's devotion, thoroughness and wisdom. The document was indeed a brave, idealistic attempt to rectify at one step the neglect of years. The imprint of Sax was on every page but, although he had come out of the examination extremely well, the model infantry band was not, as has so often been asserted, of Sax's ideal instrumentation. The sonorous effect of the family of saxhorns had been well appreciated and utilized. It is not clear just what pitches of saxophones were available at that time, which may account for only two being included. In spite of the good opinion expressed for the saxotromba, it was omitted from the infantry combination. No doubt economy had something to do with it.

Official approval of the report was given by the Minister on August 9th 1845 and published in the *Moniteur* next day. Although he had confident assurances from his high-ranking friends, Sax could hardly have expected so satisfactory an outcome. Now, no one could block the use of his instruments; their use would be compulsory by Government decree. The workshop was equipped to supply the majority of the approved instruments. In fact, he had a near monopoly which, even if only of a short duration, could earn a fortune.

All that was needed was organisation, finance and to be left alone to get on with the job. A tragedy that all three essentials were to be in such short supply.

Notes on Chapter V
Vide: Comettant, Chapters 10-14; Kastner: *Manuel général*, p.251 et seq.
1. Comettant, p.93.
2. Kastner: *Manuel général*, p.259. (footnote). A valved instrument akin to the baritone, patented by J. B. Coeffet in 1844 (Langwill Index p.27) and made by M. A. Raoux (ibid., p.128). It appears to have had an unreliable valve system and restricted air-passages due to many sharp bends in the tubing. Victor C. Mahillon: *Catalogue du Musée du Conservatoire de Musique de Bruxelles*, Ghent, 1909, Vol. 2, pp.439-441 (illustration), and Curt Sachs: *Real-lexicon, vide* 'embolyclave'.
3. In an undated letter *circa* 1843, Carafa had written to Sax praising the latter's clarinet and bass clarinet. Pontecoulant: *Organographie*, p.253.
4. *Journal des Débats*, 1st April 1845.

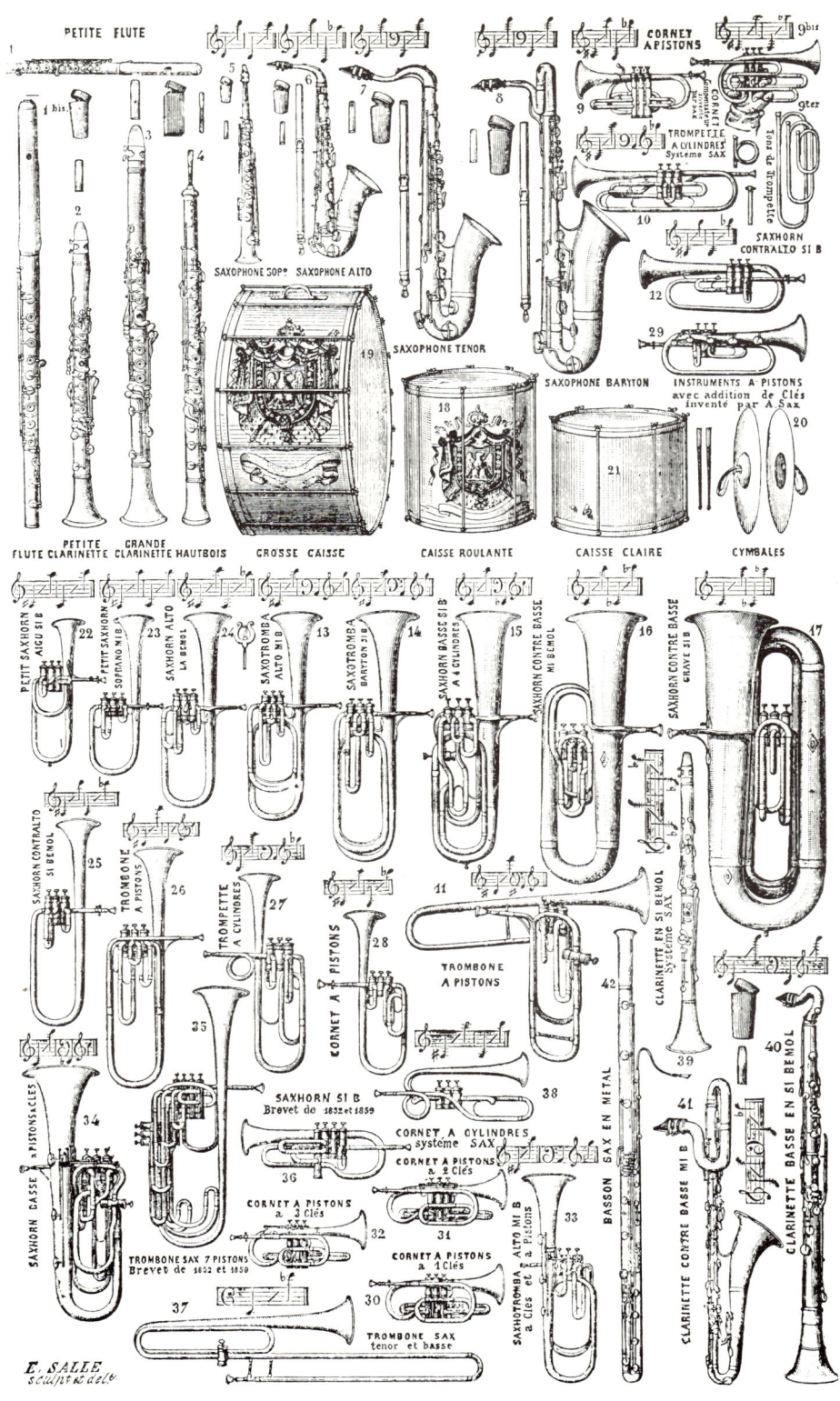

Instruments made by Adolphe Sax

VI
Conspiracies

Upholding the precept that nothing succeeds like success, Sax found himself inundated with offers of help. Still only 30 years of age, he had come from nowhere and, in just two years, had the bulk of the musical instrument business of Paris tied up neatly at his feet. Would-be investors looking for quick returns suddenly found in him an attractive proposition. How could a near-monopoly for the supply of military band instruments to an army about to be entirely re-equipped in this respect, do anything but bring rich dividends to anyone lucky enough to get a stake in it? Those ready to part with their money to this end might be forgiven for their lack of foresight. They could hardly have realised the power about to be exercised by manufacturers established over many years now, in one sweep, to be practically excluded from the business. Such men might have been expected to protest. The length and virulence of their opposition could not have been guessed at; it was to ensure that a lot of the money passing into the Sax Company's counting-house was to be dissipated on things far removed from the development and manufacture of musical instruments.

For the moment, however, Sax's financial problems began to dissolve. In preparation for the influx of work expected, the Rue Saint-Georges factory was rebuilt and extended. In place of the leaky shed there arose a lofty high-windowed structure, brilliantly lit after dark by a profusion of chandeliers and wall brackets. One end of the factory floor was effectively divided from the working area by a gigantic glass panelled show-case, taking for its frontal shape five sides of an octagon and reaching almost to the ceiling. Here was housed the comprehensive and valuable collection of instruments from which selections would be made and demonstrated to visitors.[1]

After the widespread publicity of recent events, the informal workshop concerts attracted large audiences, some people coming for instruction, some for entertainment and others for sheer curiosity to see this remarkable character who made such weird and novel constructions which commanded the approval of the highest in the land.

After the personally libellous stories put about by his enemies, anyone meeting the inventor for the first time might well have been pleasantly surprised. The arrogance and other faults in his make-up surfaced only when he was provoked. Not yet was he the embittered cynic, the outcome of years of suffering. He could be gracious to the humble, never servile to the mighty. Neatly turned out in the customary frock-coat and wing collar, his long, rather serious, visage was fringed with a close cropped beard with flowing moustaches. There was nothing in particular to distinguish him from any one of a hundred small manufacturers in the city, except when on the subject of his own wares. Then, it was not a question of gloating over anticipated profits. The man, perhaps unfortunately, had little regard for such matters. The making of instruments, inventing new conceptions and seeing them transformed into reality was enough. He was an artist through and through; if only he had had a competent and trustworthy business manager the ultimate story would have been a great deal happier.

One of his great pleasures was to be able to talk about his work to sympathetic and, if possible, knowledgeable hearers. The informal workshop concerts made a particularly valuable outlet combining, as they did, business with pleasure. In the area cordoned by the display cabinet was a raised dias, large enough to hold an upright piano with its player, together with eight or more standing musicians with their music stands. On concert occasions, the floor area would be filled with chairs, these being quickly filled until upwards of a hundred people were crammed in. Late arrivals were forced to stand at the back or in the wings.

Under the easy direction of the proprietor, Arban, his fellow musicians and, of course, Sax himself, would show off the various instruments in solos and duets with pianoforte accompaniment, trios, quartets and larger ensembles. Members of the audience had the chance to examine individual instruments at close quarters and engage the inventor in explanations of details, something on which he was never loth to expand.

Amid the blaze of fame which followed his spectacular victory on the Champ de Mars, Sax had been made a *Chevalier de la Couronne de Chêne*. The insignia had been presented by the ambassador, Baron de Gerlicke, on behalf of King William II of the Netherlands and had aroused considerable public interest so that eminent people now went out of their way to make his acquaintance.

One of his creditors was the Rothschild Bank to the extent of 2,000 francs. On the day appointed for settlement, Sax called at the Rothschild establishment to transact the business. News of his arrival was conveyed to Baron James de Rothschild who was at that moment having dinner with his brother Anthony, newly arrived in Paris from London. Interested in meeting this celebrity of the moment, the Baron invited Sax to join them. It may have been that the latter had already eaten, or perhaps his pride made him fearful of being patronised; he steadfastly refused the offer of, first, a filleted salmon-trout, then some breast of chicken and finally a magnificent hothouse peach.

The Baron, perhaps weighing up the reason for these refusals enquired whether his guest would accept anything at all. With ready wit Sax replied that he would gladly accept a share in the *Compagnie du Nord*. He must have been jesting since one of the big news stories currently circulating was the huge demand for shares in the new railway company. Thousands of would-be subscribers had been disappointed; a request for a share was tantamount to asking for the moon. Baron Rothschild, whose family were the principal shareholders, must have been taken with the answer. Perhaps feeling it a matter of honour that no guest should leave his house with a request unfulfilled, he instructed his secretary to prepare immediately a certificate for seven fully-paid shares in the railway, shares which had been issued at 500 francs but which then stood at 1,100 francs. It is also said that he cancelled Sax's outstanding debt. The great banker could be most generous when so inclined; it shows what personal charm and confidence Sax exuded to create such an impression on this shrewd man.

The friendly acquaintance thus made resulted in the Baron inviting Sax to a week-end hunting and shooting party at his *chateau* in Ferrières. The inventor, who was still a bachelor, took with him his brother, Alphonse, who was eight years younger than Adolphe and he too had followed his father's craft of wind-instrument manufacture. He had lately left Brussels to help his brother in his newly-found fortune in Paris. The party was a distinguished one but the brothers were fully at ease and were able to relax from the cares of business for a while and spent a thoroughly enjoyable week-end.[2]

Beneath these trappings of success, Sax was aware of disturbing undercurrents. His enemies had been aghast at the outcome of the Champ de Mars battle and the accepted report of the Commission. Whilst we may deplore the methods used in attempts to block the progress of the intruder, we might consider that not only had existing makers been shabbily treated by the Commission; they had been placed in an impossible situation. Most of them were faced with ruin and, in this desperate plight, it is not surprising that they resorted to desperate measures. Could he have but perceived it, Sax had gone too far in trying to corner the whole of the wind-instrument manufacturing business to himself. Did he really expect his rivals to meekly accept it all as *fait accompli* and leave him in peace? Or, if anticipating trouble, did he expect his high-placed friends to be able to deal with it without any dire effects to himself?

Any silence noticed from the enemy camp was not to be construed as acquiescence. On the contrary, they were quietly organising themselves to fight. Old rivalries between individual houses were forgotten in the need to unite against the common enemy. A Society, the United Association of Instrument Makers, was founded and legally constituted.

It had its full quota of officers — a president, a secretary and a treasurer — with a rule-book requiring regular periodic contributions from the members. The coincidental significance of its registered office being in the Rue Serpente, at No. 11, was not overlooked by Sax and his followers. From this address, a committee met regularly to consider strategy and tactics against the usurper. The first meeting of the Association took place on May 15th 1845 in the presence of the elected committee, Halary-Asté, Raoux (whose house it was), Gambaro senior, Guichard and Godefroy. All the Parisian instrument manufacturers had received a circular letter; the meeting was well attended.

It was now obvious that, with all the support commanded in the highest places, he could hardly be toppled at one blow. But they had shrewdly observed where his greatest weakness lay. Sax's basic lack of business sense had been carefully noted. Drain him of his money, drive him into bankruptcy, and no matter what decrees were passed or pronouncements made, he would be forced to dishonour his contracts. The methods they proposed to achieve this end were to prove expensive to them; hence the need for regular subscriptions.

The Association was particularly livid about the saxhorn. The granting of a patent for what was common property was, they claimed, a matter of blatant injustice. They lambasted Sax saying he was compelled to produce something he could call his own in order to justify the confidence placed in him by General de Rumigny. Lacking any originality, he was forced to adopt something in common use and pass it off as an invention. The point of view of the Paris manufacturers is rather plaintively summed up in a handbill circulated by the maker Jean-Louis Halary in 1846:

The commission appointed by the War Minister to improve and organise military music has judged it proper to add to the instruments now in use those which have recently been proposed to him. These are flugel-horns in different keys which a columnist has illegally called sax-horns in order to give them a special privilege which they cannot have, being public property.[3]

The columnist was, of course, Berlioz, who continued, in the pages of *Débats*, to extol the maker and his products to, at times, an extravagant degree. The composer was echoed by many lesser writers who found in Sax a welcome source of copy.

Sax had by 1845 advanced the development of the saxophone to a point where a patent could be applied for. As the specifications were entered, the Association launched a major offensive. A lawsuit was instigated to oppose the granting of the patent. The intention was to prove that the saxophone, far from being original, was known not only in France but in other parts of the world. Vague allusions were made to the existence of an "English tenoroon", a reference to Meikle's alto fagotto, the combination of a single-reed mouthpiece with a conical tube in the shape of a bassoon. Another example of a pre-saxophone was seen in a single specimen of an instrument which was sounded by means of a clarinet-type mouthpiece, appeared outwardly to be mainly conical and had an upturned bell similar to Sax's construction. This had been made in 1807 by one Desfontenelles, a watchmaker living in Lisieux.

Forced to defend the suit, Sax had no difficulty in defeating the two contenders No one had ever seen an "English tenoroon" whilst the Desfontenelles instrument was merely a museum curiosity. Other instruments, notably the bass clarinet, had upturned bells. This did not make them saxophones. The saxophone has an acutely tapering mouthpipe which assists in producing its peculiar tone, a feature quite different from what could be seen in the Lisieux instrument. There is no record that, at the time, anyone attempted to blow the Desfontenelles instrument. Had they done so, the point would have been proved. In the early 1930's the German saxophonist Jaap Kool took down the instrument from its place in the Paris Conservatoire Museum and was able to sound it. It was found to overblow, not at the octave as would a saxophone, but at the twelfth, showing beyond any doubt that this was an early form of bass clarinet.[4] Another low-register clarinet cited as a saxophone was the German bathyphone. An extensive search failed to produce one although, apparently, Sax had one in his collection.

The saxophone was attacked for its musical properties. Soon after it had made its first public appearance in February 1844 it had been the subject of denigration by Sax's enemies. Some called it a monster; others damned it with faint praise calling it an ingenious but simple object of curiosity, completely impractical. Scudo, critic of the *Revue des deux mondes*, declared: "The saxophones sound hollow and wrong — they are noisy and blaring". Berlioz was quick with a counterblast: *A Jupiter of Music attacks with great gusto the beautiful instruments of Adolphe Sax and puts them on the same level as instruments which offend the ear, although the Saxophone with its tender colour of sound produces exactly the opposite. This honourable and accurate and greatest philosophical critic of antiquity studies, no doubt, in the pit of the Théâtre Francais!* (That is where Scudo was a clarinettist).[5]

Since fair means had met with no success, the Association resorted to chicanery. A number of saxophones were obtained, sent abroad to have proprietary markings obliterated with false engravings, then to be ostensibly re-imported as being of foreign manufacture. As if this were not enough, it was arranged to have pictures and details of the instrument included in other makers' catalogues. Fortunately, the forgeries and frauds were not very well done and were easily exposed. On a completely different tack, the argument was advanced that Sax was trying to patent something which simply did not exist. A distinguished counsel, *Maître* Marie, acting for the Association, actually stood up in court to declare that the saxophone had never existed, could not possibly exist and was merely the trick of a charlatan.

Concurrently with this argument, the plaintiffs sought to reply on Article 31 of the Law of 1844 which stated: "No invention shall be deemed as being new when, before a patent having been taken out, it shall have been received by a sufficiently large number of the public to allow it to be made or copied". It was contended that, because Sax had played the saxophone in public and it had been revealed before the Commission for the Re-organisation of Military Bands, it was invalidated for patenting purposes. This was a more telling point.

Sax's reaction to the charges followed a predictable course. In a statement widely reported in the press, he flung down a challenge:

You say that you know the saxophone; I challenge you to make a single one. I will give you a year to make a saxophone during which time I won't take out a patent.

To add impetus to his words, and possibly to see if there really was anything resembling the saxophone in Germany, he and Arban, accompanied by Berlioz and Jules Janin, editor of *Débats*, went to to the Beethoven celebrations in Bonn. This was in August. When he returned to Paris, no one had come forward with a rival to the saxophone. After allowing further time for the challenge to be met he applied for and was given a patent for his family of saxophones on June 22nd 1846. This was immediately disputed by the Association on the grounds that the year mentioned had not yet expired. The appeal was very properly dismissed.

Despite the complete loss of this legal battle, the Association was unremitting in its underground attack. So much mud was thrown that some of its sticks to this day. As these words are being written there appears in a serious British music magazine an unequivocal statement that Desfontenelles invented the saxophone, Sax merely improving it by making it overblow at the octave instead of the fifth (sic) and by adding a brass or copper bell to the original wooden instrument.[6] Fortunately, such distortions of fact are now rare; that they occur at all reflects the virulence of Sax's enemies at the time of the original patent.

The idyllic summer of 1845 found people of note and culture flocking towards the Rhine. Musicians from all over Europe came to pay homage to the memory of Beethoven who had died only eighteen years before in poverty and neglect. Crowned heads were almost commonplace. The highlight of the celebrations was to be the unveiling of a statue to the great master, in Bonn before the Prussian Royal Family. Louis Spohr had written a cantata especially for the occasion. Among the most distinguished of the guests were Queen Victoria and Prince Albert who were staying at Bruhl castle. It was here that a most spectacular event was staged. After dark, on a glorious summer night, 1,200 soldiers each bearing a torch marched quietly on to the terrace taking up positions to form a V surrounded by a square. Suddenly, 1,200 trumpets and 300 drums crashed into a breathtaking fanfare prior to the massed bands of the Prussian army giving a concert in honour of Queen Victoria and her Consort.

Proud conductor of this magnificent serenade was a man who had more than one claim to musical distinction. In 1825, Wilhelm Wieprecht, a promising young musician of 23, had settled in Berlin and had immediately become interested in military music. Although not himself a craftsman able to build musical instruments, he was full of ideas which he had no difficulty in communicating to those who were. Stölzel and Blühmel had been known to him personally so that he had been in at the creation of the valve at a very early stage. He contributed greatly to the development of the mechanism by producing, in collaboration with Johann Gottfried Moritz, the celebrated *Berliner-Pumpen* valve, then being widely used with great success. From the very beginning he had had great faith in the valve as a means of giving brass instruments a satisfactory chromatic compass; it was mainly due to his championship that valved instruments began to get established. In 1825 he caused a great deal of interest by using some in his reconstituted cavalry band in place of keyed brass. Under his initiative, the Trumpet Corps of the Prussian Dragoon Guards, and two other cavalry bands for which he was responsible, began to use cornets, tenor horns, euphoniums and bombardons. Within a few years he had dispensed with all key-bugles.

Together with Moritz, he had designed and produced a 3-valve bombardon and a 5-valve tuba in F. The latter, with its valves arranged in sets of two and three and its inelegant unflared bell, was a resounding success when Wieprecht introduced it into his bands. Less of a triumph was his *Bathyphon*. As the name implies this instrument explored the depths of musical sound and was, in fact, a contra-bass clarinet, looking rather like a bassoon, with a metal bell and crook. Made by Ed. Skorra of Berlin and Franz Kruspe of Erfurt, it was fingered with keys on rod-axles and pitched in C two octaves below the soprano clarinet.

As an organiser of military bands, Wieprecht was second to none. In 1838, he was commissioned to carry out a complete reorganisation of Prussian bands. With Bandmasters Küffner, Neithardt and Faust, he entered into the task with such zeal that, seven years later, he had some six hundred musicians under his control which he could justly claim were the best in Europe. Berlioz had previously met Wieprecht during a visit to Prussia when Crown Prince William had, in his honour, mounted a private concert with three hundred participants. A wind-band arrangement of his own *Francs-Juges* overture and a gigantic Battle Symphony composed by Lord Burghersh, the English Ambassador, had created a deep impression.

Proud of his achievements, Wieprecht claimed no monopoly for the construction and use of valved instruments. In common with most manufacturers, he was indignant at hearing of Sax getting patents for so-called inventions which had been in use long before the Belgian had been heard of.

Well aware that Sax was making a pirated version of his valve and copies of his tuba, Wieprecht had seriously considered going to Paris and taking legal action. For the moment, however, he was fully occupied with duties at the Beethoven festival. It was during the celebrations that he had occasion to call at the Coblenz hotel apartment of Franz Liszt in connection with a Court concert at which Jenny Lind, "the Swedish nightingale", was to appear. By accident or design, Sax was present with some friends of the composer in his flat when Wieprecht was announced.

Never one to flinch from a head-on encounter, Sax nevertheless left the room only to reappear suddenly at a signal from Liszt. According to the visitor's account of the meeting, there were a number of eminent musical personages present as Liszt greeted him warmly. The composer then said, "Wieprecht, Sax has arrived!" whereupon, without warning, the German was confronted with his protagonist and given to understand that all present would like them to discuss and compare their respective instruments.

Sax played his clarinet and bass clarinet; Arban the cornet and saxhorn. Wieprecht congratulated both on their instrumental prowess and praised the bass clarinet although allowing that its size would constitute a serious impediment in military use. He was then able to name an instrument in current use in Germany to correspond with each of the saxhorns. No saxophone was available but, from the description given, Wieprecht contended that this was but a variation of his own *Bathyphon*. As a parting pleasantry, he exhorted Sax not to tarnish his reputation by seeking to claim as inventions what were really only improvements.

A completely different story is given by the Italian, Fiorentino, correspondent of the Paris *Constitutionnel,* who was present at the meeting. In a witty article he said that he found it difficult to understand why people who had spent so much time pouring scorn on Sax's instruments should now be claiming to have invented them before he did. According to Fiorentino, Wieprecht (who spoke only in German), in response to Sax's question, professed to know everything about the other's instruments including the saxophone. Affirming that he could play on Sax's bass clarinet he nevertheless grasped it awkwardly and was unable to produce a note. Amid prolific apologies, Wieprecht then admitted that he knew less about the saxhorn than the clarinet whilst the saxophone was a closed book. By way of making amends, he invited Sax to a nearby hall to hear and inspect the Prussian instruments. After the Germans had played, Sax and Arban reciprocated. According to the journalist, the bandsmen broke into a babble of excited chatter, looking enviously at the French instruments as if to say, "If we only had such equipment, what a serenade we could have given the Queen of England". Even Wieprecht was enthusiastic, embracing Sax and promising to come and see him in Paris. Fiorentino was intrigued to see "the Tuba and the Saxophone" going off arm in arm; Liszt cynically prophesied that they would not remain in tune for long.[8]

Obviously, both accounts must be treated with reservation, either side wishing to appear in the best possible light. It is hard not to feel that the meeting between the two instrument designers was contrived. Liszt must surely have expected Wieprecht to call at his apartment that morning in connection with the Court concert; it would have appealed to his waspish sense of humour to stage a contest between these two rivals on his ground.

Arranging for Sax to leave the room and then make a sudden re-appearance savours of an attempt to deliberately place Wieprecht at a disadvantage. All the same, the German seems to have taken the surprise in his stride, taking the opportunity to strongly mark the distinction between inventing and improving, and to point out that duplicates of Sax's brass instruments existed elsewhere. His ignorance of the saxophone may be forgiven; it was barely known even in Paris.

With the help of the Distin family, the saxhorn, under that name, became, to a certain extent, to be accepted in Germany. In addition to the honour bestowed on him by the King of the Netherlands, Sax was awarded the Premier Gold Medal of Prussia, placing a seal of victory on his brief excursion into Germany.

Liszt was right. Wieprecht's apparent conversion soon suffered a relapse. No sooner did the German arrive home than he published a virulent article in the 'Berlin Musical Gazette' attacking Sax and detailing the faults of his works. This brought a long and bitter rejoinder from the Belgian in which he accused Wieprecht of going back on statements made before honourable witnesses, lambasted him in reciprocal terms for ineptness and incompetence, suggested a contest between German and French musicians each using their respective systems and, lastly, challenged Wieprecht to be locked in a room furnished only with tools and raw materials, with Sax likewise confined in another, to see who could produce the best instrument.

Wieprecht was not to be drawn. Although he was prepared to help Sax's French opponents from afar, he himself abandoned the idea of taking personal action. Sensibly, he may have considered it not worth his while to spend time and money on legal wrangles when there was so much more constructive work to be done.

Notes on Chapter VI
1. *Almanac de l'Illustration* (Paris) c.1848.
2. Comettant, p.154. et seq. The hunting party included the marine painter, Jean Gudin (a close friend of Sax), an Italian prince (unidentified) and a witty character called Vatou, said to be a personal friend of King Louis-Philippe.
3. Comettant, p.250.
4. Kool: p.185.
5. Comettant, p.218.
6. *Music and Musicians* (London), Sept. 1971, p.16.
7. Vide Krager, p.47.
8. Comettant, p.250 et seq.

The Adolphe Sax Musical Instrument Factory in the Rue Saint-Georges

Bass clarinet by Desfontenelles of Lisieux (1807)
once erroneously thought to be a forerunner of the saxophone

VII
Triumphs and Disasters

As the Sax factory increased production to meet the real and anticipated demand for new instruments, some people at the War Ministry were having second thoughts. Accountants had been working on the cost of implementing the report so cheerfully accepted by the Minister. It was evident from their figures that some economies would have to be made in order to achieve, in their opinion, a reasonable budget. Concerning the number of players, 36 was accepted for cavalry bands but some of the initial allowance originally intended for new instruments was to be appropriated for the shoeing and harnessing of horses. For infantry bands, the Commission had recommended 55 men including the Musical Director. On August 10th 1845, an official announcement appeared in the *Moniteur de l'Armée* stating infantry band strengths to be fixed at 50 players only, excluding the Musical Director; 25 musicians and 25 pupils. The four instruments to receive the axe were the pairs of oboes and bassoons. These had been retained by the Commission because of their distinctive tone colours; another argument was now presented reverting to Sax's original contention that these instruments are ineffectual in the open air and going on to say that, unless their numbers could be doubled, it would be better to dispense with them altogether.

An immediate outcry, largely from manufacturers, followed the decision. It was argued that the closure of classes for these instruments at the *Gymnase* would lead to a deterioration in the number of students taking up these instruments, leading to an eventual disappearance of teachers, and players in theatre and other orchestras. The army retorted no less strongly. Already, it declared, there was an acute shortage of such players so that existing bands had difficulty in recruiting men to cover these parts. It was the duty of the *Gymnase* to train musicians for the Army and no part of its function to act as a nursery for the theatre and concert hall, especially as the city supported a perfectly good Conservatoire.

Much abuse was directed personally at Sax, alleging that he wanted to abolish the double-reed instruments altogether and eventually to have bands equipped exclusively with his saxhorns and saxophones. Whatever Sax's thoughts on the second part of the charge, it was absurd to suggest he wished for the demise of the oboe and bassoon. He made both at his factory and indeed spent a great deal of time and effort in trying to improve the very imperfect bassoon. His only contention, with which many agreed, was that these instruments in ones and twos, amid large numbers of clarinets and brass instruments, contributed nothing when used out of doors. As for the tone-colour value, the puny effect of an oboe or a bassoon solo in these conditions could be observed by anyone.

There was some difficulty regarding the initial allowance for infantry bands. The absence of this, it was felt, would jeopardise the engagement of supernumaries to improve the quality of musicianship. This could be overcome by offering better conditions to enlisted bandsmen, at the same time requiring them to serve for longer periods rather than discharge themselves into more lucrative employment just at the time when their training would be of most use to the Army. As a matter of policy, it was agreed that a general high standard of efficiency among rank-and-file bandsmen was preferable to concentrating on a few gifted soloists.

It is significant how a comparatively little thing, like not having to carry a pack in peacetime, can raise the morale of the serving soldier. The feeling that something was, at last, being done for Army musicians brought a new spirit to the ranks. Despite the cut-back in expenditure, bands were eager to seek re-equipping to fit the new order. In quite a short time, fifteen regimental bands were fitted out, with others regularly coming forward. Apathetic or ignorant Commanding Officers held some bands back; there was a strong but apparently unimplemented suggestion for the appointment of an Inspector of Bands to see that orders were carried out and to ensure that new instruments were of the quality expected.

The spirit of rivalry between bands and bandsmen is as old as bands themselves. The effort involved in trying to outshine one's neighbour often leads to improved technique if nothing else. To encourage competition, the Army toyed with the idea of arranging contests between regimental bands. Sax suggested that these should be staged twice each year, before a competent jury, on May 1st and July 31st. The champion band would be presented with a suitably engraved instrument wrought in silver and gold; the best individual bandsman would also be awarded an instrument etched with his full name. An excellent scheme, as good for business as for morale. Perhaps the expense of the prizes precluded the idea from being developed.

On the third anniversary of the 1830 revolution, the three days of celebration had been crowned with a gigantic concert of 500 instrumentalists and 300 singers. Apart from the singing of the *Marseillaise*, the result had been disappointing. Some of the blame for this was placed upon the instruments used although the real cause was probably under-rehearsal. In the same year Fétis had conducted a similar gathering in Brussels with happier results, having had five or six practices. Wieprecht too had been very successful with large contingents in Prussia. Plans began to be formulated for a concert of such proportions as to dwarf all that had gone before. Organisation was to be in the hands of the Musician's Association; to secure wide support, profits were to be donated to a benevolent fund for needy musicians. Full co-operation was promised by the Minister; Commanding Officers were asked to release their bandsmen for rehearsals which were entered into with zeal.

The celebrated violinist, Joseph Massart, was appointed Musical Director — a curious choice of such a shy man for such an ostentatious occasion. As they got down to details, difficulties became apparent. In checking the instruments available in each of the bands, it was found that only three oboes were present. Since the united bands were to aggregate 892 players, their presence was deemed to be an entire waste of effort. Large numbers of bandsmen were found to be below an acceptable standard. Not all the bands had changed to the new instrumentation; great labour and expense was involved in preparing band parts of the music to be played. Perseverance and determination swept the project forward. With the help of the Lieutenant-General in charge of the Paris garrison, men taking part in rehearsals were quartered in the suburbs and ferried to a central point by special trains.

Public response was overwhelming. On the morning of July 24th 1846, the Champs Elysées and its environs was packed with an excited crowd heading for the Franconi Hippodrome. Only seven or eight thousand were able to get inside to witness the great visual and aural kaleidoscope presided over by the Duke of Montpensier. Not all that got inside could count themselves fortunate. Some were so close to the instrumentalists of that vast orchestra as to get a very distorted hearing. Those outside heard a much more balanced performance.

The Hippodrome was a vast new arena with accommodation for between four and five thousand people. The entrepreneur, Victor Franconi, had invited Sax to equip a band of twenty-five well-paid players to demonstrate the acoustical potential of the edifice. Sax did this, apparently rehearsing them at his own expense at his own premises. Such were the acoustics of the new Hippodrome and, it was claimed, the superiority of Sax's instruments, that the sound of the small company could be heard at quite a distance along the Champs Elysées.[1] The effect, therefore, of a group nearly 36 times as large must have been deafening.

The programme followed closely the type of music which has been the staple diet of wind bands to the present day — marches, overtures, waltzes, arrangements and fantasias on popular orchestral works, penned, in this case, by Bandmasters Berr and Fessy. The Grand Finale was Berlioz's *Apothéose* from the *Symphonie Funèbre et Triomphale* transcribed to feature Sax's instruments. The effect was shattering. Once again Sax emerged triumphant to wild acclaim. The press was strong in praise of the unity achieved by the use of his instrumental families. Berlioz compared the event to a celebration of Grecian or Roman times.

Like a pedal-bass, the activities, legal and illegal, of Sax's enemies vibrated beneath the whole tenor of his life. Even at moments of greatest elation, he was always conscious of these sinister undercurrents. Yet, if he was never to be allowed any completely unalloyed satisfaction, at least his blackest despair was tempered with tangible signs of appreciation from those who valued his work. Few men could have, for such a long period, experienced such extremes of triumph and disaster simultaneously. No opportunity was ever lost by the Rue Serpente conspiracy to make life difficult, embarrassing and costly for the inventor. Intimidation and bribery were constantly in use against his workmen, making the maintenance of a permanent skilled workforce a matter of perpetual worry. Nevertheless, he was able to command the loyalty and support of a few good men at supervisory level and high-quality production was maintained.

At times, the disloyalty of workmen who, at outside instigation, smuggled drawings or sabotaged production got so bad that the inventor was driven to seek a desperate remedy. A well-meaning friend had pointed out that the Melun Central Prison was full of able-bodied men doing nothing productive as they served out their sentences. Why not set up a branch workshop in the prison? By so doing, there would, under the eyes of the guards, be no smuggling and no sabotage; at the same time, favourable rates could be negotiated for the labour. The prison authorities favoured the project. Sax spent a lot of time and effort in setting up the workshop and training suitable prisoners. The scheme worked well; all three parties to it appeared to be happy. Trouble arose when some of the convicts were released.

They arrived in the Rue Saint-Georges demanding work at normal rates of pay; when this was refused they simply demanded money. The proprietor promptly sent them packing only to have them return in force attempting to extort money with menaces. They reckoned without Sax's stubborn resistance in the face of any sort of intimidation. He stood up to them and again they had to leave empty handed. Of course, this was the end of the experiment; the problems created were greater than those solved.[2] Writers heavily in favour of Sax tried to insist his methods in this venture were entirely philanthropic. His enemies were equally adamant that he did it to exploit a source of cheap labour. The truth, as usual, is probably somewhere between. Naturally, he was happy to cut costs; happier still at the security offered. At the same time, he would undoubtedly have gained some satisfaction at being able to help some of the dregs of society to perhaps make a new start in life.

Sax was warm hearted to a fault. Bitter as he was against his detractors, he responded often with touching gratitude to any apparently genuine approach. This fact was not lost upon the opposition who put in his way such confidence tricksters against whose wiles the inventor was no match. Because of the constant flow of lawyers' bills and problems in keeping production going at the factory, finance again was becoming a problem. But Sax was not one to forget old kindnesses. His great champion, Berlioz, was deeply moved by one particular gesture. After the Paris production of "The Damnation of Faust" has proved disastrous, the composer, now almost penniless, was preparing for a contracted concert tour of Prussia. Despite his pressing problems, Sax scraped together 1,200 francs in gold for his friend.[3]

Berlioz continued active support for Sax and his work in the columns of *Débats*. From here it is possible to trace some of the varied activities upon which the inventor was engaged. The popularity of the workshop concerts had outgrown the meagre space available; the demand for instruments meant that every inch of factory space was needed for their making and the two hundred or so workmen employed. To bring alleviation on both counts, Sax was able to acquire three artists studios which formed part of the Rue Saint-Georges building and turn them into a concert hall seating some 400 people. This was opened in 1847. Although the hall abutted the street the Rue Saint-Georges was, at the time, a quiet pedestrian precinct where carriages could not pass. The quietness appealed to both artists and audience so that the concerts were well attended. Shortly afterwards, however, the tranquility was shattered when the city authorities caused an opening to be made into the Rue d'Aumale, thus making the Rue Saint-Georges available to wheeled traffic. The resultant noise was enough to render the hall unusable for music and activities had to be transferred elsewhere.[4]

Early in the same year, a saxophone class was established at the *Gymnase;* by the Autumn, first and second prizes had been awarded to five of its students. The instrument found favour in many places. Following the Champs-de-Mars contest, two regimental bands, the 9th Dragoons and the 45th Line, had been equipped with Sax's instruments. Both appeared before an appreciative Royal Family at the Tuileries.

At one occasion at Neuilly, the 45th Infantry Band was playing incidental music during the Royal dinner. The band had recently brought in a saxophone to augment its instrumentation this had a solo melody to play in one of the pieces. King Louise-Philippe had his attention compelled from the food and petty talk by this new and intriguing sound. He wanted to know all about the instrument and requested that the solo be repeated. From then, by all accounts, the King could be numbered among the saxophone's admirers.

The new tone colour commended itself particularly to composers. Meyerbeer's new opera, *Le Prophète*, was staged in Paris in April 1849. The composer was, of course, well acquainted with Sax's bass clarinet which he had used extensively in the last two acts. Berlioz had not failed to praise the music, the instrument and its inventor in his column. Meyerbeer had the highest regard for Sax; after the opera's favourable reception he wrote: "Sax is not only an instrument maker, he is a distinguished musical performer; his theoretic knowledge resulting from conscientious study added to long practice in his art, has allowed him to achieve the greatest improvements and inventions which have brought him so great a reputation".

To the inventor himself, he penned a long letter in which he regretted not having known of the saxophone soon enough to include a part for it in the opera. There is a suggestion, however, that the real reason for the omission was opposition from orchestral players.

Unfortunately for both monarch and inventor, there was little time left for the one to enjoy the music of the other. The evening of the 23rd February 1848 was apparently calm and normal when Sax escorted an aunt and niece to see the Paris illuminations. In the Rue de la Paix they saw a number of insurgents armed with guns and sabres; nevertheless, they pressed on as far as the Boulevard des Capucines. Near the Foreign Office, however, they were suddenly engulfed by a noisy crowd confronting a group of soldiers, and experienced the horror of seeing the soldiers take aim and fire indiscriminately into the crowd. Sax had to search among the dead and dying for his two ladies until he eventually found them severely shocked, covered with blood, but otherwise unhurt, and was able to get them safely home. It would seem that later, in June 1848, Sax himself took up arms against the insurgents.

Events were moving against the King, helped forward by a revolutionary committee which actually met in a house close by the Sax factory in the Rue Saint-Georges. The day after Sax's gory experience the King abdicated and within three days he and his entourage had fled the country.

For Sax this was high calamity. Not only had the deposed King always received him kindly and shown an interest in his work; his chief *aide-de-camp*, General de Rumigny, had been a true patron, friend and protector. The General unquestioningly accompanied the Royal Family into exile; the extent of his former protection became abundantly clear as it was removed with his departure. The situation in Paris was close to anarchy. Such proceedings as were conducted in the Chamber of Deputies were rowdy and uproarious. Those who had been in some way connected with the former monarch were open to ridicule and persecution. Sax, who was considered a King's protégé, came in for vindictive attack.

Amid the confusion, the Association of the Rue Serpente managed to get a vital piece of legislation through the Chamber. The 1845 decrees for the reform of military bands were revoked. The saxhorn, chief source of bitterness among other instrument makers, was abolished by a pointed paragraph in the new Order which stated: " . . . there must be given back to a number of instruments, wrongly designated under the name of the maker who manufactured them, the family name which they should never have lost".

Bands reverted to their former instrumentation; instruments of Sax's manufacture already on order were cancelled by the Ministry; others lately delivered were returned. The factory premises were soon stacked high with unwanted instruments.

During the unrest created by the revolution, Sax was approached by one of his most skilled hands, a valve-maker, and asked to attend a workshop meeting of his employees. Certain proposals were to put to him in the name of the Society for the Rights of Man. At the meeting it was explained to the proprietor that, as the moment for the emancipation of the worker had come, they wished for the business to be run in the future on a co-operative basis. Sax agreed and said that he would willingly have entered into such an agreement previously without waiting for a revolution. Then they got down to details.

"Do you want to be paid daily?", asked Sax.

"Yes", they all agreed.

"Do you want all wages to be equal so that everyone receives the same?"

The lower paid workers said, "Yes"' the higher paid, "No".

Then it was agreed that there should be equality within certain grades of skill. They agreed that Sax should receive the remuneration of a top-grade skilled man. This was fixed at 48 francs a day; a journeyman would receive 10 francs a day and unskilled workers 3.50 francs. This was practically the same as the scale already existing.

Sax then asked if they would wish to share in the profits of the business to which there was a ready affirmative. When, however, he mentioned possible losses, this notion took them by surprise. They wished to be shareholders in the company but, by way of putting up capital, pointed out that the only asset they possessed was their skill and their labour.

The proprietor showed how the difficulty could be overcome; he would stop an agreed sum out of the wages of each shareholder each week and, at the end of the year, the company would be wound up and any profit distributed. The point about possible losses seemed to trouble the men; they asked what would happen in these circumstances.

"In that case", Sax replied, "you will have lost the money you have invested and will still owe me something".

The meeting asked for time to consider and saw, probably for the first time, the problems as well as the advantages of ownership. Nothing further was heard of the matter.[5]

With a large bill for wages to meet each week for his 191 employees and with work at a standstill there was a clear case for closing down the factory and dismissing the whole staff. The maker was loth to let his trained workmen go but there really seemed to be no alternative. Before he could act, however, there came a request from a business associate that he should stay his hand. Unemployment was rife in the troubled city; for political reasons it was desirable that Sax should keep his work-force together if a way could be found. The maker was glad to co-operate; some sign of favour in political circles would be welcome at this time.

To implement the plan, Sax's acquaintance passed over 30,000 francs without requiring or accepting a receipt, thus making it appear that an outright gift was intended rather than a loan. The money allowed Sax to pay his workmen but, since there was practically nothing to do, the payments were in the nature of a "dole". From the manufacturer's point of view there was no difficulty; he probably considered he was merely administering someone else's charity.

As the political atmosphere began to clear, Sax, little knowing he was sitting on a time-bomb, welcomed with relief the election of Louis Napoleon as President. The manufacturer congratulated himself at being able to hold his company together during those troubled days; now that order was being restored, he too looked for some restoration of his previous good fortune. Things augured well and he obtained a gold medal at the Paris Exhibition of 1849 despite the fact that his old antagonist Raoux was on the jury. An even greater accolade was imminent. The name of Sax featured in the Honours List prepared by the President. Surely the inventor was to know no prouder moment than that when he was appointed to the Legion of Honour. He was to find the future Emperor hardly less interested and appreciative of his works than was the deposed Louis-Philippe.

Such honours were naturally not appreciated by the opposition; not only in Paris but, in the case of the Gold Medal, from beyond the borders of France. The Austrian and German makers were incensed at Sax having the premier award of the 1849 Exhibition. Girand, Director of the

Austrian Music Academy, was joined by eleven professors from the Paris Conservatoire and five other notable musicians in an open protest at the Gold Medal going to Sax. Their point of view was expounded by a contemporary military commentator, Captain C. Raynard: *The Austrian instruments are known for their beauty of metal, purity and sound. The military bands of Austria and Germany are far better than the French orchestras. Could we praise them more? It is all the more regrettable that the Austrian brass instruments did not receive a higher medal as their system is superior to the French one. Some exhibits excelled themselves in fine technical details and were by far the best in the Exhibition. We do not wish to say anything against Ad. Sax's inventive ideas but it seems that the results of his genius were not very successful.* One of Girand's arguments was that, if traditional instruments were to be displaced by Sax's homogeneous constructions, composers' intentions would be thwarted.[6]

On the day of the coup d'état of 2nd December 1851 which placed Louis Napoleon firmly in control of France, Sax had another brush with death. Rising methodically at six and living, as it were, on top of his work, he had already put in a good day's work before he breakfasted at eleven. This was the best time of day to catch him; he welcomed company at a repast which never varied from steaks, fried eggs in butter, Bordeaux and coffee. This was followed by liqueurs and cigars, the latter being bought wholesale and kept for years so that he was able to boast that they cost him "only a penny apiece". Breakfast lasted a considerable time and was his one big break during the day. After it he would, more often than not, work well into the night.

On the morning in question he was breakfasting at the house of Brandus, the music-publisher, in the Rue Richelieu, with many friends and acquaintances including Davison, music critic of "The Times". A commotion was heard and the party were startled to see a number of soldiers forcing their way into the house. One of Brandus's men-servants went forward to remonstrate and was summarily shot dead. The troops insisted that they had been fired upon from the house. Sax, Davison, Brandus and some others were hustled into the street where the officer commanding, being assured that they had fired upon his men, ordered them to be shot.

Before the act could be carried out, a general arrived. He recognised Sax as a fellow music lover and was able to recall that Sax had fought bravely against the insurgents in June 1848. Sax and his friends were told to get away as quickly as possible while the troops were "mopping-up" in the street.[7]

As Sax's fortunes once again improved, the time-bomb was quietly ticking. The explosion was triggered off in 1852 by events far removed from immediate affairs. The benefactor who had helped Sax keep his factory going during the troubles had died. His daughter and heiress defied the wishes of her family in her marriage. A squabble broke out between members of the family, to be fought out in the Courts. As details of the estate were sifted, 30,000 francs remained unaccounted for. Someone remembered Sax. He was approached by the executors and, in his usual open way, freely and immediately admitted to having the money. He then did an extremely foolish thing. Instead of first seeking legal advice he, on the mere verbal assurance that no one would press for payment, signed a document acknowledging that the sum had been a loan. The same day he received an official order to repay the debt in full with interest within twenty-four hours.

Sax was horrified to find himself, by one rash act, in a terrible position. The money had long been spent for its original purpose; it was quite impossible to find such an enormous sum, certainly not in a single day. Remonstrations with the creditors produced no softening in their attitude. The alternative before him was to become bankrupt or be arrested for debt. He had, not long before, been in London for the Great Exhibition. In far less happy circumstances he again crossed the Channel a few hours before the law was to take its course. From London, he corresponded by letter without having the slightest effect. There being no other course, and in the deepest despair, he returned to Paris and filed his petition in bankruptcy.

Notes on Chapter VII

Vide Kastner: *Manuel général*, pp.276-329.
1. Comettant, pp.242-3.
2. *ibid.,* pp.170-183.
3. Barzun: *Berlioz and his Century*, p.244.
4. Comettant p.242.
5. *ibid.,* pp.319-320.
6. V. F. Cerveny & Sohne catalogue and price list, c.1895, p.94.
7. *St. James's Gazette* (London) 12th February 1894, p.12

Exhibition of Industrial Products — Musical Instruments —
L'Illustration, 11th August, 1849

VIII
Litigation

It was by no means certain how far the declared enemies of Sax had a hand in the chain of events which brought him to insolvency. They undoubtedly knew of the circumstances by which he was able to keep his factory open during those troubled days; they could never be accused of lethargy in exploiting a weakness to their advantage. Even so, Sax played right into their hands with his gullibility, showing he could have managed his own ruin without the aid of virulent foes. After the heights of success, to be plunged into the depths of failure was enough to depress the most philosophical nature.

The Association of Instrument Manufacturers had pursued him relentlessly in and out of the Courts almost from the moment he had first set foot in Paris. As in the case of the saxophone patent, the inventor usually won the actions brought against him. Yet they were hollow victories in terms of the time and expense involved. The association judged its tactics to a nicety and, although Sax was fond of quoting a saying he attributed to one of Napoleon's marshals — "Victory goes to he who can fight an extra quarter-of-an-hour" — it was never certain that he would be the one on his feet at the end of the day. Immediately an action was lost in a lower Court, an appeal would be made to the next highest, until the case was finally decided in the Supreme Court. After that, the whole process would begin again with something else. The sum of legal costs to either side may be imagined.

Before the suit against the granting of the saxophone patent had run its course the Association was already preparing the ground for what was to become a massive series of lawsuits and appeals which were to occupy Sax and his adversaries for many years to come.

It should not be thought that every manufacturer without exception was ranged against Sax. In certain instances he was, because of the inadequacy of his own factory, able of necessity to pass out lucrative work to others. Two Strasborg manufacturers, Charles Finck and Charles Roth had, early in 1846, applied for and been given licences to manufacture to Sax designs.

The inventor's first inkling of fresh trouble came through the action of a certain manufacturer who was acting as a sub-contractor to Sax in making valves. A normal, pleasant business relationship was suddenly shattered when the manufacturer turned abusive, accusing Sax of plagiarism, refusing to make any more valve components for him and declaring that he would henceforth make them on his own account. It was obvious that this was the work of the opposition, but, while the inventor was busy going to law over what he considered to be a flagrant breach of contract, the President of the Lower Civil Court of the Seine, at the *Palais-de-Justice* was reading another application to commence legal proceedings. This was dated 3rd March 1846 and was in the names of instrument manufacturers Raoux, Antoine Halary, Gautrot senior, Buffet junior and Gambraze. The text of the application ran:

The said persons, acting in their own names and as representatives of all the instrument manufacturers of Paris and the departments, being represented by Maître Lavaux, have the honour to inform you, M. Président, that M. Sax, a Belgian manufacturer, who arrived in Paris in 1843, on 17th August 1843 and on 13th October 1845, took out invention patents for instruments called bugles-à-cylindres *and* saxtrombas, *and which, since this time, M. Sax, helped by powerful protectors, has extolled these instruments, substituting the name of Saxhorn and had obtained, following a decision of the Minister of War dated 31st July 1845, that the Saxhorn should be included in the composition of instrumental military bands; the complainants have not been able to see with indifference this glorification of a pretended new system, called the*

Sax system; it is important to all French musical instrument manufacturers that the general public should know that the Sax system, which is vaunted by him to be a new system, has nothing new about it; it does not constitute any new invention and that the qualification of the Sax system is quite simply a lie; that the instruments for which M. Sax has taken out patents have been known for a long time in the trade, both in France and abroad; that the complainants have interests in the nullification of these patents which is open to them under Article 30 and 34 of the law of 15th July 1844; they request urgent action on this question which concerns to a high degree a complete branch of their industry; they request your permission to announce to M. Adolphe Sax, manufacturer, living in Paris, Rue Neuve Saint-Georges, No. 10, that from three days time, and without any chance of conciliation, to understand that the patents of invention obtained by him on 17th August 1843 and 13th October 1845 for the instruments described above shall be null and void and shall not be taken out by him again; that he should be forbidden to use in his publicity and his prospectuses the term Sax system, since this indicates an invention which does not exist; that he should be fined the sum of 100 francs as damages to our interests at each contravention of this judgement and, of course, costs.

On receipt of a registration fee of 3 francs 30 centimes, the President allowed the summons to be served within 3 days of 28th February 1846. Having served the writ on Sax, the Association was in no hurry to bring the case to a hearing and nearly a year passed before it was ready.

During this time, Sax printed and distributed a prospectus which expressed without trace of modesty, his own opinion of himself and his work:

The various instruments either invented or improved by M. Sax are immensely superior to the old instruments used by European armies.

Their superiority has been recognised and even stated in print by the Commission appointed by the Minister of War to reorganise military bands in France.

The Commission only pronounced this verdict after a long and profound examination of the instruments, and during the examination, the Commission heard instruments from Germany, France and Belgium.

The contest which took place in the Champ-de-Mars in April 1845 proved the superiority of M. Sax's system as far as sonority, power and trueness of sound was concerned. One can judge advantages of using his instruments in military bands.

The prospectus went on to explain that, although Sax tried to keep his prices competitive with his rivals, his use of superior materials meant that they inclined to be a little more expensive. It ended by saying that Sax was willing and able to sue any who infringed his patents and counterfeited his instruments, and all such instruments would be seized.

The circulation of this document incensed the Association to reply in the pages of *Moniteur de l'Armée* on 20th July 1846.

We cannot allow M. Sax's circular to pass without reply. For more than ten years these instruments have been known in Germany, and all French manufacturers have been making similar ones.

Some of these models were shown at the Exhibition of 1844.

M. Sax cannot be allowed to take out patents for instruments which he has not invented and which were known in the trade before the appearance of his; therefore he cannot hold a monopoly for them.

Therefore, the manufacturers have made a demand before the Tribunal of the Seine for the annulment of his pretended patents.

We take this occasion to remind bandmasters of military bands that, by letters of 17th April and 3rd November 1845, the Duke of Dalmatia and Lt.-Général de Saint-Yon, who is today Minister of War, formerly declared that there should be no monopoly in the manufacture of musical instruments for anybody, and that regiments are completely free to buy instruments of their own choice.

The Delegates of the French Manufacturers
Raoux, Halary, Gautrot senior, Buffet, Gambaro.

A concert in the Sax factory in honour of a visiting 'eastern potentate'

A demonstration of Sax's instruments before an invited audience at the Rue Saint-Georges factory
Almanac de l'Illustration 16th July 1864

G. A. Besson took an independent line and issued a counter-prospectus:

M. G. Besson is recognised as the only creator in France of several new systems of manufacture, of improving instruments such as ophicleides, trombones and valved cornets — notably instruments with large short valves and straight cylinders which are inappropriately termed Saxhorns.

Besson claimed that, during the period from 1841 to 1843, he supplied such instruments to many regiments and that, from 1843, Sax had claimed the profits and the glory from those instruments. In addition, Besson wrote to all regimental Commanding Officers and to members of the Ministry of War, claiming precedent over Sax's "inventions", saying that Sax had deceived everyone and, in addition, was a Belgian. Large posters were printed and displayed, stating that G. Besson & Cie were the only people recognised in France responsible for the construction and improvement of ophicleides, trombones, valved cornets and instruments with valves to which Sax had given his name.

Pending the hearing of the case, Sax's patents were automatically invalidated and the instruments in question could be made by others without fear of retribution. At the same time, the Association went to considerable pains to collect evidence. Manufacturers beyond the borders of France were circularised and encouraged to join in the fight against Sax. French manufacturers received the following request:

Paris, 2nd September 1846.
Sir and dear brother,
I have the honour to announce to you that the Committee in the interests of our defence desires each musical instrument manufacturer to send to it documents or any arguments which could be favourable to our cause. I beg you personally to send me all particulars.
As soon as manufacturers have sent me this information, the defence will consult it and take from it any arguments which would help the cause.
I ask you to make all possible haste because this must be finished for the 8th of September.
(signed) Gambaro.

Chief among Italian makers to be approached by the Association was Guiseppe Pelitti who made excellent valved bugles of many sizes which were known under the generic name *Pelittoni*. In the summer of 1846, M. Joubard, Director of the Belgian Industrial Museum and a friend of Sax who claimed to have influenced the inventor in earlier days by "pushing him by the shoulders towards Paris", was in Milan. Chancing to pass Pelitti's establishment, he saw in the window instruments which struck him as being familiar, and was tactless enough to ask the Italian, "Why do you make Sax's instruments in Milan?" Pelitti indignantly retorted, "It is Sax who makes my instruments in Paris!" — and went on to accuse Sax of visiting the establishment of Pelitti's friend in Germany and of copying every one of the instruments he saw there. In fact, this seems to have been a case of mistaken identity (the alleged counterfeiter was described as "short and fat" whereas Joubard was able to say that Sax was "tall and thin"); the Italian showed Joubard a letter from the French maker, Guichard, offering to pay Pelitti's expenses in going to Paris to take part in the action against Sax. Joubart conveyed all this intelligence to Sax in a letter dated 7th September 1846.[1]

Early in 1847, evidence for the Association's case was nearing completion and a final meeting prior to the hearing was called:

Sir,
The Committee will meet on Monday, 1st February at 7 p.m. at the house of M. Blanc in the Rue Rougemont 13, Faubourg Poisonière. The subject of this meeting will be the lawsuit against M. Sax, and M. Blanc will need all the necessary documents for the success of this lawsuit. Paris, 27th January 1847.   (signed) Gambaro.

It does not appear that Pelitti responded to the invitation; nevertheless, the case came on in February 1847. *Maître* Marie was leading counsel for the plaintiffs, *Maître* Chaix d'Est-Ange represented Sax.

Marie opened elequently and convincingly, pleading for the annulment of Sax's patents of 1843, 1845 and 1846. He dismissed with scorn the idea that Sax had invented or improved anything, saying that it was common knowledge that such improvements and inventions were in existence long before the patents were granted. He considered Sax to be a vulgar intriguer and that his object in seeking to improve military bands was nothing but a pretext to obtain a monopoly for the provision of their instruments. Further, he contended, the so-called inventor was a petty, vain, ridiculous person who would take out a patent for the most impractical and impossible thing.

Turning to Sax's supporters, he directly accused the President of the Commission for the Re-organisation of Military Bands, General de Rumigny, and its secretary, Georges Kastner, of being in league with Sax, supplying him with money and being shareholders in his company for the express purpose of securing a monopoly. Kastner in particular came in for abuse, being ridiculed as a rich dilettante who would naively give his help to anyone who requested it.

Returning to the General, Marie pointed out that the Military members of the Commission consisted of serving officers who were subordinate to de Rumigny in military discipline.

This attack brought an immediate response from the General. In a letter to the Court he firmly denied any shareholding interest in Sax's business. It is true, he wrote, that he had given the inventor a small amount, not exceeding 1,000 or 1,500 francs, in order that the process of instrument manufacture might not cease, but this was in the form of an interest-free loan, repayment of which would be waived if the beneficiary continued to be in financial distress.

De Rumigny went on to stress the defects in existing military band instruments, stating that, during his missions in Prussia in 1842 and again in 1846, he found similar shortcomings in German instruments. Furthermore, there were gaps in instrumental families which needed filling. The Commission, composed of eminent civilians as well as distinguished officers, had been unanimous in accepting Sax's new instruments and, whilst he understood the alarm of existing manufacturers, he could not go out of his way to pity them.

As for making money out of Sax's instruments, the General felt it to be beneath his dignity even to deny the charge. But, he added, if the attacks continue, he would most certainly bring an action for defamation of character.

For his part, Kastner submitted to the Court an affidavit, dated 1st March 1847, formally denying Marie's charges, stating that he had never been financially interested in Sax's enterprises or any other industrial enterprise either in France or abroad.

Maître Chaix d'Est-Ange made a telling speech in defence of Sax, describing him as a man who was reduced to such penury as to contemplate the pawning of medals gained at many Exhibitions. The advocate produced Sax's patent specifications to the Court, underlining in detail the various points of novelty and ingenuity. He finished his plea on Sax's behalf by saying:

This is not only the case of Sax and his adversaries; it is the case of art and industry. This case concerns the destinies of all those who take part in the music of France. By your judgement you have to declare whether routine can possibly be allowed to put a stop to progress. I hope that you will never come to say, 'You shall go no further'.

In the session of 23rd February 1847, *Maître* Etienne Blanc, on behalf of the plaintiffs, again insisted that the patents be nullified. By way of fresh argument, he endeavoured to show Sax as a charlatan because the so-called inventor had made no attempt to impound the instruments he considered to be counterfeits. (Sax submitted that the cost of this operation and the consequent lawsuits would, for him, have been out of the question). Secondly, Blanc went on, the Association had previously written to Sax stating that, in spite of the patents, they were going to continue to make the instruments specified in them. In spite of this provocation, subsequently renewed, Sax had apparently kept silent throughout. This was not, the counsel claimed, the action of a man who had a legitimate claim to protect.

On 9th March 1847, M. Gaujal, Deputy King's Procurator, summed up:

M. Raoux and his colleagues have just asked the Court that M. Sax's patents should be made null and void. In making this demand they are doing it not only in their personal names but as representatives and delegates of all the brass instrument makers from Paris and the departments; that is, they claim to represent the entire making of brass instruments. This is not possible.

A corner of the Sax factory

The Sax factory in full production

Nobody in France can plead through a procurator. In terms of law, you cannot maintain a pretention of this kind. However, if one gets to the bottom of things, one realises that it is not only the five complainants who are appearing before you; it is a complete branch of our national industry which is interested in whether M. Sax's patents stand or not, and have an interest in seeing them terminated. It is a vital question for the industry. It is also a vital question for M. Sax. For him above all it is a question of honour. It is a question of laying claim to his own inventions. It is also a question of his very existence, of his past and his future, the fruit of his work and his fortune. There is, therefore, great interest on both sides.

It is also a question of morality. This word has been bandied about constantly during this trial and had been used by the advocates on both sides. I want to talk for a few minutes on the situation in which Sax found himself before this trial started, and particularly I want to talk about the alleged illegitimate protection that he had received from a highly placed official and even from the Minister of War.

If one is to believe the complaints, the contests instituted in 1845 to reorganise military bands were not true contests. Obviously, they were organised without good faith and with partiality, and the result of these contests was only due to the interested influence of General de Rumigny who, although a sleeping partner in the Company by Shares organised by M. Sax to exploit his patents, nevertheless became president of the commission organising the contest, and appointed two colonels to serve on this commission. Let us examine this.

First of all, if the Minister of War had intended, as the complainants state, to damage national industry and concede a monopoly to M. Sax, what was to stop him, I ask you, from doing this openly and outright? If the Minister of War had enough evidence in his hands to show the relative value of Sax's instruments compared with others, what was there to stop him making an immediate pronouncement under his responsibility as Minister and to give Sax a monopoly? Was the Minister of War obliged to hold such a contest? Was he bound by the report of the Commission which was formed to judge the contest? Certainly not! Thus it was obvious that the holding of the contest and the instigating of a commission to judge the contest was, on the part of the Minister, proof of his impartiality; not only impartiality, but of good faith towards our national industry.

Gaujal then went on to ask whether the Minister, the Commission, or any member of it had been guilty of partiality. His argument was that each person was distinguished in his own particular field and of such standing that such a breach of conduct would be unthinkable. It was calculated insult to suggest that de Rumigny's subordinates had been influenced by him.

The Deputy King's Procurator went on to say that, in the case of the patent of 1845 where the plaintiffs insisted that the instruments had previously existed, where was the proof? Such evidence as had been given should be discounted. Testimonies given by rivals in the profession must always be regarded with suspicion.

With regard to the search for witnesses in Italy and Prussia, he said:

You go where it is convenient for you. They who say what you want, you bring along. Those who don't say what you want, you drop. Therefore you are not bringing impartial witnesses. These witnesses, whenever they made their depositions previously, made them before particular magistrates chosen by the complainants in this case. Therefore, you may make witnesses say exactly what you like.

What exactly has the research proved? There is some talk of an invention dating back to 1816 by M. Hetzel which was perfected in 1828 by M. Wieprecht and was re-perfected in 1835, not only by M. Wieprecht but by M. Moritz both of whom were musicians at the Court of Prussia. But are these two men disinterested and impartial? Certainly not! Messrs Wieprecht and Moritz are saying: 'There is an instrument which M. Sax is declaring he has invented: he is deceving you because we have invented it'. It is evident that if you ask Messrs. Wieprecht and Moritz if M. Sax has surpassed them in the art of perfecting brass instruments, they will never agree that he has. Therefore their arguments are not valid.

Concerning the saxophone, Gaujal went on:

Two main objections have been made against the saxophone. The first is that it is unplayable;

that it is nothing; that it is an adulterated instrument, a strange mixture of the clarinet and the ophicleide; M. Sax is not showing a saxophone; he has never made one. The second objection is this: M. Sax cannot take out a patent for the saxophone because he already presented the saxophone at the contest held on the occasion of the reorganisation of military bands. He displayed his instrument to the public and he did this before taking out his patent, and by doing so he makes it public property which cannot be taken back as private property. This is an extraordinary argument, having said that it doesn't exist!

The tribunal notes that these two objections are contradictory and that one destroys the other. M. Sax can reply by using the first to contradict the second and the second to contradict the first. Indeed, if the saxophone is not able to be made, it has never been made; therefore M. Sax cannot have made it known to the public; therefore he cannot have published it before taking out a patent for it. That is evident!

On the other hand, if M. Sax published the saxophone before taking out the patent, then the saxophone is not unthinkable. Therefore it cannot be, as had been said, a fantastic and derisory instrument. M. Sax's adversaries ought to get together and decide which of the two objections they will choose. The choice is rather difficult since no one could have any confidence in either argument.

The case against Sax was dismissed but, despite the possibly questionable tactics and confused presentation of the Association, it is hard not to concede the point that they had received a raw deal, at least in respect of the valved-bugle patents. The summing-up had been clearly biased in favour of the inventor, some of the arguments were fatuous beyond belief, the ranks and positions of certain great personages connected with the case had been blatantly used as a bludgeon.

An appeal was immediately filed by the Association. Because of the technical nature of much of the evidence put forward in the Courts, many questions had to be referred to arbitrators, thus making for delay and more expense. It was alleged that the Association tried to influence the judgement of the arbitrators by bombarding them with false information and half truths. When the Appeal Court met to consider the case, it had before it an arbitrators' report dated 2nd November 1847 and signed by Boquillon,[2] Savart and Halévy:

M. Sax has encountered obstacles and difficulties; he is in a country which prides itself on its hospitality which encourages strangers with favour, particularly when they are bringing useful inventions into the country. He is in a country which is a patron of the arts, which likes artists, which understands and honours them. If, because of envy and rivalry, M. Sax has met with difficulties and discouragement, we hope he will remember that such things are always powerless against true merit and, in any case, justice is always present and knows how to protect legitimate right.

The report then went on for 66 pages and reached the conclusion that the instruments described in the various patents had been, or were able to be, made and were perfectly patentable; they were sufficiently well described in the specifications so that, on expiry of the patents, others could make them as well as Sax; the instruments were new in as much as a change of form gave them properties which other instruments did not have. "Finally", the report concluded, "these instruments are not public property".

The appeal had hardly begun when it had been suspended because of the 1848 revolution. When it reconvened, the atmosphere had completely changed and was now hostile to Sax. Marie had become Minister of Justice and the case against Sax was led by *Maître* Lioville. The report of the experts was disregarded and it was held on 19th August 1849 that the properties of a musical instrument's tube with regard to its proportions and the angles of the valve tubes did not constitute a patentable invention. The patent of 1845 and part of that of 1843 were declared void, but the saxophone patent was upheld as was the part of the 1843 patent relating to slides.

This verdict satisfied nobody; both Sax and the Association appealed against it. This appeal began in 1849 and continued into the early part of 1850. Marie, who had meanwhile lost his high appointment, once again appeared for the plaintiffs while Chaix d'Est-Ange was retained for Sax.

The president of the Court, M. Poultier, delivered his verdict on 16th February 1850. He upheld the decisions of the earlier judges on all points, saying that the details submitted by Sax were insufficient to fulfil the conditions essential to the validity of a patent. Sax's immediate response was to lodge yet another appeal which was accepted in 1851. The particular point of this appeal was that the proportions of an instrument's tube were of paramount importance and that the descriptions he had given in his patent specifications were indeed patentable. It was February 9th 1853 before Advocate-General Rouland gave the Court's ruling. This was a complete about-face. The appeal was upheld — he *had* supplied sufficient information in his drawings. The verdict of the 16th February 1850 was over-ruled; the Association members were ordered to pay costs.

Inevitably, the case was taken further; this time to the Imperial Court at Rouen. The subject of proportions was close to Sax's heart. His father had realised the vital part played by balanced measurements in the construction of a good instrument; Adolphe had had these facts instilled into him from his earliest recollection. In his 1845 specification for the saxotromba, he had taken the unusual course of laying down precisely in figures the dimensions of the cones for each individual piece in the family. During the course of the Rouen hearing he eloquently made known his views:

Proportions are the laws which lay down an instrument's shape and give it its sound, its quality of tone; these are proportions. These proportions are different for each kind of instrument; it is these which make a horn different from a trumpet, a bugle from a saxotromba. And my enemies dare repeat to the Court what they said to the experts; that, far from being a fundamental law, proportions are of no importance and they are prepared to adjust them to the whims of players. But while denying the necessity for proportions, these unfortunate people are obliged to give way, for without them they could not manufacture. Only in following a routine laid down by an employer, a product of dogmatism or of trial-and-error, they are making proportions without knowing it, as M. Jourdain did prose. (the last was a reference to a character in Molière's play, *Le Bourgeois Gentilhomme*.)[3]

The Court had to decide on two points of litigation, whether the 1843 patent, already invalidated in respect of angles, should not now be declared invalid in respect of slides; and whether the 1845 patent concerning valved-bugles should be upheld. The question of damages for Sax would also be considered.

The case did not come until the following year. Marie, for the Association, made a point that Sax could have little faith in his inventions since he had taken out his patent for the minimum period, five years. Dufaure, for Sax, replied that the fee for a five-year patent was 500 francs; for 10 years, 1,000 francs; and for 15 years, 1,500 francs. Because of Sax's constant impecunious state, he could not afford a longer patent, much as his inventions warranted it.

On 28th June 1854, the President of the Court, M. Frank-Carré, delivered his summing-up. He dismissed the demand of the manufacturers asking for the nullity of the patent of 1843 — that is concerning the suppression of angles — and declared this patent to be valid; dismissed the demand for the annulment of the patent of 1845; condemned Raoux and his fellow plaintiffs to pay 10,000 francs damages to Sax for all the causes of prejudice they had made against him and to reimburse him for losses sustained through counterfeiting. He further condemned them to pay all of the costs of the first trial and the appeals. The summing-up concluded that the actions had been brought by men who were better placed than anybody to appreciate the merit of his inventions. These trials should be considered as an undue vexation. They had lasted for several years and had caused a prejudice against Sax for which reparations were due to him.

After eight years, this was the last word in this particular case. The Association appeared to have suffered a calamity; yet there was some satisfaction in the result even for its members. They had caused Sax endless worry with those time-consuming cases. Furthermore, if he wanted the restitution awarded him, he would still have to fight for it.

Notes on Chapter VIII

Vide Comettant, p.216 *et seq.*
1. Pontecoulant: *Organographie* 11, p.513.
2. *ibid.,* p.279; Boquillon, physisist and librarian, replaced Spontini, the Court's first choice who was subsequently unable to act.
3. Fétis, p.416.

The Sax factory
Work in progress on the upper floor

The Sax bass clarinet was a huge success.
In comparison, a rival's instrument was said to have sounded like a kazoo!

IX
Abortive Inventions

It was in 1853 that Sax's father and mother left their home in Brussels and came to live with their eldest son in Paris. Now at the age of sixty it is likely that Charles Sax felt the strain of running a business alone to be too much. For the next twelve years he was to work with his illustrious son; even though their roles were now reversed, it is inconceivable that they did not receive mutual help and comfort and, in the light of yet another tragedy which was to overtake Adolphe almost at once, the presence of his parents must have been a great consolation. Details of his family life are scanty. His younger brother Alphonse was still with him, the two sons and a daughter who died in 1856 being, together with the parents, all that remained of the once large family.

Sax did marry, but the date of the marriage and the name of his wife cannot now be ascertained. It is possible, although by no means certain, that the wedding took place from the residence that Sax occupied for many years, being part of the factory at No. 10 Rue Saint-Georges in the 9th *arrondisement* of Paris where it seems that many of the civil records pertaining to birth, deaths and marriages have not survived. The date of the marriage lies somewhere between the years 1847 and 1856. In the former year, Berlioz noted that one of the charges often flung at the inventor by his enemies was that, not only was he a Belgian and a foreigner, but in addition a bachelor, while they were all good family men. Some time within the next nine years, Sax was married, a point proved from a poignant letter dated May 23rd 1856, written by Berlioz to Theodore Ritter. Morbidly noting his almost continual attendance at the cemetery, the composer tells how Sax had recently lost a child and, three days later, a sister. He did have other progeny; reference can be traced to two sons who carried the profession of musical instrument maker into the next generation.

Continuing the lifelong pattern of alternating (when not concurrent) good and bad fortune, a new and most gruelling trial lay imminently ahead. This time his enemies bore no responsibility although the less compassionate among them might well have rejoiced that the Deity must surely be on their side. In 1853, when aged 39, a dark spot on his lip was causing the inventor growing concern.[1]

Several doctors were consulted but all they could recommend, unhelpfully for such a busy man, was rest. There was, at this stage, no pain and otherwise Sax was in good general health. By the next year, the spot was more pronounced and many remedies were tried without success. The infected part of the lip had become hard and difficult to move, making the mastication of food an increasing problem. Gradually, over the next five years, the spot grew larger until by 1858, its size was alarming. The doctors diagnosed melanosis, an exceedingly malignant cancer characterised by the blackening of the skin in its vicinity. The tumour was deeply rooted in the jaw; if left to take its course, a particularly horrible and painful death was inevitable. The only possible hope lay in a hazardous surgical operation in which the infected parts, including the diseased lip, would have to be removed.

A more cruel choice could hardly be imagined; between hideous disfigurement and a choking death. Fortuitously, the proposed operation was postponed to allow Sax to appear in Court during his interminable lawsuits. In desperation, grasping at the slightest hope of finding a more hopeful alternative, Sax listened eagerly to the advice of his friend Oscar Comettant. There was, Comettant had heard, an Indian doctor in Paris who had gained a reputation for being able to cure diseases given up as incurable by the rest of the medical profession. Dr.

Vries, nicknamed "Dr. Black" because of the colour of his skin, was not qualified in the accepted sense. In that respect he was a "quack" but his treatments did seem, in many cases, efficacious.

Sax's infection was examined; Dr. Vries upheld the diagnosis but promised a cure within six months without recourse to surgery. On 6th June 1858, the inventor was placed on a strict diet with the minimum of liquids, and given a medicine extracted by a secret formula from Indian herbs. Although the treatment was begun immediately, no spectacular cure resulted. Sax's condition deteriorated; the tumour was restricting his throat and feeding had to be carried out by means of a tube. In this seemingly hopeless plight, the patient was led to make an attempt on his own life. This was fortunately thwarted; Dr. Vries, who never ceased to be reassuring and optimistic, persevered with his method. Then suddenly, in 1859, some six years after the black spot had first appeared, it began to diminish. Within a few days, by 17th February 1859, it had gone completely leaving his lip as clean and healthy as though it had never been infected.

The effect on Sax, his family and friends, may be imagined. To be plucked back from the brink of death in this fashion was nothing short of miraculous. In gratitude, a great banquet was organised in honour of the Indian doctor. This was held in the magnificent hall of the *hôtel du Louvre*. To it were invited those distinguished in the arts, science, literature and the armed forces. Amid the lavish splendour which typified the high regard Sax was held in by many of his contemporaries, the Band of the Imperial Guard played, by special permission of the Emperor. Under the baton of Mohr, it was in high form playing marches, fantasias and overtures including the overtures to Herold's *Zampa* and Weber's *Oberon,* and the march from Meyerbeer's *Le Phophète.* Berlioz was especially delighted with their rendering of his *Carnaval Romain* overture. In proposing a toast to the conductor he came out with a pun on his name and the recently receded Spectre of Death: "To Mohr (*mort*) the living man, let us drink to Mohr!"

Present at the banquet was the celebrated Dr. Velpeau who had been consulted originally on Sax's case. Being of a liberal turn of mind, he was intrigued by the Indian's achievements and wished to know more. He placed under Dr. Vries' care a number of pauper patients, inmates of the Charity Hospital, all suffering from diseases pronounced as incurable by legitimate medical authorities. This time, there were no spectacular recoveries but at least no one died under the Indian's ministrations and it was claimed that, after two months treatment, many felt better.

Conservative medical opinion was not impressed and, although Dr. Velpeau might have wished to persevere a little longer, he was forced to call a halt to the experiment under pressure from his colleagues. He read a paper to the Academy in which the Indian doctor's methods were condemned and he was removed from his place at the hospital. Contrary to the best diagnoses of the time, it was at this time stated that Sax had not really had a cancer at all; but supporters of the deposed medic were quick to point out that, immediately after his departure most of the patients died. This is hardly surprising when one considers their pitiable state and advanced ages; Dr. Vries might consider himself fortunate that they obligingly survived during his term.

At the height of his fame, "Dr. Black" ran a lucrative practice where fashionable patients would wait for four or five hours for his attentions. Berlioz, who had abortively consulted the doctor himself, was prevailed upon to compose a piece especially for his projected health centre. Such condemnation from the highest medical authorities spelled the end for the unqualified doctor; less than three months after apparently curing the incurable he was removed from the scene. As for Sax; the good people of Dinant must surely have shaken their heads knowingly — "the Ghost" walked again!

Except for the most desperate moments of his illness, Sax never ceased to apply himself to his work. Amid all the worries occasioned by his enemies and, at times, by his own foolishness; even during the terrible years of the cancer, he was busy with new ideas, new designs, new inventions. In April 1852, Halévy's "The Wandering Jew" was produced at the Paris *Opéra*. For the stage action a number of instruments of helicon form to resemble the Roman *buccina*

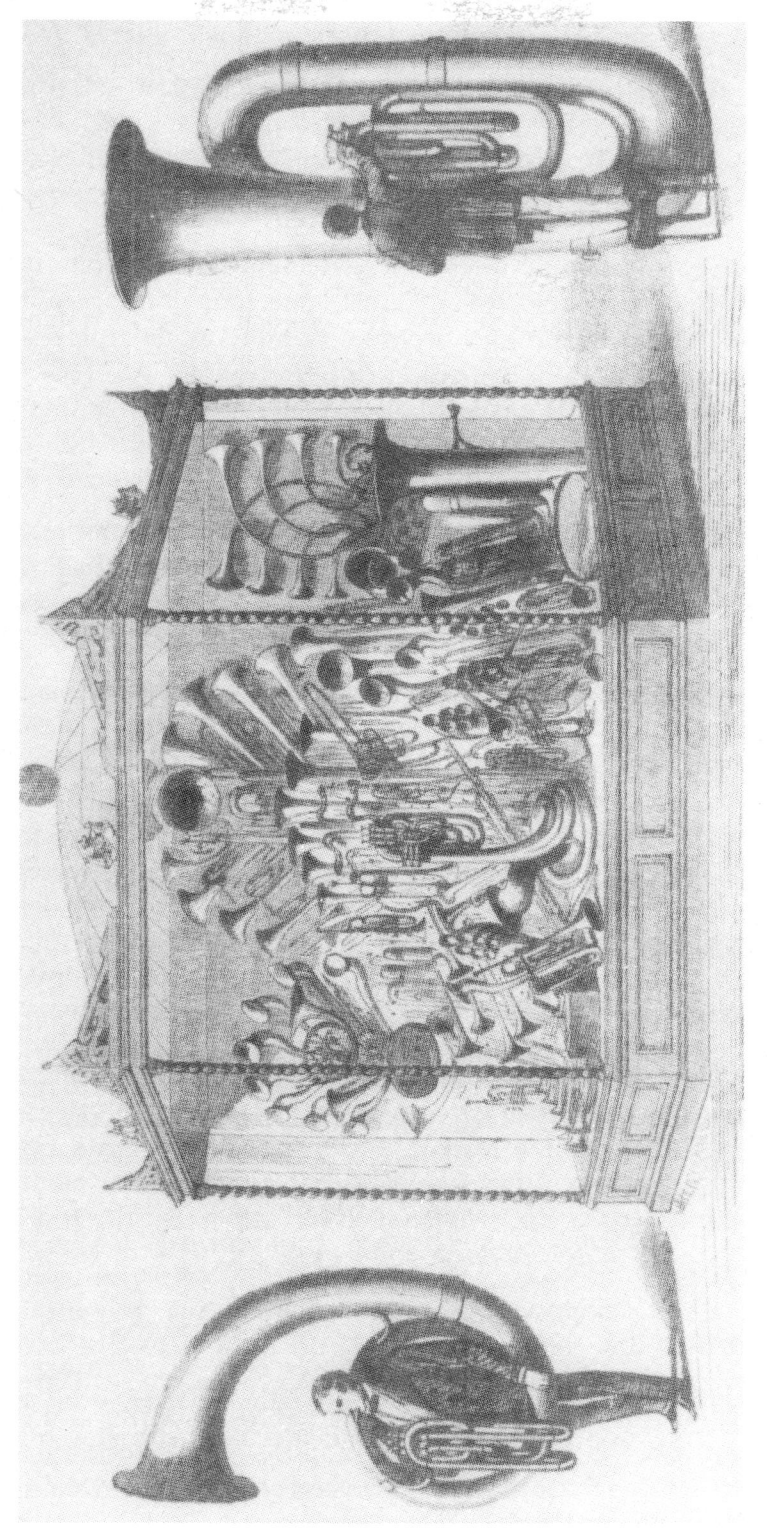

Sax's gigantic showcase, flanked by two more 'monstrosities'.

"Excuse me; may one visit the interior of this establishment?"
Le Journal Amusant, 1855.
This concerns the showing of the EE-flat saxhorn-bourdon at the Paris Industrial Exhibition of that year.

were needed. Sax designed a series of valved instruments in this shape to which he gave the name saxtuba.[2] Their appearance in the opera caused something of a sensation. The enhanced volume of sound of which the instrument was capable was credited to the reduction in the number of sharp bends in the tube. Saxtubas were tried out in military bands where their career was meteoric. When the massed bands of thirty regiments, 1,550 players, assembled in the same year on the Champ-de-Mars for a presentation of colours by Napoleon III, it was said that twelve saxtubas dominated the entire ensemble. Comettant, echoing a sentiment expressed many years before by Madame Dacosta, expressed the view that "the trombone, beside the saxtuba, is nothing more than a kazoo!" One can but speculate on the effect produced by these mighty coils of brass. One thing is certain; their fame was exceedingly short lived. The trombone was never in peril and, by 1867, its rival had completely disappeared.

Another more significant development in brass instrument design which occupied the inventor at that time was the question of intonation when two or more valves are used in combination. It will be readily appreciated that, as the first valve brings into use additional tubing calculated to lower the pitch of the tube by two semitones, no intonation problems should arise with either the open or the valved note. Similarly with the second and third valves when used independently, lowering the pitch by one and three semitones respectively. Difficulties arise when more than one valve is depressd at a time. It is desired to lower the harmonic g' by five semitones to d', the only way it can done on a three-valved instrument is by depressing the first and third valves together. The first valve will give a note two semitones lower. When the third valve is operated, the additional tubing brought into play is measured to lower by three semitones *the original length of tube*. Since the first valve tubing has already lengthened this, the third valve tubing is therefore not quite long enough making the resulting note sharp.

With the smaller instruments the discrepancy is scarcely perceptible and is corrected instinctively by the ear and lip of the player. Instruments of the tenor, bass and contrabass registers do experience real tuning difficulties too great to be adjusted by other than mechanical means. From about 1850, many correcting devices were made and patented. They were of varying degrees of efficiency, none being entirely satisfactory until the appearance in 1874 of D. J. Blaikley's "Compensating Pistons" which automatically brought in extra tubing when valves were used in combination.

Sax tackled the problem in his own individual way with a basically simple idea. The slide trombone had remained practically unchanged in principle for more than 300 years. Yet, particularly in the 19th century, many makers saw the slide as something old fashioned and inefficient which ought to be superseded by the valve. The biggest reaction against the valve trombone came, and still comes, from the players themselves. This is not the usual conservative opposition to change and few would disagree that the executants are right in generally preferring the magnificent slide instrument with its open tone and capacity, in common with bowed instruments, of sounding every graduation of pitch within its compass. Sax was no exception in this trend of thinking. He made both slide and valve trombones, sometimes attaching a single valve to the slide instrument to extend its compass to the fundamental, having all the potential inherent in the present-day tenor-bass model. In addition, he made a trombone with a slide and three valves which could be played by either method or both combined.[3]

In his quest for good valve intonation, Sax looked to the seven slide "shifts" from which, using the harmonics produced from each, the slide trombone gets its full chromatic compass. The tuning of each note is always capable of being perfect since the slide may be placed with the minutest precision in the position to give this result. The inventor, then, built a trombone with a fixed length of tube, calculated to give the notes of the seventh, or most extended, position. With the addition of six valves which would always be used independently and never in combination, he devised a system whereby each valve would cut off a portion of the tube in lengths to correspond exactly with the seven positions of the slide. By obviating the need for the operation of more than one valve at a time, accurate tuning of each note was achieved.

The tube of the entire instrument was bent in a practical fashion to allow three horizontally placed valves to be fingered with the right hand in the usual way, with the remaining three valves arranged vertically in front of the player for which he would use his left hand. The complete instrument aroused a good deal of interest but never gained general acceptance. For one thing, its weight did not commend it to the marching musician. Again, as has been said, players preferred the intimacy of the finely adjustable simple slide to this complex piece of mechanism. On the other hand, there is no doubt that the trombone with *six pistons à tubes independants* was capable of being much more facile in execution than the ponderous slide. Musical exercises were written which, it was claimed, were impossible to perform on anything in brass but a six-valved instrument.[4] The technique, though, was quite different from that of three- and four-valved instruments with the usual descending valves. Considerable mental dexterity was required from the musician; the least hesitation in selecting the correct valve could result in, at best, faulty intonation — which it was designed to correct — or, at worst, performing disaster. Instrumentalists, especially those with reputations to uphold, do not take kindly to anxieties when they are performing; this fact must have seriously militated against the instrument's possible popularity.

The inventor used his influence to have his six-valved trombones and saxhorns tried out in bands of the *Garde Républicaine* and of the Guides. The *Gymnase*, now being closed, had its classes in military music transferred to the Conservatoire. The six-valved system was included in the syllabus as it was at the Brussels Conservatoire under the professorship of H. Seha, a one time inspector at the Sax factory.[5]

The proprietor at this time held the post of Musical Director of the stage brass band at the Opera. In this position he was able to include his own instruments among the number and used saxhorns in Rossini's overture "Robert Bruce" and in Meyerbeer's *Le Prophète*. Halévy's *Le Juif-errant* of 1852 had a contingent of saxhorns and four saxophones. In 1857, with the help of Gevarte, Director of Music at the Academy and a loyal supporter of Sax, the instrumentation of the band was changed to include six-valved instruments. The score of Ambrois Thomas's opera *Hamlet* contains a fine trombone solo in the first act. The inventor saw this as a showpiece for his new instrument and had it played on his six-valved trombone. Thomas is reported to have extolled the instrument as "the last one of the most admirable of M. Sax's inventions which seems destined to revolutionise the family of brass instruments".[6]

The ultimate failure of the instrument cannot be attributed in any way to Sax's enemies. It lay in the fact that players simply did not like playing it. Victor Mahillon, assiduous worker on the problems of wind instrument construction and a fellow Belgian sums up the position: "The system is perfect if we consider only the theoretical side. There is not a musician who does not jump at the first sight; but on the practical side it presents difficulties."[7] Sax managed to retain his six-valved trombone in the Opera band for many years although the soloist in *Hamlet* went back to his slide trombone at an early opportunity. Military bands soon dispensed with it. There was one survivor, as Pierre tells us; a son of the inventor who, as a musician in the Band of the *Garde Républicaine*, continued to play on six valves long after everyone else had given them up.[8]

As an instrument maker of superlative skill matched with a fertile mind, it is surprising to find such an impractical streak in the character. He was so often carried away with the ingenuity of his work that he became oblivious of the practical disadvantages in terms of such things as weight, portability and cost. The six-ascending-valve system, an original invention which even his sternest critics do not deny him, was a case in point. We have noted that the weight was a disadvantage; the drawback was accentuated by the addition of a seventh valve to carry the compass down to the fundamental. Not content with independent tubes using a common bell, he made a bizarre construction with seven independent bells! These rose wraithlike above the player's head and could be pointed in any direction. The contraption was the equivalent of seven separate trombones! Not only was the weight intolerable, the problem of transport in a suitably designed carrying case and the effort of assembling and dismantling did not endear it to the potential player. A patent for the system was obtained in 1859 but no one seemed eager to infringe it.

Throughout the most prolific period in his life, Sax was taken with the problems of constructing large instruments of the contrabass register. The early years in Paris saw him grappling with a low clarinet pitched in E-flat an octave below the alto clarinet. In view of the success enjoyed by the bass clarinet it is surprising to note the failure of his contrabasses. It must be said that the problems inherent in building a satisfactory bass are amplified in even larger instruments. The earliest recorded contrabass clarinet was Streitwolf's bassoon-shaped 19-key model of 1829 made in F or E-flat. It was apparently very cheap to make; despite glowing praise from Spohr and Fétis, nothing came of it. Next came Sax with his E-flat *clarinette-contrabasse* some five or six years after the bass. This was a compact design made completely of brass with a long coiled crook and an outward turned bell. No one appears to have been impressed with this either.

Sax also made a true contrabass, a *clarinette-bourdon* pitched an octave below the B-flat bass clarinet. Here he was no more successful than Dumas whose *contre-basse guerrière* appeared in 1808 and rather less than his protagonist Wieprecht, whose *bathyphone*, as we have seen, found a place for a time in Prussian military bands. Sax could hardly have made many contrabasses; none were listed when his instrument collection was sold in 1879.

The brass family, too, received attention in his quest for depth of sound. The original group of saxhorns ended with the E-flat contrabass, an instrument hardly different from the E-flat bass in general use in brass and military bands today. A logical further step was the addition of a BB-flat contrabass a fourth below, introduced in the early 1850's although similar instruments in 16ft. C or 18ft. B-flat had already been in existence for some years. The lowest note obtainable by using the three valves of a normal BB-flat bass is about as low as the average ear can discern. Notes with very slow vibrations are felt rather than heard so that the fitting of a **fourth valve to carry the compass complete down to the fundamental is of dubious utility.** The difficulty in appreciating differences in pitch among very low notes is illustrated in an important work for brass band by a composer eminent in that sphere. On a final quiet chord, the BB-flat basses are required to sound E-flat, a semitone below their normal compass. A note on the score instructs how the note is to be obtained; it "may be lipped without the use of valves".[9] In other words, the difference in pitch from what should be the fundamental and a note a fourth above is considered to be indistinguishable.

If this premise is accepted, the building of even larger brass instruments, although possible, is an impractical exercise bordering on the absurd. Yet Sax pioneered these gigantic sub-bass constructions, introducing his *saxhorn bourdon* in EE-flat at the Paris Exhibition of 1855. As if that were not enough, Gilson tells of a **Sax instrument in the *Musée des Arts et Métiers*** in Paris, a sub-bass in B-flat pitched an octave below the BB-flat bass! Standing in its coiled form some 6½ ft. high, this monster was supposed to require no more effort to play than a small or medium saxhorn.[10] At this distance in time, this device for producing little more than subterranean rumbles must show Sax at his most impractical.

As might be expected, the general public were vastly amused by these elephantine serpents. Typical of the reaction of the humorous press is a cartoon of 1855 in *Le Journal Amusant*. There is depicted an innocent visitor to the Exhibition standing beside a towering coil enquiring of the attendant if he might visit the interior of the establishment. Sax was unbelievably touchy about his colossal basses. Lashing back at humourists he threatened, "Next year, I shall exhibit an instrument with the diameter of the *Colonne de Juillet* and I shall call it 'Saxothunder'".

Passion for the sub-bass extended to the saxophone. Berlioz, in his "A Treatise on Modern Instruments and Orchestration" of 1854 lists six sizes only, adding that "M. Sax is about to produce a seventh, a double-bass saxophone". The patent of 1846 specifies eight sizes including a contrabass in FF and EE-flat, pitched an octave below the baritone, and another in **CC and BB-flat, an octave below the bass.** Kastner mentioned the former in 1843; there is no traceable mention of either during the inventor's lifetime except for **Lavoix** who, in his 1878 "History of Instruments" specifies both with the rider, "little used". There is no reason to think that Sax saw the project for either contrabass realised, either by himself or any other. This is paradoxical since the EE-flat contrabass saxophone is by no means an impractical instrument and might have been more worthy of his attention than the sub-contrabass saxhorn of similar pitch. The task of actually building monster saxophones is one which would surely have appealed to the inventor. It can only be supposed that one or other of his multifarious schemes always found precedence.

Of all the ideas for gargantuan musical instruments to formulate in his brain, none was more bizarre than a project for an "orchestra-organ". While still in Brussels he had set down his ideas and the *Revue et Gazette Musicale de Paris* had a paragraph on the subject in its edition of June 13th 1841. The organ was to be powered by steam being forced against huge vibrating steel bars at about four or five times the normal atmospheric pressure. Steam was to be supplied by an ordinary railway locomotive with the organ mounted in front on a truck. "Such an organ would cover the noise of the engine and wheels, and drown even thunder" the notice concluded. It would seem that Sax's imagination had been fired by the newly-discovered power of steam locomotion; his idea was that the steam organ would add splendour to many railway inaugurations then taking place, as well as adding to the gaiety of other public festivals.

Thus far the project, if sounding a little quaint to modern ears, was not too unreasonable. The crowded years which followed his settling in Paris pushed the idea into the background only for it to be revived fifteen years later in 1860. This time the organ was to be of colossal dimensions and to be mounted on one of the Paris hills so that the entire populace might hear the music with the utmost clarity. On second thoughts, to use a mere natural promontary seemed to the inventor hardly adequate for his ambitious scheme. What were needed were man-made towers of great engineering skill in keeping with the enlightened age.

Sax stated his ideas precisely:[12] "I shall need four immense towers, higher than the Pantheon or Nôtre Dame and joined by bridges, making a gigantic platform. Once my towers are built, I shall construct an apparatus using all the principal methods of producing sounds known to date. Steam engines will put huge cylinders in motion, compressing air at five, ten or even fifteen times its normal atmospheric pressure, in reservoirs or regulators, to distribute it to the high or low stops of the instrument. Add to this an enormous set of triangles, cymbals, big drums, kettledrums on which elephant hide has been used instead of sheepskin. Add to this metal ropes the size of cables which will hold the suspended bridges; stretch these ropes over an opening from which compressed air will make them resound at will and with unequalled power. Imagine a hundred other ways which I will spare you".

The music cylinders were to be shunted on a railway truck to a position under the organ. One cylinder would then be mounted into place ready to play an entire symphonic movement or operatic excerpt, after which it would be removed and replaced. If Sax had been allowed to proceed with the notion he would have become the innovator of mass background music with a vengeance — except that, with all the power at his disposal, he had no intention of having his music overlooked. How the inhabitants of the city would have reacted to having music forced into their ears is an interesting speculation. Even the most ardent music-lover has the right to choose when he will listen and when he will be quiet.[13]

Friends of the inventor evidently found the whole idea a huge joke and a good deal of banter was indulged in; but Sax reacted violently to the levity. Seeing him in deadly earnest brought dismay. How could he be talked out of the scheme without giving offence? It was his friend, the noted sound engineer Savart who eventually put it so nicely. Taking the inventor gently aside he said in all seriousness, "I'm no longer making fun: you are right: nothing is easier than this. But keep your idea to yourself because if you put it into practice before another fifty years of progress, they'll lock you up in a madhouse".[14]

Diplomacy worked; Sax was content to concentrate on other more pressing matters in the knowledge that his ideas were far ahead of their time and it might be hoped that posterity would appreciate them more. Thus an assault on the eardrums of Paris was averted.

Trombone with six ascending valves
An ingenious attempt by Sax to achieve perfect intonation

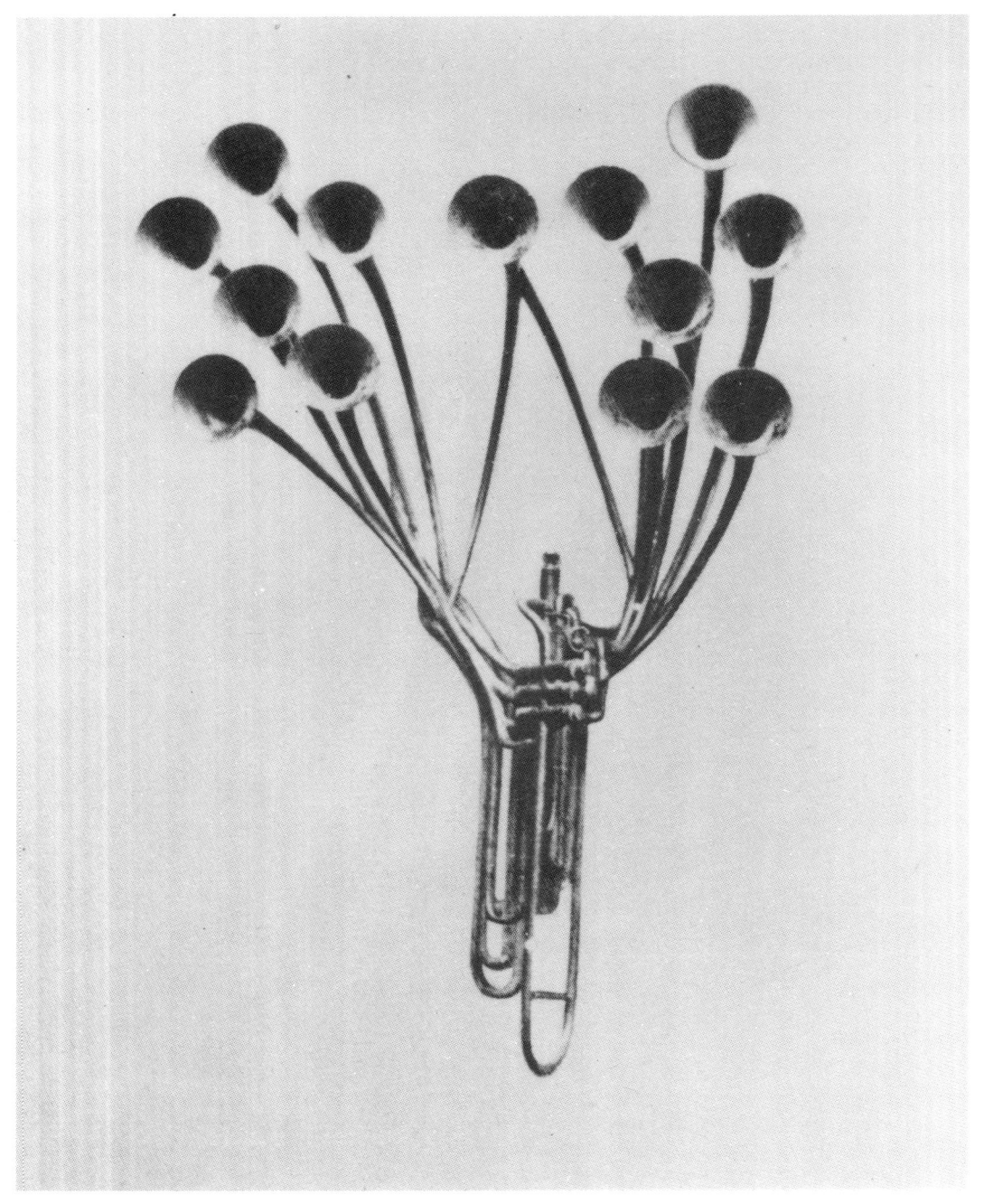
Trombone with seven valves and thirteen bells
Sax's ingenious ideas were often severely impractical. In achieving theoretical acoustic perfection, he creates formidable problems of technique, weight and transportation — including a rare riddle for the case-maker!

Notes on Chapter IX

1. *Vide* Comettant, Chapter 46.
2. Fétis, p.422.
3. *ibid.,* pp.420-1.
4. These were written by a Frenchman, De Meersman, who cleverly arranged pieces for a band of 25, all playing 6-valved instruments. Led by Sax the group gave concerts in Paris and went on publicity tours, mainly in Belgium — Gilson, p.11.
5. Gilson, p.16.
6. Ella, John: *Musical Sketches at Home and Abroad,* London 1869, (3rd Edition 1878, pp.304-5.)
7. Pierre, C: *La Facteur,* p.134.
8. *ibid.*
9. Eric Ball: *Songs of the Morning* — suite for brass band, S.P. & S. Ltd., 1937.
10. Gilson, p.13.
11. *Vide* Berlioz: *Traité,* 2nd Edition, 1854, p.284. Lavoix: *History of Instruments,* 1878, p.127. Sachs: *Handbuch der Musikinstrumentenkunde,* 1920, p.342, mentions "Subkontrabass in B" giving the range (in *Die modernen Musikinstrumente*) as A-flat to c.
    Frederick Fay Swift, writing in *Woodwind World* (U.S.A.) Dec. 1972, p.18, mentions a sub-contrabass saxophone he saw in Clark's Music Store, Syracuse, in the late 1930's, displayed as "The World's Largest Saxophone". "It was a contra-contrabass and we believe it was the only one made. We walked up a four-step ladder in order to reach the mouthpiece. Everything functioned. Some of the pads were as large as pie plates".
12. Comettant, pp.267-272.
13. Even Comettant (p.272) was dismayed at the scheme, pointing out that Sax had no hope of raising the 8-10 million francs for the project's estimated cost and, in any case, the Prefect of Police would have to be won over.
14. Brenta, p.74. Sax's friend Savart appears at one time to have been a Colonel of Engineers. He could not have been the distinguished physicist Felix Savart, of 'Savart's Wheel' fame, who died in 1841.

Saxhorn bourdon in EE-flat
Shown by Sax at the Paris Exhibition of 1855

X
Counter-Actions

Despite his ever present troubles, 1854 was, at least, a year of relative good fortune. The attitude of Napoleon III to Sax was gratifying and did much to uplift his spirits. Years before, Charles Sax had been appointed Imperial Instrument-maker to King William I of the Netherlands; in April of that year a similar honour was bestowed on the son, that of Musical Instrument Maker to the Household Troops of the Emperor. In addition he became the Emperor's private Director of Music. Some parts of his recommendations for the reform of military music had been a long time in reaching fruition. The improved conditions for serving musicans outlined in the original report and subsequently approved by the Commission and without which there could be no hope of bands worthy of the honour of France, were at last realised. In August, at a time when there were no less than two hundred established military bands in the country, the Emperor published a decree giving service musicians a new deal and a proper career structure.

In June, the Imperial Court at Rouen upheld all of Sax's patents and allowed the patentee to take action against any breach. With the lethargy of the law, he was kept waiting for many months for the written decree of the Court; when it eventually arrived, on December 29th, he was ready with a counter-attack against any and all who had infringed his patents and thus deprived him of business. A formidable force assembled under his initiative; fourteen police commissioners and fourteen bailiffs assisted by twenty-four clerks. Fourteen of his major manufacturing rivals, including Besson, Halary, Raoux, Labbaye, David and Gautrot, received sudden and simultaneous visits and a number of instruments were impounded for use as evidence as the inventor began legal actions in reverse.

However, when the alleged counterfeiters were brought to Court, they soon demonstrated that they still had some shots left in the locker. They declared that the seizure of the instruments was illegal, arguing that it had not been preceded by the caution required by the Law of 5th July 1844 which applied when the plaintiff was a foreigner. Caught on a technical point, Sax offered to return the instruments and seize them over again after the statutory caution had been given, but a judgement given on 3rd May 1855 would not allow this. Sax immediately appealed, got the verdict reversed, issued his caution and, on the 25th and 26th May 1855, visited the house of Gautrot where the instruments had been placed and seized them for the second time.[1]

To return for a moment to 1852 and the imminent bankruptcy, unexpected relief was at hand. Emperor Napoleon III, now firmly in power, looked with favour on the unhappy inventor and showed that his earlier achievements had not been entirely forgotten. A number of influential admirers, including the Emperor, assisted in making arrangements with Sax's creditors: as a consequence, the manufacturer was able to return to the Rue Saint-Georges and again begin to make musical instruments.

With undiminished resilience, he immediately re-established himself as a powerful force. He announced plans by which he intended to make the Band of the Imperial Guard the finest military band in the world. He again opened up his workshop to a dazzling and influential cross-section of Parisian life; the band, equipped throughout with the latest models of his instruments, gave a splendid performance. The effect on the audience was electric; a eulogistic report was passed to the Emperor who commanded that the band play for him at the Tuileries. The musicians numbered among their ranks five saxophones and twenty saxhorns of various sizes.

Although by now he had many years experience of the workings of the law, he was not deterred by the prospect of spending more time and money in the courts in what he saw to be his best interests. If he had been content to stop at the point where existing wrongs were rectified, his action might have been understandable. Unfortunately, his treatment in Paris had left him bitter, so that he was prone to see an affront even where none existed or was intended. At least two of his lawsuits can only be described as mean and rather petty.

The first of these concerned a new musical instrument which had been patented for use in military bands. There were many among the musical fraternity who, whilst agreeing with the inadequacy of the oboe and bassoon in the open air, deplored the removal and absence of the double-reed sound from the military aggregation. One such was Bandmaster Sarrus of the 13th Line Regiment. Sarrus designed a family of conical instruments, operating on the shortening-hole system and sounded by means of a double reed in the manner of the oboe and bassoon. In the use of brass and the adoption of a wider bore with larger note-holes, the inventor sought to overcome the lack of sonority inherent in established wooden instruments when used out of doors. To get his plans executed, Sarrus approached the noted Paris maker, P. L. Gautrot who not only agreed to make the prototypes but, calling them sarrusophones after the inventor, took out a patent in 1856 and a year later published a Method for them.

The original family of five sarrusophones were named similarly to their saxophone counterparts: B-flat soprano, E-flat alto, B-flat tenor, B-flat bass and E-flat contrabass. Later, an E-flat baritone and contrabasses in C and EE-flat were added. Again like the saxophone, the sarrusophone's compass extended, in the case of the smaller instruments, from b to f'''; a lower extension to b-flat and another upwards to g''' came with later developments. The keywork, on rod axles with finger plates, had a marked and not surprising resemblance to that of the saxophone. Sarrusophones from the alto downwards had two or three U bends terminating at the blowing end in a crook with a double reed. The similarity to the saxophone in so many respects was apparently too close for Sax's liking. He immediately commenced an action against Gautrot for an infringement of his saxophone patent.

It is quite likely that Sarrus had received his original inspiration from the saxophone family and felt that the idea could well be applied to a similar group with oboe-like characteristics. Since the instruments were intended for robust outdoor use with enhanced carrying power, the use of brass together with larger proportions would naturally follow, as would the adoption of finger plates to cover the large tone holes. Some similarity to the saxophone was therefore inevitable. Nevertheless, the sound of the instrument had nothing in common with Sax's invention; the Courts were quick to see that, in spite of any superficial similarities, the two instruments were entirely different. Sax lost his case.[2]

The verdict must have given Gautrot, a bitter opponent of Sax, keen satisfaction. What is there to say that the maker of the sarrusophone did not take up the invention without an idea of getting back at Sax? Free of legal restraint, a determined effort was made to get the new instrumental family accepted into Army bands. Bandmasters generally were not adverse to giving the work of their colleague a hearing. For a time, a section of sarrusophones took their place alongside their distant cousin saxophones, between them giving the tone of French military bands a distinct and peculiar *timbre*. It looked as though such oboes and bassoons which had survived must now finally be displaced as musical circles showed increasing interest in the new creations. As late as 1890 "The Musical Times' was saying that "its introduction into the orchestra is probably only a question of time".[3]

However, the instrument did not make the headway for which its inventor and maker had hoped, despite vigorous pushing by Gautrot. It was said at the time that Sax used his considerable influence in the military musical sphere to jeopardise a fair trial for the sarrusophone. Undoubtedly, Sax would not have been idle in this respect; yet the sarrusophone was still being made long after Sax's influence had waned. Of the melodic

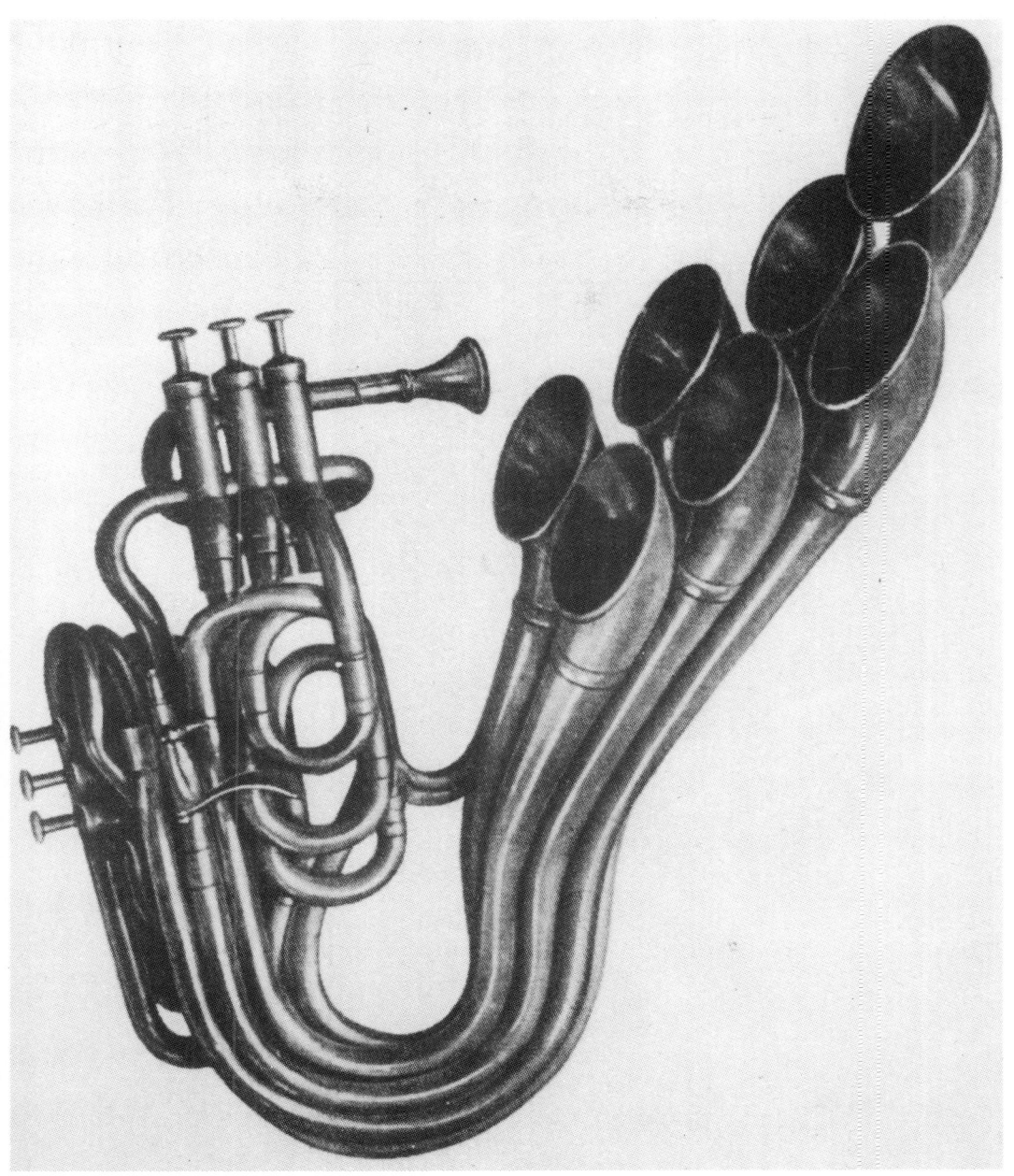

A trombone by Sax, having six ascending valves and seven independent tubes and bells
An original and ingenious idea, but one which imposed on the player a difficult technique and an inordinate weight.

Sarrusophone *versus* Saxophone
Bandmaster Sarrus of the 13th Line Regiment designed his family of sarrusophones which were sounded with double reeds and were intended to replace oboes and bassoons in the open air.
They were made by Sax's arch-enemy, P. L. Gautrot. Sax sued him in the Courts — and lost!

instruments the alto in particular was well favoured. The reedy sonorous power of the contrabass attracted attention from the orchestra; in 1867 Saint-Saëns used it to replace the contrabassoon and, some years later, paid personally for two to be made for use in his compositions.

The real cause of failure of six of the instruments, from soprano to bass, was the tone. In achieving the required volume, Sarrus completely destroyed the pure tone of the oboe and the muffled dryness of the bassoon. In the hands of the ordinary bandsman, the sarrusophone had a coarse, blatant tone which, after a time, offended sensitive ears. George Miller, writing in 1912, gives the viewpoint of the military bandmaster: "Their tone is altogether too nasal for Western ears, though probably far-Eastern countries ... with their curious ideas of voice production, would admire them, particularly the altissimo variety." Notwithstanding the recommendation, there is nothing to show that the sarrusophone ever made a deep impression on the Orient.

If Sax had any justification for seeking to suppress a rival instrument, it is difficult to find any for another action brought in 1866. Marie-Constance Sass was a fellow Belgian from Ghent. She came of a poor family but was endowed with a remarkably rich voice. After early years of struggle for recognition she became a pupil of Madame Ugalda and, at the age of 21, appeared as a soprano at the *Lyrique* in Paris in 1859.

A year later, she had a part at the *Opéra*. Her magnificent voice and acting ability brought rapid success. Among many operatic composers, Wagner had a high regard for her; she sang the part of Elizabeth in the disastrous Paris production of *Tannhäuser* in 1860 where she and Sax were fellow artistes, he being the Musical Director of the stage brass band.

Continual personal success and exposure to good living gave Mlle. Sass not only a voluptuous bulk but a certain professional vanity. She convinced herself that "Sass" did not look good on opera and concert posters. She conceived the idea of making a slight adjustment to "Sax". Although she and the inventor had worked in the same production, their roles were so completely different that the lady might well have been oblivious of the name of the stage bandmaster. Unless there is more in the incident than has since come to light, it is difficult to see how her change of name could have affected the original holder adversely. Many a man might have been flattered. Not so Sax. No doubt he was so embittered by the ceaseless actions of his enemies that once again he saw antipathy where none was contemplated. Berlioz did nothing to help. In a report on the *prima donna* in *Débats*, his sardonic humour bubbled over: "Her rich and powerful voice has great carrying power, reaching the furthest corners of the great Opera hall. It is like a Sax contrabass crossed with a saxophone".

Although Sax was embroiled in more than one lawsuit at the time, he unhesitatingly started proceedings against Mlle. Sass to prevent her usurping his name. Unaccountably, the court found in his favour and issued an injunction. The singer then thought that "Saxe" would serve her purpose as well and even approached King John of Saxony (Saxe) who had no objection. But Sax had. Again he contested the assumption in the Courts and again was given the judgement on the dubious grounds that the final "e" is silent! The result gave Sax a queer satisfaction. He was not unaware of popular feeling against him; in justifying himself, a dry sense of humour appeared. "After all", he wrote, "she didn't need me to make herself heard." Poor Marie Sass! In 1864 she married a baritone named Castlemary and thereafter styled herself "Sass-Castlemary". In later life her glorious talent left her; in 1907, just before her seventieth birthday she died in destitution.[4]

Among the actions instigated by Sax there was one concerning a counterfeited saxophone which has about it a distinct element of situation comedy; this had taken place many years before in 1850.

An infantry-regiment musician named Barlès had been intrigued by a friend's saxophone and desired to have one for himself. Being stationed in Lyon, he approached a brass-instrument maker in the town, one Rivet, and asked if he could make another instrument to the pattern of his friend's specimen. Rivet said he could and apparently performed the remarkable feat of producing the replica within a week.

Some time later, Barlès was posted from Lyon to Paris and, finding his instrument in need of repair, enquired locally as to a suitable establishment to which to take it. He was directed to the Rue Saint-Georges.

The musician could hardly have anticipated his reception. He found himself the recipient of a tirade from Sax, quickly followed by a writ, coupled with Rivet in a lawsuit for the infringement of the saxophone patent. The result was in little doubt. The Police Tribunal, however, dismissed the charge against Barlès since he had obviously — as Sax ought to have perceived — acted innocently and in good faith. Why else should he have taken the instrument to Sax?

Rivet first insisted that he had not actually made the saxophone but had merely sold it on behalf of Sax. Sax was able to prove that the brass used in the manufacture was of inferior quality, allowing it to be sold at a price well below the price charged by Sax. The point was appreciated by the Tribunal; Rivet was fined 100 francs with 60 francs costs. The saxophone was confiscated and given to Sax together with damages of 100 francs.[5]

After the 1854 judgement in favour of Sax and the seizure of instruments a year later, the members of the Association were debarred from taking further action against the inventor in respect of his patents. Predictably the Association were not prepared to remain impotent for long. Among the manufacturers from whom instruments had been confiscated was Rivet. He had taken no part in the long civil action and thus was not prevented in bringing an action himself. He was not, of course, in a financial position to take such a course but, with the backing of the Association, he became an acceptable front for their activities.

Early in 1856, Rivet brought an action against Sax regarding a 4-valved bass which, he claimed, had preceded the one patented by Sax. The true status of Rivet did not go unrecognised. The Advocate-General, Roussel, made a remarkable speech to the Court:

Rivet is a manufacturer of musical instruments on a very small scale. Only one suspect bass with four valves is found in his workshop. Who is this Rivet? Why is there this Court case with **considerable costs against him which relate so little to his fortune and his personal business?** *We can find the cause of this in a document which ought to be brought to the eye of the Court. M. Rivet is no other than a tool of M. Gautrot. This is incontestable. Here is the document, and the Court will judge the importance of Rivet in this case:*

I the undersigned, Gautrot Snr., a musical instrument manufacturer living 60 Rue Saint-Louis, in the Marais, in Paris, declare this present that I guarantee to M. Rivet, musical instrument manufacturer living in Lyon, passage de Largue No. (?), and I personally undertake through all courses of justice to pay all his costs whatever they may be, whatever the result, from **unfavourable verdicts in the lawsuits going on at the moment between the said Rivet and M. Ad.** *Sax, also an instrument maker of 50 (sic) Rue Saint-George in Paris, on which the verdict must be pronounced on the 13th March instant.*

Signed in Paris, 13th March 1856.[6]

The Court found in favour of Sax; Rivet had to pay Sax damages with costs.

Returning to the attack behind Rivet, the Association brought forward evidence to show that instruments similar to saxhorns had been in existence prior to the date of the saxhorn patent. These included a family of eight valved instruments, somewhat like valved trombones with upright bells, called *Clavicors*. In the drawings offered to the Court, these look uniform and efficient although in practice it is doubtful that the actual instruments reached the perfection depicted by the draughtsman.

Next the Court was shown a set of *Néo-altos* in F, E-flat and C, corresponding to the tenor and baritone saxhorns, a 4-valved bombardon in B-flat similar to the bass saxhorn, and a contrabass bombardon in E-flat, with three or four valves as with the contrabass saxhorns. These, it was claimed, were being made by several Parisian manufacturers in 1845 and it was from these that Sax had copied his designs.

On this occasion, Marie was in Court, not as counsel for the plaintiff but as Imperial Advocate. He was as generous towards Sax as hitherto he had appeared vindictive. After going over the points at issue in the judgement of 8th April 1855 he ended with a eulogy in favour of

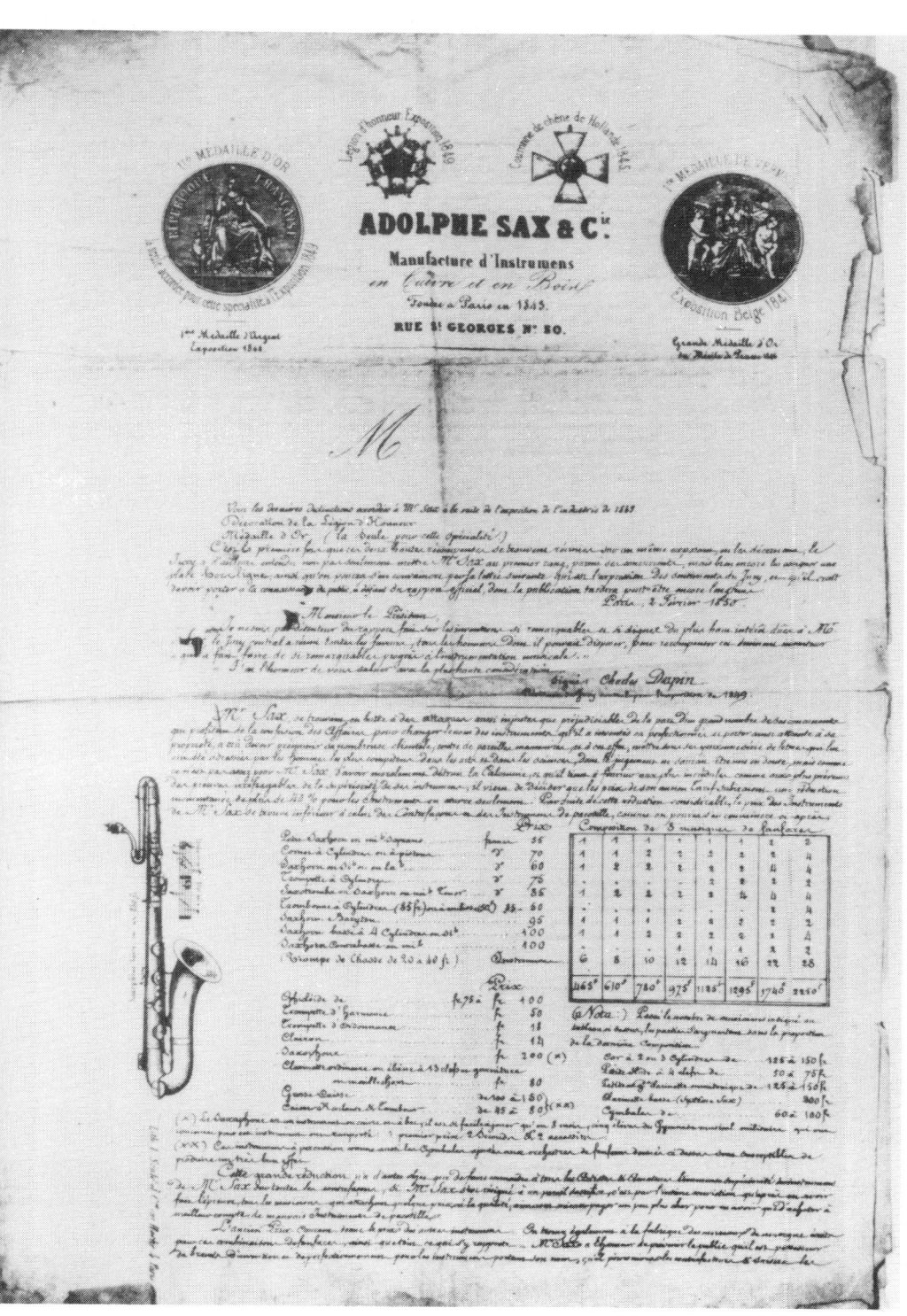

Prospectus and Price List
issued by Adolphe Sax and Company — 2nd February 1850

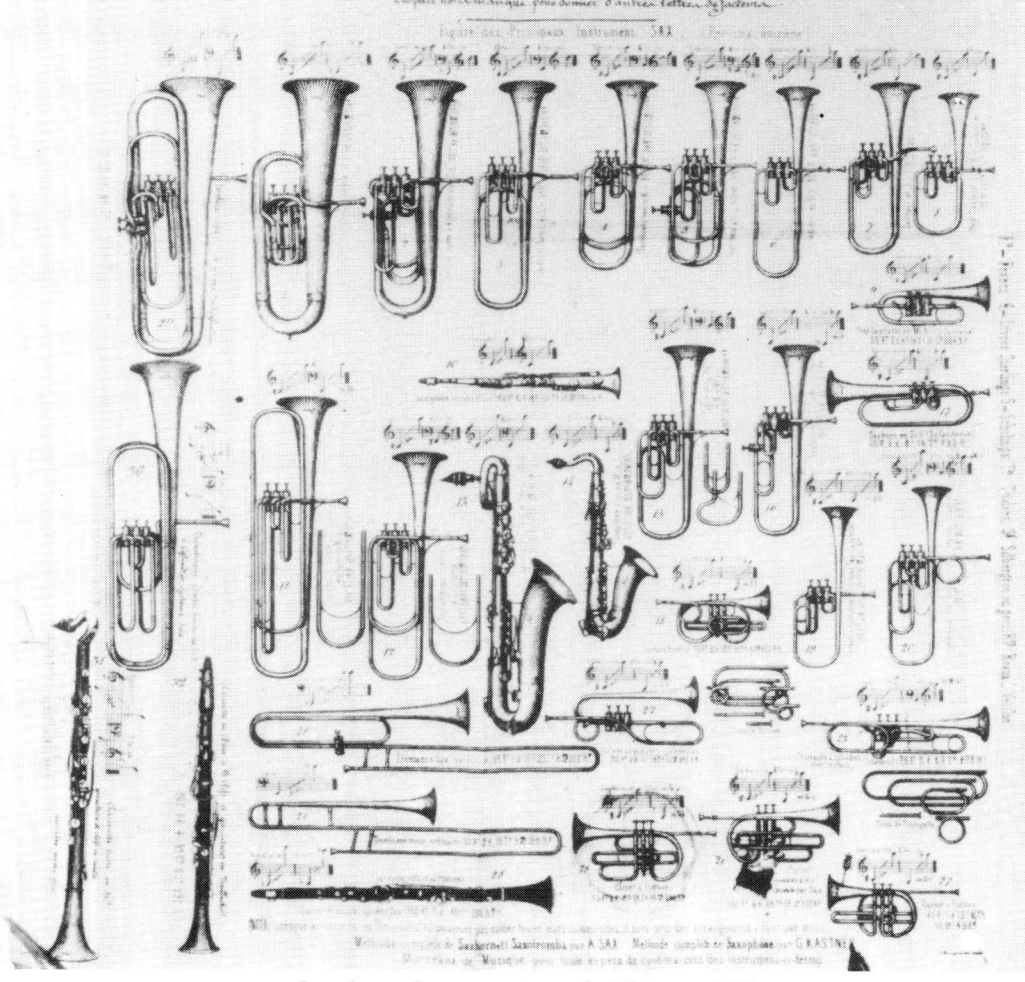

Page from a Sax prospectus — 2nd February 1850
with testimonials from Gasparo Spontini, Ambrois Thomas and Charles Finck.

revolution in musical art. France, he declared, needed inventors such as Sax; his important discoveries deserve the protection of justice.

On 24th April 1856, the Tribunal returned a judgement against Rivet who was again compelled to pay damages and costs to Sax. Sax recognised Gautrot as the biggest and most talented of his adversaries. Switching to the offensive after the Rivet cases, he sued Gautrot for patent infringements, his counsel, Dufaure, demonstrating Sax's large losses at Gautrot's hands. Marie was back as advocate for Sax's enemy. The Tribunal, on 12th June 1856 found against Gautrot, ordering him to pay Sax 2,000 francs damages, the profits from the sale of counterfeit instruments and to pass over to Sax all such instruments, complete or incomplete, then in his possession. Gautrot was also ordered to pay all costs and the cost of publishing the judgement in five Paris newspapers and in 27 newspapers in the departments all of Sax's choice.

Gautrot, whose aim was to prolong the dispute for as long as possible, filed an appeal which was heard on 6th and 27th February 1857. It was dismissed. The case was then taken to the Court of Amiens where the ubiquitous Marie, demonstrating his impartiality and his willingness to ardently serve the cause of whoever paid his fee, this time appeared *for* Sax. On 24th December 1858, the appeal was again dismissed.

The patents held by Sax gave him little protection against plagiarists. When seeking redress in the Courts, he found himself against a severe impediment. The Association of United Instrument Makers was not recognised in law as a corporate body. Therefore, the inventor had to take action against each member individually. Having secured a judgement, Sax found that appeals against it would then be passed from Court to Court; and, again, having endured the process with one manufacturer, the plaintiff was compelled to begin again in the next. As each was sued, he could rely on every possible help from his colleagues. For Sax, as soon as one adversary was despatched, there was another to take his place in a seemingly endless succession. The cost of all the actions he was involved in up to the end of 1858 amounted to nearly 200,000 francs.

In spite of the awards made against the members of the Association, they received a good deal of protection through a weakness in the Law of 5th July 1844. Article 42 stated that, however many counterfeits were made, there could be no more than a single fine of 2,000 francs. Sax's supporters contended that the profits from the sale of pirated instruments more than compensated for the expenditure in the Courts. Thus a war of attrition could be carried on almost indefinitely. The opposite view was, of course, that these instruments were falsely patented and, if they could not be made generally, many manufacturers would be ruined by having nothing to make.

As a postscript to the years of lawsuits against the inventor, the Courts appreciated that he had been deprived of the normal rights and privileges bestowed by his patents during the time they were being contested. In view of the Rouen Court finding entirely in his favour, and by way of compensation, an Act was passed and a decree published in 1860 extending the validity of all Sax's patents by five years. This was an occurrence so rare as to have happened only twice in France in the whole of the 19th century. Here was a chance to recoup from the wasted years; any average businessman would have exploited it to the full. But Sax was not of that breed. Time and time again, golden opportunities for making fortunes slipped through his fingers. Nowhere is this more evident than in his attitude to the reformation of pitch, a question occupying a Government Department at the time.

The need for standardisation of the pitch had been forcing itself with increasing urgency on the attention of musical authorities. In days when communications and travel were difficult, so that the joining together of different bands of players was a rare event, the fact that the note A in one part of the country differed completely from an A elsewhere did not often matter. With the enlargement of bands and orchestras, and increasing opportunities for meeting and intermingling, the difference in pitch between one group and another could be awkward and embarrassing.

The British Army had undergone a chastening experience in 1854 during the Crimean War. At Scutari, on the Bosphorus, 16,000 men of the Army of the East, *en route* for the Crimea, were immaculately turned out in review order. The occasion was the official birthday of Queen Victoria. The General Staff was gratified and Allied attachés and staffs impressed by the impeccable marching and drill of the troops. Hands and weapons flashed to the salute as drums heralded the playing of the National Anthem by the massed bands. Fiasco! An unbelievable cacophony made those in command squirm with mortification; at the same time, surely, bringing a suppressed twitch to the lip of many an oppressed private. No one had thought of rehearsing the combined bands in anything so simple as "God Save the Queen" or of checking to see if all had the same band parts. There was a multitude of differing pitches, keys and arrangements which, as one staff officer observed with masterly British understatement, "rather spoilt the effect of the review". Its immediate effect was to stir the War Office into recognising the need for some standard and was the direct cause of the Royal Military School of Music being established at Kneller Hall three years afterwards.

In France, standardisation in military music had progressed further since a school of music had been established for some time. But, although there had been previous efforts to bring about uniformity of pitch, the matter was far from being resolved. A commission was set up by the French government in 1858 to settle once and for all the question of a standard pitch. Auber, Berlioz, Halévy, Meyerbeer, Rossini and Ambrois Thomas represented the musical element, together with two physicists and four other holders of distinguished office.

The commission first investigated the various pitches then in use in Europe. Discrepancies were staggering. In London, for instance, pianos were tuned as far apart as $A=455$ and 434 cycles per second according to whether they were to accompany instruments or voices. In 1700, the pitch in Paris had been 404; currently it was 448. On February 1st 1859 the Commission issued its recommendation that, irrespective of temperature, the standard pitch for France should be $A=435$ c.p.s. A Bill was passed adopting the report and giving it legal status.

This piece of news must have set every wind instrument maker rubbing his hands. All existing instruments would immediately become obsolete; those which could not be adapted would have to be replaced. Such a stimulus to trade comes but rarely. As a leading manufacturer with a large tooled-up factory, Sax was in a powerful position to make a quick fortune from the circumstances. Amazingly, he seems to have been opposed to the reformation. Perhaps the trials of the passing years had wearied his spirit in the mere making of merchandise to sell, although even if it had, he could have left much of the routine to his experienced supervisors and inspectors. As it was, the chance went by without any substantial reflection on the inventor's fortune.

Interest in pure invention did not wane. At least he felt the need for all instruments within the same combination to have a common pitch and, among his minor inventions of the time, he produced a small instrument for sounding a true A. The idea was probably for use instead of a tuning fork which is too quiet for practical purposes, or when an oboe, which usually sounds the note for the orchestra, was not present. It cannot be construed as yet another example of his antipathy towards the oboe, for he not only made and sold oboes of the conventional pattern, but spent a good deal of time and effort in trying to improve the bassoon.

The bassoon had always presented makers with its own peculiar and difficult problems. To get the six primary note-holes of an 8ft instrument within the span of a hand, early makers drilled them obliquely into the thick walls of the wooden tube. As far back as 1820, Charles Sax had been among the first to experiment by drilling in the correct acoustical positions, effecting the operation by means of keys and rods. He exhibited such an instrument at Haarlem in 1825; later he applied the system to a metal bassoon for which he took out a patent in 1840. It was no doubt the partial success of these instruments which prompted the son to continue on the same lines. For the London Exhibition of 1851, he included a brass bassoon with 23 keys, which caused considerable interest when demonstrated by the Belgian bassoonist, Friedrich Baumann, then settled in England. Theobald Boehm, whose key system had revolutionised the flute and which various makers were attempting to apply to other woodwinds, heard Sax's bassoon in London. On his way home, he called at the Rue Saint-Georges, examined the instrument closely, and congratulated the inventor.

Adolphe-Edouard Sax (1859-1945)
... *carried on an instrument manufactory in the Rue Myrha after his father's bankruptcy and death.*

SAXOPHONE

"Our third illustration represents a new Musical Instrument, the invention of M. Saxe, whose fame is already known in this branch of art; it is appropriately named after the inventor — the *Saxophone*."

— *The Illustrated London News,* July 7, 1849

Despite the excitement, Sax's construction was not taken up. It was shown but not played in London in 1862. Fétis says that, as a result of the 1851 demonstration, Boehm was led to collaborate with Triébert in a laterally-bored, key-rod operated bassoon for which the latter received the Prize Medal in 1862. This was an efficient, but heavy and expensive model; only a few were made, some being stamped "Marzoli" after a notable player who appears to have been a part of the collaborative team. No doubt Sax had other pressing matters on hand, or else felt that Triébert's instrument was ahead of his own conception. H. Lavoix, who credits Adolphe Sax with having the original idea for making acoustically correct bassoons in 1840, says that Sax first thought of designing his own instruments after seeing the work of J. B. J. Willent-Bordogni, eminent player and one-time professor at the Brussels Conservatoire. He notes that, by 1878, the Sax-bassoon had been developed no further.[7]

All the ingenious ideas tried at this time and later, seem to have come to grief because they tended to alter the tone of the bassoon too much to be acceptable. Although Sax contended that the basic characteristic tone of an instrument is not altered by the material of which it is made, modern opinion is that resonant wood does vibrate in sympathy with the air column, which metal does not, and, by enhancing the upper partials, subtly influences the tone colour. Of all wind instruments, this is most applicable to the bassoon, where the thick walls and obliquely bored holes play their part in producing a "true" bassoon tone. Later makers followed Sax in trying metal for bassoon construction, notably Lécomte whose instrument had projecting tubes to simulate oblique borings, and an experimental Heckel. None succeeded in ousting the traditional wood.

Sax does not seem to have devoted much attention to improving the oboe and the flute; he might have been gratified to know that, many years afterwards, oboes would be made with finger-plates in imitation of saxophone keywork, for the benefit of inveterate dance-band "doublers". Constant Pierre, no admirer of Sax, hints that the inventor experimented, without success, to improve the flute,[8] of which it will be remembered, he had been trained as a player. To judge from Kastner's pictures, the flutes he offered were of the accepted cone-Boehm kind with all tone-holes covered.

At the height of its fame the factory at Rue Saint-Georges offered such a comprehensive range of instruments as to accommodate almost every wind instrumentalist. Percussionists, too, were catered for in a catalogue which illustrates bass, tenor and side drums with sticks and cymbals. As music was becoming more chromatic, Sax saw the difficulties experienced by timpanists as they laboriously endeavoured to retune their instruments during the course of a performance. His *timbale-à-pistons* did away entirely with the bass "kettle" which he considered superfluous. In its place, he put a graduated tube over which the skin was stretched, the piston mechanism giving instant access to any note within the range. Sax claimed that his invention was accurate and was not affected by humidity. Like so many of his revolutionary notions, it found no favour.

Drums had been included in the collection of Sax instruments displayed at the Great Exhibition in London 1851. It would appear from an exhibit by Augustus Knoche of Munich, that mechanical kettledrums, heavy, expensive, but easily tuned by hand or foot, had been in use in the Royal Orchestra of Munich for the previous ten years, these being among many other similar attempts forestalling Sax in this field.

"The Illustrated London News" of August 23rd 1851, devotes more space to Sax than any other wind instrument manufacturer:

The show of brass wind instruments in the French department is exceedingly good, and the great number and variety exhibited would seem to indicate the penchant of our Gallic neighbours for anything of a military character, even to the manufacturers of drums and trumpets. First and foremost amongst the foreign exhibitors is M. Adolphe Sax of Paris (No. 1726), well known in England and on the Continent as the inventor of Sax horns so beautifully played by Messrs. Distin. M. Sax has succeeded in giving to his horn a soft, full, clear and musical quality of tone which was before considered almost unattainable on that instrument; and, from scarcely ever heard but in an orchestra or a military band, has, in the hands of Messrs. Distin. become an agreeable variety in the concert room. The instruments exhibited by M. Sax in the Nave, from the Sax horns and the cornet-à-pistons to the immense trombones, are characterised by the greatest beauty and finish, as well as elegance of form. The kettle and side-drums are also fine specimens of those instruments.

The author of the review obviously considers the saxhorn to be an "improvement" on the French horn. Of course it is not, being an entirely different instrument which has suffered in comparison in the same way as the cornet has for so long been castigated for not being a trumpet. In view of the scarcity of good French horn players, and the comparatively easy technique of the saxhorn, the latter was often pressed into service for the former. Even Wagner was forced into this position at the notorious Paris production of *Tannhaüser* on March 13th 1861.

At this time, Sax had advanced his reputation as an executive musician by obtaining the directorship of the Opera stage band. He had a group of sixteen players who were kept busy, since few operas did not feature grand marches led by a band on stage at impressive entrances. The musical director on these occasions saw no reason why he should not use the appearance as a showcase for his instruments. Wagner gave precise directions to the Opera directors as to his instrumental requirements back-stage. For the First Act, he needed twelve horns, to be doubled when the players came on stage for the finale. "As there are not enough horns in Paris", he wrote, "M. Sax should be asked to substitute for them instruments of like tone, perhaps saxophones". His naming of the saxophone as a suitable replacement for the French horn is surprising for one noted for his attention to detail in orchestration, since the two instruments differ widely in character. Writing later in his autobiography, his account of the position differs somewhat from his Opera note: "For instance, it was impossible in the whole of Paris to find the twelve French horns which in Dresden had so bravely sounded the hunting call in the First Act. In connection with this matter, I had to deal with the terrible man Sax, the celebrated instrument-maker. He had to help me out with all kinds of substitutes in the shape of saxophones and saxhorns, moreover he was officially appointed to conduct the music behind the scenes. It was an impossibility to get the music properly played".

Here there is no word of doubling the horns and this time he mentions saxhorns as well as saxophones. If a substitute is imperative, the saxhorn is a much better proposition; one can only conclude that Wagner was rather vague as to the identity of the saxophone. In 1932, W. F. H. Blandford cleared up the point by corresponding directly with a son of the inventor who had continued with his father's post as musical director of the Opera band. M. Adolphe Sax junior replied: "I think I can assure you that the help given by my father consisted in using the saxhorn and not the saxophone".[9] With a characteristic lack of generosity, Wagner lashed out at everyone and everything because things had gone badly with the production. The stage-bandmaster who, in all probability, had done as competent a job as was possible in the circumstances, did not escape.

Although this event may have engendered some bad feeling between composer and inventor, it has been suggested that Wagner's ideas for orchestral reform were influenced by Sax. In the latter's proposals can be sensed the sweeping conceptions of Berlioz. They were based on whole families of instruments being represented in place of haphazard, incompatible groupings, particularly in the woodwind. He advocates groups of six homogeneous instruments for each of the woodwind parts, in addition to six different sizes of stringed instruments.

With the passing years, the saxophone attracted increasing attention. In order that there should be an adequate supply of proficient players, Sax was obliged to add the role of teacher to his already diverse activities. In 1857, he was appointed Professor of Saxophone at the Paris Conservatoire, a post he held until the troubles of 1870 brought about its abolition. Six years before, he had written "Methods" for both his principal families, saxhorns and saxophones, in which he proposed that all instruments, whatever their pitch, should play from music written on the treble stave. Because of the identical fingering, a player of one size, when switching to another, would have nothing to re-learn, having only an adjustment of embouchure to cope with. This system holds good in British brass bands until this day; although saxophones from the baritone downwards used, for a time, the bass clef, it has long been common practice for all sizes to conform with Sax's original idea. But for this, the amount of "doubling" for which dance-band saxophonists are noted, might have been severely restricted.

The saxophone was not slow to cross the Channel; its first appearance in an English concert hall was probably in November 1850 as "The Musical World" of 16th November 1850 reported. It was first known under the names of "Corno-musa" or "Zouave". On this occasion it was said: M. Soualle plays solos on the Corno-musa, a new instrument, in M. Jullier's Quadrille designations, accompanied by a harp". The instrument was mentioned again in the next week's issue. Soualle, a Belgian clarinettist, occasioned a rather facetious note in "The Musical World" of 10th January 1852 when the novelty was described as "a large instrument with the reed and mouthpiece of a clarinet which bristles with keys, and the bell of a horn. It has a rich mellow tone, a compound of the clarinet and the cornet. It seems to be a musical monster, neither fish, nor flesh, nor fowl — a red herring!"

The quaint names were soon dropped. Later issues of the journal commented that the saxophone "produced a great effect" when Soualle played "a fine instrument of the clarinet kind" at a Wednesday concert at the Exeter Hall.

Another Belgian clarinettist, Wuille, was brought over to play for Jullien. He played saxophone solos at Ella's Musical Union on which "The Musical World" of 12th June 1852 discoursed: "Lastly, his versatility was demonstrated in a fantasia of his own composition on the saxophone, one of the most remarkable of M. Sax's inventions with which the audience was particularly pleased".

Jullien had five saxophones in his touring wind band of 1856 and Soualle, Wuille and Demange were all featured as soloists at the Jullien concerts of the 1850's as the Distin family had been earlier with their saxhorns. Observant readers of the "Illustrated London News" would have known of its existence some years before. The issue of July 7th 1849, in reviewing the Paris Exhibition, carried a woodcut of a tenor saxophone with the information this "represents a new Musical Instrument, the invention of M. Saxe (sic), whose fame is already known in this branch of art; it is appropriately named after the inventor — the Saxophone".

In the same year, Henry Distin was offering saxophones for sale from his Cranbourne Street establishment. An advertisement in a November 1849 issue of the "The Musical World" stated that drawings and prices of saxhorns, cornets and saxophones etc. were to be had for two stamps from Henry Distin's Music Warehouse.

Although British Army bands did not take to the saxophone with the same enthusiasm as the French, it does seem that certain bands were quick to adopt it in ones and twos. Henry George Farmer, the military-music historian, asserts that Bandsman Henry Rigby was playing a saxophone with the Royal Artillery Band as early as 1848 and that he was a featured soloist on a programme printed for Newcastle concerts in September 1855.[10] The Band Accounts show that there were two alto and two tenor saxophones in the inventory for the year 1856-7.

As far as Sax was concerned, the latter years of the sixth decade saw him still in high standing with many influential friends and patrons. In particular the Emperor, Napoleon III, never failed to show him consideration. In 1857, during one of the inevitable financial crises, the Emperor gave him an order for six silver trumpets for use by his personal guard. These instruments were remarkable in themselves. Fétis describes them: *By means of a detachable part added to the basic instrument, this can be transformed at will to soprano, alto, baritone or bass with the full chromatic scale in each of these registers; with the result that it is possible to play instrumental music in harmony on instruments which are themselves confined to the harmonics of the basic sound.*[11] This would appear to mean that the trumpets were equipped with a detachable valve component similar to that which he had applied to the bugle in 1849 and which will be mentioned in the next chapter.

Other marks of Royal grace were given him. In additon to the Cross of the Legion of Honour and the title of Imperial Instrument Maker, he was appointed, in 1858, Private Director of Music to the Emperor.

Notes on Chapter X

1. Comettant, p.307.
2. Macgillivray, J. A.: *Musical Instruments Through the Ages*, p.262.
3. "The Musical Times" (London) 1st December 1890, p.722.
4. Brenta, p.80. (footnote).
5. Comettant, pp.353-5.
6. *ibid.*, pp.356-7.
7. Langwill, L. G.: *The 'Boehm Bassoon: A Retrospect*, Galpin Society Journal XII, June 1959, pp.63-65.
8. Pierre, C.: *Les Facteurs*, p.351.
9. Letter to "Radio Times" (London), 30th December 1932.
10. Unfortunately Farmer did not publish these programmes. He apparently wrote an article under a *nom-de-plume, The First British Saxophonist*, for the "Musicians Journal" July 1931, p.5, but even the British Museum is unable to trace this issue.
11. Fetis, p.421.

Saxophones from sopranino to bass
Kneller Hall collection

E-flat alto saxophone, among the instruments which gained First Prize at the Paris Exhibition of 1867.

XI
Decline

Sax was always a keen participator in the many exhibitions of the time, realising their value in terms of publicity and advertisement despite the cost and trouble. It was his aim not only to display a comprehensive selection of his wares but to introduce a novelty or two to capture interest. At the London Exhibition of 1862, for instance, he had on show cornets, saxhorns and saxotrombas fitted, in addition to the three valves, with two, three, four and five keys. This reversion to keys in the style of the obsolete key-bugle is curious. Valves are obviously superior to keys in this type of instrument; yet there may have been some who retained a regard for certain aspects of key technique.

Up to 1850, many English cornopeans were fitted with "Macfarlane's clapper key", named after its inventor, a one-time cornettist at the Drury Lane Theatre. This was a closed key opening a hole located about a foot to the rear of the bell, operated by the left hand and permitting the use of shakes. A modern player can perform all possible trills and ornaments with valves alone; Sax's valves were efficient and by no means sluggish so that the inclusion of keys ought not to be on account of shakes alone. From the inspection of a patent abridgement of 1859 it would appear from a drawing of an contralto (B-flat) saxhorn that all five closed key-pads were placed close together at the widest part of the bore, the very largest being but a few inches from the rim of the bell. The accompanying text states: "By the provision of lever keys, the main tube is not interrupted, the tones melt together quicker, and softness is given to trills".

The purpose of the keys would therefore seem to be in the producing of a sort of *portamento* effect somewhat reminiscent of the "half-valve" technique of jazz trumpeters. In addition, their presence would facilitate the production of high notes, particularly on the widely-tapered instruments, as well as acting as compensators for correctness of pitch. Fétis says that, at the London Exhibition of 1862, these key-valve instruments "roused the greatest interest among the jury as well as many artists by the charm of their mellow sound, pure in the top register as well as by the perfect effect in the execution of groups, trills and portamento".[1] Despite the interest and praise, nothing came of the key-valve combination.

The life of Adolphe Sax can be seen as a vista of rapidly succeeding peaks and depressions. In following its course we can see the last summit was scaled in 1867 when the inventor was but 53; for the next twenty-seven years until his death, the path lead steadily downwards. Before we reluctantly descend with him, it is well to take stock of the many ingenious, sometimes brilliant, often harebrained schemes, notions and inventions with which he was at some time concerned and which have not so far been mentioned in this narrative.

"The bugle", once said Berlioz, referring to the military signalling instrument, "is only fit for the ears of savages". In 1849, Sax did something to help music-loving buglers get more satisfaction from their simple piece of equipment. He patented an attachment to give the bugle a full chromatic compass. To effect the conversion, the mouthpiece and shank were removed from the bugle and a lightweight valve set substituted. Comettant says — and we may wonder if he fully grasped the implication of his words — that these attachments could turn an ordinary set of bugles into a fully chromatic consort ranging from soprano to contrabass "without varying the size of the instrument in any way from the ordinary bugle".

The invention was called "clarion-Sax"; the attachment was to be carried in a specially-designed calfskin case. It is interesting to note that, some 15 years later, Henry Distin was endeavouring to get the British Army interested in his "new invention"; an ingenious chromatic attachment which would change an ordinary bugle into a band instrument.[2]

He was constantly working on the improvement of brass instruments and valve systems. Unusual conceptions of design occupied him; seven-valved duplex instruments combining in one mouthpiece and bell the characteristics of a saxhorn and a saxotromba, or two pitches of the same instrument an octave apart. Several patents were taken out for valve modifications, including airtight, dustproof designs, compensators, new plans for springs and a rod-and-fingerplate device allowing pistons to be fingered with either hand. To overcome the effects of moisture in wooden tubes, experiments were carried out with metal linings. Key-pad seatings were designed to obviate hollows under the pads, caused by the thickness of the tube. Nor was his interest limited to conventional wind-instruments. Fétis includes in his list of inventions[3] a set of Panpipes.

Just as Charles Sax had devoted some of his inventive energies to instruments other than wind, so the son registered various patents in this field. Among modifications for bowed instruments were experiments in new shapes and proportions, a sound-box for improving volume for the cello and a double-bass to be tuned in fifths and to play an octave below the cello. He designed a pianoforte with enhanced power for orchestral use and a plan for piano tuning by means of one master screw instead of multifarious pegs. And, between working on practical instrumental improvements, he evolved what was claimed to be a simpler system for writing musical notation.

Sax had a strong predilection for the parabolic shape. Many ideas of his were based on the parabola which, he maintained, possessed perfect acoustical properties. At the World Exhibition of 1867, he exhibited models of kiosks, at least one of which, in the Waux-hall in Brussels, was actually constructed. There was also a model of a concert hall with a special platform intended to improve orchestral resonance. He expounded his theory: "All theatre and concert halls are defective and only partly obtain their objective; that is, being given a fixed place for the platform, stage or orchestra pit; to direct the sound towards another fixed place — that occupied by the audience".

To meet those requirements, Sax adopted the idea of the parabola; an egg-shaped interior with the artists at the top with all sound waves diverging from this focal point in line parallel with the parabolic axis. Mathematically sound as this may be, it falls down because of the impracticality of placing a large choir or orchestra exactly at the focal point. Just how far a musician could be from this point without spoiling the effect is not clear since such a hall has never been built. Nevertheless, the idea is an ingenious one, scientifically reasoned and worthy of consideraton. Some years later he patented another parabolic design. Émile Paladilhe required a very deep-sounding bell for use in his opera *La Patrie*. To overcome the difficulty of getting a large, heavy, conventional bell into the orchestra pit, Sax made a small instrument shaped from sheet brass which ideally met the requirement. In 1861, he made a triangle which was used in Berlioz's *Harold*. *"Its shape"*, wrote the composer, *"is in the image of God, like all triangles, but more than other triangles, and more than God in particular, you will find it plays true"*.

The faculty of Sax for invention and innovation stretched beyond the confines of music into the everyday world of labour. Kastner relates that, at the age of eleven, Sax, with an early leaning towards things mechanical and mathematical, had thoughtfully appraised problems in connection with landslips in his native region. He proffered advice as to how they might be prevented, being so efficacious as to prompt the chief beneficiary of the advice to urge the seeking of a patent. Another plan of his of a like nature was for preventing falls of earth whilst digging wells.

With the population of Paris growing, he submitted to the City Council plans for opening up the plain of Saint-Denis as a new suburb, being connected to the main centre by means of a huge tunnel to be driven from the Saint-Lazare area through the Montmartre heights. During the height of his troubles following the fall of Louise-Philipe and the temporary suspension of business, Sax found consolation in the new railway. He perceived that engine signal whistles were often diffused in the wind in a way that could render them inaudible at the point where they most needed to be heard. The method which emerged from his thoughts sought to direct the sound towards any desired point irrespective of weather conditions.

For every notion of clear-sighted, practical application, there would be at least one conceived in fantasy. None was more crazy than his plan for the "Saxocannon". As the allied generals bungled their way through the Crimean War, their armies were encamped outside Sebastapol suffering cruelly from cold and disease. The bitter winter of 1854 persisted into the following year without any sign of surrender from the besieged garrison. With the tools at his ready disposal, it could be facetiously conjectured that the inventor might have taken a leaf out of Joshua's book and marched round the walls with a contingent of saxhorns, saxotrombas and saxtubas. Although this solution lay in the apparently conventional use of a piece of artillery, the idea had just about the same chance of success. Since ordinary guns were unable to pierce the defences, Sax reasoned: "If men were a hundred times stronger than they are, our artillery weapons would be for them only what pistols are for us". He then proposed plans for a monster mortar of a size that would be appropriate for supermen. It was to have a bore of eleven yards diameter and to fire a shot of some 550 tons! It would be manufactured and transported in sections and assembled in an advantageous firing position. Because of the recoil and consequent danger to anyone in the vicinity, its designer proposed to operate the firing mechanism at a safe distance using the newly-acquired power of electricity.[4] The idea, if it ever got as far as the general staff, was never taken seriously. If it had been, and had worked, Sebastabol might have preceded Hiroshima by nearly a century as a monument to the destructive nature of man. Better by far to be remembered for the saxophone than for widespread carnage.

It may be reasonably supposed that Sax was never able to see the practical difficulties in the way of his proposals. He would be genuinely disgusted that others would not provide materials, finance and authority to carry them out, no doubt attributing their reluctance to spite and vindictiveness, or, at best, to lack of imagination. He appreciated that he was not alone in so suffering. He met inventors in other spheres and found that they had similar problems. This led to the publication of a paper setting out the need for a School for Inventors where those with aptitude and talent would be trained in the theories and techniques, and helped to bring their original ideas to fruition. There would be examinations in which specific problems would be set for the student to solve. With such a grounding, it was contended, an inventor would be able to face such difficulties that an unenlightened world would surely place in his path, with a strength born of confidence in his own ability. And, at the end of a long life dedicated to the cause of innovation, the inventor would find solace and comfort in old age in the Sax Home for Poor and Elderly Inventors.[5]

Two significant clues as to Sax's personal character emerge from this publication. As a reason for establishing the School, he felt it would stimulate in inventors a desire for fame; something which, for him, meant more than wealth or comfort. Secondly, despite the comprehensive nature of his paper, he omits all reference to patent law and possible legal consequences arising out of the action of pirates or vindictive parties. For one who took and gave so much offence in this matter it would appear that, by not thinking of pointing out these dangers to the novice, the master himself had not fully learned the hard lesson.

In 1864, Sax exhibited at the Industrial Exhibition in Bayonne. The next year saw him at Oporto in Portugal where the jury awarded him First Prize in direct competition with the large Austro-German brass manufacturer, V. F. Červeny, although both received a Medal of Honour. Červeny was so incensed at getting only the Silver Medal that the catalogue of that house thirty years after the event was still carrying attacks on Sax, referring to the Prussians and Austrians as *real army musicians, always ready to oblige, whereas the Paris Guard ... has nothing military to show but their uniforms.* This condemnation concludes: *One can only hope that, from now on, the Military Administration will not trust H. Sax's inventions.*[6] *Foreign bands who know nothing of them, gained more success than artists of the Paris Guard who are, in fact, completely equipped with Saxhorns. The result shows that the monopoly given to H. Sax twenty years ago is regrettable as it was on the point of annihilating an important branch of the industry which is far from doing well where art is concerned.* With due sympathy for the German point of view, much of this might be classed as Teutonic sour grapes; bands, at least to the west, were finding the products of Sax greatly to their liking.

At the Paris Exhibition of 1867, Sax achieved his greatest distinction. Here his display included at least one specimen of every musical instrument he had invented or improved, the centre-piece being a magnificent alto saxophone plated with fine gold. For this collection he received the *Grand Prix*, the highest award ever given for his work.

The terrible years when he had the cancerous tumour of the lip must have instilled into the patient a deep regard for medical matters. Doubtless he pondered the imperfections of the human frame and searched the recesses of his mind for ways of remedying them.

From careful observations, he reached certain conclusions. Tuberculosis he declared, was rarely found among military musicians. This was due to the beneficial effect of playing wind instruments. The one instrument he excepted was the oboe where the player is compelled to conserve lungs full of air whilst playing. He advanced a breathing system for strengthening the lungs and extolled the healthy virtues of playing and singing for all. However, even his crony Comettant shuddered at the idea of "1,000,000,000 inhabitants of Europe all singing and playing trumpets together".

1862 brought Sax another serious illness, this time an infection of the lungs. Medical advice was that he should seek to live somewhere where the air was cleaner than in the centre of Paris, preferably close to the pine forest.

As so often happens, what is the best medical solution turns out to be the most impracticable. Sax felt he could not leave his factory for any length of time. He therefore thought of a way whereby if he could not go to a pine forest, the pine forest or its equivalent should be brought to him.

By the standards of the day it was thought that tar, creosote and similar products contained antiseptic properties. To diffuse their vapours about his rooms the inventor made a rectangular metal box, the lid of which had six parallel vertical plates. When the lid was closed, the plates dipped into the prepared solution; it could then be opened and adjusted by a spring to any desired height according to the intensity required, the process being repeated as evaporation became complete.

Sax received personal benefit from the box and was pleased with his air-purifier. With his usual sense of proprietary rights, he named the box *Goudronnière Sax* and sent a sample, with a paper, to the academy of Science. For once, an extra-musical notion of his aroused interest. Dr. Velpeau, who has been consulted about the cancer, approved the idea, as did a number of his colleagues. One of these eminent men recommended the "tarbox" to Louis Pasteur. From Alais on February 9th 1866, the great scientist wrote graciously to the inventor, thanking him for his useful fumigation box, telling him that he had passed it on to a director at the War Ministry. Pasteur was obviously more interested in Sax's method of spreading the antiseptic than in the agent in the box. He goes on to ask the inventor to send two more boxes of exactly the same shape, this time empty, as he wished to fill them with his own substances for research purposes. To be the supplier even of empty boxes to so great a man would have given Sax immense satisfaction.

The inventor had a great belief in the liberal use of antiseptics in combating disease. He saw that the blowing of wind instruments called for a high standard of hygiene and was a ripe field for their application. He submitted patent plans providing wind instruments with an inner double jacket for the reception of **antiseptic** liquids. As an alternative, he proposed that the inner tube of an instrument be coated with suitable substances so that the performer would automatically inhale impregnated air as he played. He wrote a paper which might have been taken seriously on the beneficial effect in strengthening lungs and preventing consumption, to be found in the regular playing of a wind instrument.

Brother Alphonse, too, was concerned with respiratory and similar matters. In 1865 he published a semi-advertising booklet, vastly amusing in retrospect, entitled "Exercises of the lungs: instrumental music from the point of view of health, and the establishment of women's orchestras".[7] The two brothers, reunited with their father worked together for some years in the Rue Saint-Georges, the younger man devoting much of his time to work on ascending pistons. Around 1860 it appears that Alphonse set up business for himself as a brass instrument maker at No. 5 (*bis*) Rue d'Abbeville. At the time of the 1862 London Exhibition, quarrels broke out between the brothers regarding the ascending valve system and the fact that the Exhibition jury awarded an identical prize medal to both of them. It could be that the older man resented his brother, a mere maker, being ranked with him the inventor. Alphonse was a skilled craftsman in his own right as is testified by much of his inventive acumen, some of his instruments have novel features, such as a trumpet with two ascending and two descending pistons on a system known as *saxomblatarique*. Pierre complains that Alphonse is given less than justice and takes Fétis to task for eulogising Adolphe to the total exclusion of his brother. It is hinted that Alphonse had other interests beside musical instruments; the establishment did not last long.[8] By 1867 he was no longer to be found in the list of Parisian manufacturers and nothing further is heard of him until his death on June 26th 1874.

The break-up of the once large family was completed on April 26th when Charles Sax died. The loss of his father must have affected Adolphe considerably. He was never unmindful of the debt owed for his early training and the opportunities for developing his natural bent. Despite the vicissitudes of his life, who can say that things might often have been worse but for the father's wise counsel. Inevitably, the triumphs of 1867 were tempered with troubles and griefs. One of the greatest blows to his personal pride happened ten years before. With the help and patronage of the Emperor he had quickly recovered from the 1852 bankruptcy. This painful episode soon dwindled into the past and was seldom thought of again. It was therefore a great shock to be reminded suddenly that an undischarged bankrupt was not considered worthy of being a member of the Legion of Honour. For seven years it had been his greatest pride to wear its cross; it could well be that his enemies had eventually pointed out the position. Sax protested that the settlement with his creditors had been mutually acceptable and entirely honourable. By a curious oversight which the President of the Chamber of Commerce confessed had not happened in a hundred years, his discharge from bankruptcy had never been recorded in the official publication. The administrators of the Legion felt duty bound to rigidly observe the conventions although it had taken them five years to appreciate the situation. In consequence, Sax was humiliated and dishonoured by being removed from the Order.

The Franco-Prussian War of 1870, the Siege of Paris and the disaster suffered by French arms at Sedan brought an end to the Second Empire and to Sax's patron, Emperor Napoleon III. Close friends and allies in early struggles were passing from the scene. Kastner, Berlioz and Fétis all died within a span of four years; the inventor must have felt singularly isolated since much of the enmity engendered in former years still persisted. The extended patents had now expired without the inventor being able to make much capital out of them. Other makers, less inventive but more skilled in business, were quick to take advantage of the lapsed patents. They were turning out saxhorns at a steady rate; orders on the Sax factory dwindled.

Sax exhibited in London in 1869 for what seems to have been the last time abroad. The troubles of 1870 brought about the closure of both the *Gymnase* and the saxophone class. The effect of this was to deprive the inventor of a useful source of income and to jeopardise the success of the saxophone. A new instrument, to attract students, must have adequate teaching facilities if it is to become established.

Financial affairs became entangled to an alarming extent. Being unable to make a success in business with everything in his favour, the effects of those years sounded the death-knell of his days as a leading manufacturer of musical instruments. Creditors were apprehensive and pressed firmly for payment of debts which at last it had to be admitted would never be paid. In 1873, for the second time, bankrupty came to the unfortunate man.

The post of Musical Director at the *Opéra* was still his, and for some years remained his only stable source of income. Cast down as he certainly was, his mind continued to grapple with innumerable problems and their possible solutions; many of the plans and inventions previously mentioned belong to the period. But on this occasion he could find no way again of making arrangements with his creditors. Bankruptcy proceedings went their full course. The Rue Saint-Georges factory, scene of so many triumphs and disasters over the years, was closed. Stocks of instruments together with tools and equipment of the trade were sold to appease creditors. The final stroke of dissolution came in December 1877 when the famous collection of musical instruments was put up for sale. The printed catalogue listed 467 items consisting of many rare and valuable specimens together with many examples of blatant infringements of Sax patents. A number of the pieces went back to the inventor's native land; some to Renaix into the collection of the wealthy César Snoeck, others to the *Musée Instrumental* of Brussels. The Paris Conservatoire Museum acquired many fine specimens.

For ten years after the sale, Adolphe Sax, who had held the centre of the stage for so long in his colourful, controversial role, slipped away into obscurity. He even gave up the Opera conductorship, being succeeded by his son Adolphe who held the post for many years. Without this income, the proud, independent man must have been entirely dependent upon his family. His sons carried on a manufacturing business at a greatly reduced level, possibly assisted by the ageing father. Up to the outbreak of the Second World War the Sax Company continued in business at No. 84 Rue Myrha.[9]

All through the 1880's, the Courts were still arguing many outstanding lawsuits; where the money came from to pay the lawyers is not clear since the plaintiff had little to spare. Likely, the fees were to be settled when indemnities awarded him against his adversaries were eventually paid. But after 26 years of waiting, the amount of those indemnities, as decided by experts, had never been published.

In 1887, at the age of 73, there came one final outburst from this unhappy man. In the press he voiced a poignant last "Appeal to the Public" in which he outlined his plight. *I am sorry that I cannot have even a few hours peace in a life eaten up by worry.*[10] His sorry position did not go entirely unnoticed. There were at least a few musicians who remembered the old man and appreciated the debt owed to his work. It was left to the composer Paul Jean Lacôme[11] to organise a petition, supported by Chabrier, Massanet and Saint-Saens, which was addressed to Henry Roujon, Director of Fine Arts. This resulted in a small pension being awarded which helped to alleviate a little the discomforts of his last years.

Antoine Joseph, always known as Adolphe, Sax died on the 4th of February 1894 in his eightieth year. With the removal of the plaintiff, the last of the lawsuits in which he had been involved for a half a century was concluded. All his life he had desired fame and peace. In attaining the first he had forfeited the second. Now he was at peace, with any claim to lasting fame in the hands of a fickle posterity.

Notes on Chapter XI

1. Fétis, p. 420.
2. Comettant, pp. 357-2; Binns P.L: *100 Years of Military Music*, p.69
3. *Vide* Fétis, p.421 *et seq.*
4. Brenta, p. 78.
5. Comettant, p. 532.
6. V. F. Červeny & Sohn catalogue and price list c. 1895, pp. 96-8.
7. "Gymnastique des poumons: La Musique Instrumentale au point de vue de l'Hygiène et la Création des Orchestres Féminins par M. Alphonse Sax Junior" — Paris 1865.
8. Pierre C: *Les Facteurs*, p. 259.
9. Gilson, p. 18.
10. Brenta, p. 82.
11. *ibid.*

Alphonse Sax (1822-1874)
Adolphe's younger brother worked with him in Paris until a bitter quarrel separated them.
Alphonse set up on his own as a skilled craftsman and innovator, but was even less a businessman than his brother.

Sax's kettledrums — 'sans kettles'

XII
Influence on Clarinet Design

The event of Sax's death was merely a punctuation in the obscurity of his later years. Long before his demise he was already largely forgotten and his permanent removal from the scene caused little comment. His instruments, particularly his clarinets, saxhorns and saxophones, lived on to be made by many who, in any case, had blatantly infringed his patents during his lifetime just as he himself had freely borrowed from the ideas and designs of others. Compatriot critics, writing shortly after his death, were not particularly kind, tending to denigrate everything, or at best, damn with faint praise. There were others, however, following the pattern of Sax's early supporters, who were wont to credit him with too much; with having invented practically everything of worth concerning wind-instruments in the 19th century, even down to the principle of the valve. With such extravagances on both sides, a balanced view must be sought with care.

In the preceding narrative it will have been observed that the majority of the inventive projects engaged in by Sax were dead before he was. It was R. Morley-Pegge who pointed out — perhaps a little unkindly — that nothing now remains of Sax but his name attached to the E-flat tenor horn and "that not unmixed blessing, the saxophone".[1] In terms of material legacies this may be so, although to have invented one completely new instrument which eventually became the most popular wind instrument ever is no mean achievement upon which to hang a reputation. If we leave it at that then we are not giving credit for the influence that this inventor had on others of his time and immediately afterwards.

Sax was primarily a woodwind player but our links with him through this instrumental category are nowadays very tenuous. In his lifetime he enjoyed a fair measure of success with his woodwind innovations, particularly with the bass clarinet. In tracing forward the outcome of his work following his death, let us first examine those woodwind ideas which did not realise their author's dreams, if for no other reason that we might finish the chapter on a more successful note.

When the outstanding acclaim of his bass clarinet is noted, it seems strange that Sax, despite huge efforts was unable to produce an acceptable model of lower pitch. Here he was in good company for no one else had any better luck until almost at the end of the century when Richard Kohl of New York produced a widely praised contrabass clarinet in B-flat said to be 16-ft. in length. In the 1930's the German house of G. Hüller made an attractive blackwood model and, in the same decade, came W. Heckel's simple compact model in metal. Metal, too, has been favoured in the E-flat contra-alto and the BB-flat contrabass clarinets designed by Charles Houvenaghel for Leblanc of Paris. The same house has also produced an OCTO-Contra-Alto clarinet with 12-feet of effective tubing and pitched two octaves below the E-flat alto clarinet,[2] capable of sounding a 32-ft. C of only 38 vibrations a second and claimed to be the most expensive wind instrument ever made! The *système intégral*[3] of this inventor seems to have overcome all the problems which beset Sax and other early makers; these large clarinets are eminently practical and effective in use.

Despite the efficiency of the modern contrabass clarinet it has not, as yet, become a serious rival to the contrabassoon as the standard foundation of the orchestral woodwind. The only real threat, indeed, has come from another metal contrabass, the "double-reeded saxophone" over which Sax was defeated in the Courts. For many years, a section of sarrusophones could be found alongside the saxophones in French military bands, imparting a reedy texture to the ensemble. As their novelty decreased, all members of the family, from sopranino to bass, gradually fell into disfavour until the band of the *Garde Républicaine* was left with just one large contrabass in C. They never really caught on in England and, by the time early this century when Sir Thomas Beecham needed one for a performance of Joseph Holbrook's *Apollo and the Seaman*, composer and conductor had to scour Paris to find what appeared to be the last of the French sarrusophonists.[4]

Sarrusophones were more popular in America where at one time their manufacture was encouraged by the U.S. Government. It was not unknown for the occasional specimen to be found among the masses of tubing surrounding the saxophone sections of early dance orchestras and there is a recollection that a sarrusophone replaced the contrabassoon in the Pittsburg Orchestra as late as the 1940's. Contrabass sarrusophones in E-flat were certainly being made by Conn[5] in the 1930's being offered with an alternative single-reed mouthpiece. In this form the instrument has some affinity with Meikle's alto-fagotto of vague memory, which was once cited as the forerunner of the saxophone.

Much of Sax's early inventive energy was devoted to the soprano clarinet. As a competent player of a far-from-perfect instrument, it was not unnatural for him to first turn his blossoming powers to its improvement. It has been said that he did this because, being aware that Klosé and Buffet had joined forces to apply Boehm's flute principles to the clarinet, he felt constrained to do something in opposition. While this reaction is not out of character, it is equally possible that Sax had doubts as to the possible efficacy of the Boehm method as applied to the clarinet that, with some improvements, the existing instrument had a better chance of success.

It was towards the end of the 17th century that Johann Christoph Denner, a flute-maker of Nuremberg, rediscovered a principle previously known to the Greeks. By opening a small hole at the top of a simple cylindrical pipe which had a compass roughly corresponding to the lower register of the modern clarinet, a second register a twelfth above the first could be sounded. This acoustical phenomenon at once gives the clarinet its characteristic *timbre* and its large compass as compared with the oboe and the saxophone, both of which are conical and overblow at the octave. At the same time it gives rise to a problem which has taxed the ingenuity of makers from Denner's day to this: how to satisfactorily bridge the gap between the registers. In fact, this is done by a series of tone-holes and keys at the top of the instrument, but considerable onus is placed upon the player to "humour" good tone and intonation from this throat register. Without delving too deeply into the difficulties encountered in the fingering across the "break" — between b'-flat, the highest note of the lower register, and b'-natural, the lowest note of the higher register — it may be said that the clarinet, above most instrumens with the possible exception of the bassoon needed a big investment of effort and ingenuity to bring it to within hailing distance of perfection.

A considerable leap forward was made by Ivan Müller, of whom it was said that, if Denner invented the clarinet, then Müller re-invented it. A virtuoso player of Russo-German parentage, he spent much of his life in clarinet design. Some time before 1812 he reached a pinnacle of achievement with a 13-key model. After years of frustration at the hands of ultra-conservative musical institutions, his instrument began to be taken up by leading players and eventually won widespread acceptance. It was the Müller clarinet that Sax, father and son, manufactured and which Adolphe played.

Excellent as was Müller's product, it still left a number of problems to be overcome. There was still much for someone like Sax to ponder; being a player himself he was fully aware of the shortcomings; being a craftsman beside, he had the means at his disposal to do something about them. Whilst accepting the general principles of Müller's clarinet, he set about resolving the remaining difficulties. One of these was (and still is!) the "stuffy" nature of the tone in the throat register. This is particularly true of the b'-flat where the speaker hole doubles in duty as a tone hole. Sax's idea was to take the b'-flat and a' out of the throat register and to give alternatives in the upper register. The patents of 1840 and 1842[6] show that he lengthened the tube to give two extra semitones — e-flat and d-[7] at the bottom which, with the speaker hole open would produce the required notes a twelfth above although with a different and, it was maintained, a satisfactory tone quality.

In this expedient, Sax was not original. Some fifty years before, Anton Stadler, for whom Mozart wrote some of his most sublime music, had a "basset" clarinet descending to C although this was because of the player's love of the low register tone. More importantly, William Gutteridge of Cork designed a clarinet descending to d in 1813, not long after Müller's model had made its appearance. In ingenuity, Gutteridge's conception far outshines even Müller and if he could have found a maker capable of building a reliable instrument to his specifications, this would more than probably have become the standard clarinet of the day.

This idea for facilitating fingering across the break is, theoretically, a very good one. Strangely, it has never found wide favour, perhaps because, in the course of time, makers have improved on the finer points of construction so that the throat tones are not now so inferior as they once were. The alternative fingering possible on modern instruments, too, make the crossing of the break much less of an ordeal than hitherto. The "full-Boehm" system includes the low e-flat, making it possible, at least in theory, to play parts written for the A-clarinet on the B-flat instrument. Nevertheless, the vast majority of clarinets now in use in all sorts of musical combinations go no lower than the traditional e with which most players seem content.[8]

Rendall[9] lists other attempts at improvements tried by Sax. The c'-sharp key, fingered with the left-hand little finger, opens another poor note of long standing. For technical reasons connected with the bore, the main body of a clarinet needs to be made in two parts, fitting together on a tenon. It is just at this point that the c-sharp hole must be drilled. If sited too high to avoid the tenon, poor intonation is inevitable. Sax's work on the accurate positioning of this hole led to the use of a long tenon, a feature which still survives. Success was, however, not entire since modern makers still grapple with what is one of the less entrancing notes of the compass.

To facilitate the production of notes in the extreme top register Sax introduced a holed plate to reduce the diameter of the vent hole. He further fitted a second speaker-key which, according to Berlioz, made the notes of the high register "as pure and smooth ... almost as easy as those of the medium". A covered cup over the open g' hole was borrowed from the Lyons clarinet maker, Jacques Simiot. Sax also fitted gilt-metal mouthpieces to counteract the effects of excessive dryness and moisture prevalent in wood. None of these innovations survive today.

With a view to avoiding the inherent disadvantages of wood as a manufacturing medium, Sax was, quite early in his career, attracted to the use of metal. His brass clarinets were efficient and popular, especially in rough usage of service life and in the extremes of climate experienced on foreign stations. Clarinets in metal had been made more than thirty years before Sax; the type that he made consisted of a narrow tube to the dimensions of the bore, with the tone-holes projecting above the outer surface in bushes. Brass clarinets have had occasional vogues over the years being once found in dance bands of the early years and even today occasionally in military bands. On the whole, clarinettists have preferred the greater expressiveness of wood to the durability of metal although the subtle difference in tone will sometimes commend itself to a distinguished player for a special effect or occasion.

The most helpful and lasting of Sax's clarinet improvements was the addition of a pair of ring keys (known as a *brille*) to the lower joint of the instrument. A ring-key encircles an open hole without covering it. As a finger descends on to the hole, the ring key is of necessity depressed. This action, by means of a pivot and axle, enables a hole lying some distance away from the finger to be closed automatically. Such keys had been applied as early as 1808[10] and were a feature of Boehm's 1832 flute. In 1840, Sax placed ring-keys around the holes covered by the second and third fingers of the right hand. The old b/f''-sharp side key, a serious obstacle to facile fingering, was discarded, and previously faulty intonation around this part of the compass corrected. Thus, the Müller key-system, with the addition of Sax's ring-keys, became the "simple-system" clarinet which, with further small improvements by subsequent makers, enjoyed favour over a long period.

The "Boehm" clarinet took a long time to become established and the "simple-system" gave ground only slowly. Because of the eventual overwhelming success of the Klosé-Buffet system, Sax's work in this field has not always received the credit it deserves. All the same, what he did with Müllers construction, coupled with his own light, well-designed keywork, inspired other Brussels makers to persevere on similar lines. His influence on Eugene Albert, with whom he worked for a time, and on Charles Mahillon, was considerable. Not so many years ago, "simple-system" clarinets were still in general use even professionally. Now, only the occasional specimen in the hands of a learner or possibly a diehard maintains the link with Sax.

The bass clarinet as originally designed by Sax and now incorporating many subsequent developments has been a consistent success. True it was never popular in Germany where the tone was considered too big, so that a narrower bore with a smaller reed remained in favour. But in France, Britain and in many other countries, echoes of Sax are still to be heard through the French-pattern instrument. His keywork has, of course, been superseded by the Boehm system, automatic speaker mechanism is now common, the upturned bell requires no extraneous reflecting gadget and the metal crook has a more alluring curve. Yet the straight design and the proportions which give that luscious tone can undeniably be traced back to the Belgian inventor.

Notes on Chapter XII

1. Grove, 1954, IV, p.667.
2. *Woodwind World* (USA), Sept. 1971, p.6. (Valued at $3,700).
3. Macgillivray, J. A.: *Recent Advances in Woodwind Fingering*, Galpin Society Journal, XII, June 1959.
4. Beecham, Sir T.: *A Mingled Chime*, pp.98-9.
5. Conn Corporation (USA) catalogue, c.1930, p.72.
6. Brevet Belge. Ad Sax., Ordre No. 160. Brevet No. 5034, 16th April 1840. Brevet Belge. Ad Sax. Ordre No. 1631, No. de l'indicature 1326, 4th August 1842.
7. *Vide* notes by R. B. Chatwyn, 21st February 1935, Adam Carse papers, Horniman Museum, London.
8. There is also the question of the additional weight imparted to the instrument which many players consider a serious drawback.
9. Rendall, F. G.: *The Clarinet*, pp.96-7.
10. Rev. Frederick Nolan of Colchester, *vide* Rendall, p.19.

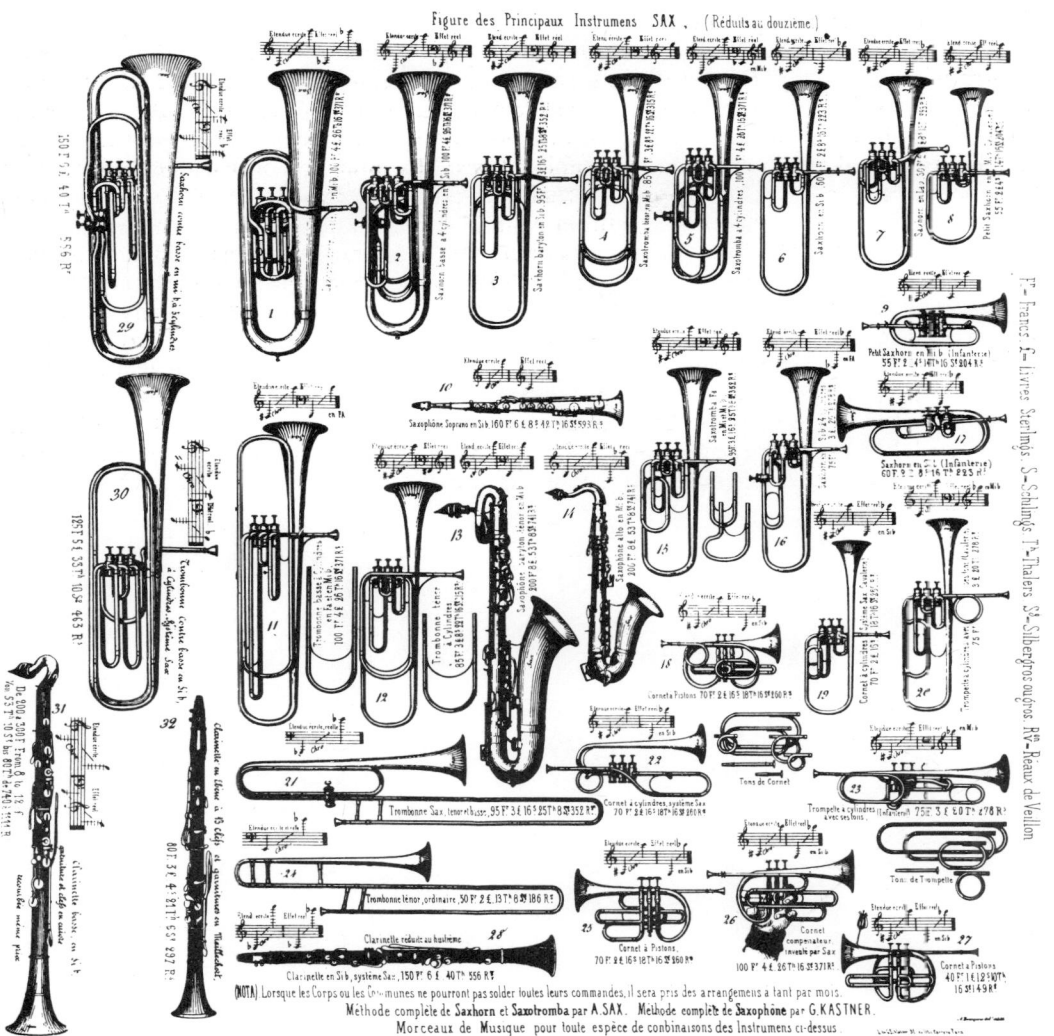

A handbill of Sax's products, about 1850.

The Swindon Citadel brass band of The Salvation Army (*circa 1920*), with its octet of saxophones.

The combination of a quartette or of the entire family of saxophones is simply marvellous; they make beautiful and smooth that which before was harsh and rough and they blend most perfectly with the brass. They bring to a band a tone quality which when once introduced can never be dispensed with. — Dr. Charles Vincent, "The Brass Band and How to Write for It" (1908).

(Saxophones) combine so well with the other instruments that there is really no reason for objecting to them on account of their relation to the "reeds". — Harold C. Hind, "The Brass Band" (1934).

XIII
The Nebulous Saxhorn

Those concerned with the violin, the French horn, the flute, the guitar in its many styles, the highland bagpipe and indeed any orchestral or band instrument will find in print a wealth of detail in the form of methods, tutors, treatises and studies which leave few, if any, aspects of the subjects uncovered. The search for anything comparable on the saxhorn would be long indeed. This is surprising surely when many musicians would recognise the name as applying to a musical wind-instrument and those who play in wind-bands might well point to the alto bugle in E-flat and the tenor bugle in B-flat and positively identify them as saxhorns. What, though, of the wide-bore bugle in B-flat; and the smaller one shaped like a trumpet? Are these, too, not saxhorns? It is at this point that someone will surely ask, "What exactly *is* a saxhorn?" A question with a devious answer.

We can say, as did Sax's opponents, that a saxhorn is merely an illegal name given to instruments already well established before the world had heard of Sax. Conversely, we may insist, as did Sax's supporters, that a saxhorn is a valved bugle built to the superior proportions and specifications of its designer, being so superior to former bugles as to warrant being called an invention. Posterity has passed an ambiguous judgement.

As might be expected, the name has endured longest in France but even there it seems to be dropping out of favour as witness the reply recently given by a French village bandmaster when asked the instrumentation of his band. He replied that he had E-flat and B-flat bugles but no saxhorns! In the English-speaking world the term is recognised as applying to one or two members of the bugle group although it never appears in any modern printed score In Austria and Germany, where, it is claimed with some justification, the instruments really were born, the old names are retained.

All this has led to an irritating confusion of nomenclature so that the same terms can mean different things to different people. A "tenor horn" in England is not what it is in Germany; "alto horn" has a meaning in America but not in Britain; "baritone" means something different on either side of the Atlantic; "althorn" is applied equally to two instruments of different pitches. Through this situation, confusing to the knowledgeable, utterly bewildering to the layman, we will try to place the various members of Sax's saxhorn family in relation to their precursors and successors.

Perhaps the instrument most readily identifiable as a saxhorn is the one in E-flat which Sax called alto or tenor. A conical valved construction of this pitch was certainly in existence by the second decade of the 19th-century, long before Sax. Wieprecht had them in Prussian bands and it was his colleague Moritz who first put them into the upright form as we know today. The *clavicor alto* and the *néo-alto* were also of this shape and pitch, the latter being contemporary with, and the former preceding by many years, the saxhorn. It can, therefore, be readily appreciated why a hornet's nest was stirred when Sax patented what he claimed to be a new invention.

The E-flat saxhorn retained that name in British brass bands until about the time of the First World War; after that it was known as, "tenor horn" and nowadays is designated generally merely as "E-flat horn". In almost every other country it is regarded as an alto instrument which is more appropriate with regard to its tone and pitch. The modern E-flat horn follows closely the shape and proportions adopted by Sax. The upright bell — "tuba shape" — is standard in Britain, the three piston valves being sited sometimes within and sometimes on top of the upper loop. Bells curving forward are common in the U.S.A. and in Germany they can be found in characteristic oval shape fitted with either piston or cylinder valves. They have been made in trumpet style.

Just as the cornet has, in its time, been severely criticised because it was used as a substitute for the trumpet, so the E-flat saxhorn has suffered in being compared with the French horn. In fact, it is a beautiful, expressive and full-fledged instrument in its own right and deserves to be judged as such. The French horn, among brass instruments, has no rival in regard to compass, dynamic range, expression, virtuosity and tone. In return, a would-be player must address himself to a study of its formidable technique. Less than a fair amount of dedication will not yield satisfactory results; but such application is often beyond the resources of the amateur part-time instrumentalist whose daily work must of necessity take precedence. If amateur wind-bands throughout the world had had to rely on the French horn for inner harmonies, progress over the years would have been greatly decreased.

The E-flat horn has not been used in British military bands except as an unofficial substitute for the French horn. It plays, however, a vital part in the brass band. Unfortunately, the instrument lacks the glamour of the cornet, the trombone and the euphonium and an exponent must resign himself solely to brass band work as this combination is its last haven. Too often it is played with a nondescript tone to give the impression that the player is really a half-hearted, frustrated cornettist. In the hands of someone who has studied the E-flat horn for its own sake and can produce a full-bodied tone, the potentials of the instrument are revealed.

A standard brass band in Britain has three independent parts for the E-flat horn, marked "Solo", "1st" and "2nd". The principal player is an important passage soloist but all too rarely gets a chance to show off his instrument's capabilities in a featured solo. In America, the instrument is often referred to as a "peck horn",[1] at once a tribute and a condemnation. In marches, waltzes and similar rhythmic pieces, someone has to peck away at the after-beat notes to the basic plod of the bass. This donkey-work usually falls to the lot of the secondary horns and they do it very well even if endless repetitive bars will eventually drive the players to distraction. The French horn, despite its immense superiority in other respects, will not do this half as well. In fact, as Sax contended, the more aristocratic instrument loses much of its effectiveness out of doors and on the march.

Tenor saxhorns in D-flat were once popular. There were two in the Cyfarthfa band of 1847 and no less than 122 were to be found in a band of 1,390 players which assembled after the first Crystal Palace contest in July 1860. Other varieties around this pitch have appeared from time to time, the most lasting being the "tenor cor", an alto-tenor horn usually in F and E-flat, sometimes with an extra slide to put it into C. The idea has been, apparently, to deceive the eye as well as the ear since it is twisted into a circular shape to resemble the French horn, nevertheless being fingered with the right hand. Under the exotic name of "mellophone", it gained great popularity in America, being found in jazz and dance-bands in the early pre-saxophone days, thereafter becoming a "double" for trumpet players. Nowadays, it has virtually disappeared from this venue of music-making.

The solo repertoire of the E-flat horn is slight and undistinguished. There exists a sonata for alto horn and piano by Paul Hindemith but even this appears to have been annexed by the alto saxophone.

Much of what has been said about the E-flat horn applies to an even greater degree to its bigger brother in B-flat. This was originally called *saxhorn basse en si bémol* and actually supplied the bass part in the celebrated Distin quintet. However, it is not really a bass instrument; the narrow bore makes the production of the lower notes difficult. The name was later transferred to the wide bore instrument of the same pitch and the smaller version renamed *saxhorn baryton* or *tenor*. Since the middle and upper notes are the most effective parts of the compass, it really is a tenor voice and in America is known merely as "tenor". It shares with the E-flat horn the term "althorn", is known in Germany as *"tenorhorn"* and in England as "baritone".

Instruments of this pitch and roughly the same proportions existed before Sax. There was a *néo-alto* in C and *clavicors* in C and B-flat. Wieprecht used them extensively; none were essentially different from Sax's construction. The modern B-flat baritone looks very much like, and is easily identifiable with, the original saxhorn of this pitch. It was introduced into British military bands, probably through the enterprise of Henry Distin, in or soon after 1845. Easy to blow and finger, light to carry on the march and with a pleasant, if neutral, tone. the baritone had a distinguished career both as a supporter of inner harmonies and as a prominent soloist, specialising in tenor arias in operatic selections and in sentimental ballads. With the rise in fortune of the richer-toned euphonium and saxophones, the light, dry voice of the baritone gradually lost favour. In 1921, the Directors of Music of the combined British services met in conference at Kneller Hall, condemned the baritone for lack of characer and unanimously agreed to banish it in favour of the tenor saxophone. For some time afterwards, the baritone continued to be found particularly in marching bands but it is now practically extinct in this medium.

As with the E-flat horn, the B-flat baritone finds its last refuge in the British brass band. Here, for some decades, it occupied the same harmonic position as it did in the military band. Again, the full, fat tone of the euphonium led to its eclipse; it now keeps its harmonic importance but rarely gets the chance to shine as a soloist. There are two independent parts for the baritone in the brass band score, designated "1st" and "2nd." The second baritone is almost entirely relegated to harmonic support with the horns. The principle part requires a player of fair accomplishment who is often required to execute florid passages through the higher register. The light tone lends itself admirably to accompaniments but, in the light of oft-repeated criticism of the brass band for its lack of tonal variety, the baritone's almost total neglect as a soloist is more surprising.

There is little glamour in being a baritone player. Those who are tend to play a part rather than study an instrument since any with such inclinations will certainly gravitate to the more versatile euphonium. The result of this is that the best tone that the baritone can produce is seldom cultivated. Its solo repertoire is practically non-existent. A brief moment of glory occurs at the opening of Mahler's Seventh Symphony where the unbiased hearer must agree that here is sound which cannot be exactly duplicated by any other instrument.

The instrument suffers too from its nondescript name, a noun when it should be an adjective. The term "baritone", when placed after a musician's name, can signify a singer, a brass instrumentalist or a saxophonist according to the context.[2] The ambiguity and confusion which can arise from this was humorously brought home to the writer when, some years ago, he was instructing a hitherto unmusical gentleman in the elements of brass instrumental technique as applied to the B-flat baritone. What he lacked in ability he made up for in enthusiasm. Proud of his modest achievement he came one day in wild excitement requesting that tickets be secured for a forthcoming concert he had seen advertised. The poster had stated: *Dietrich Fischer-Dieskau — baritone —* and he wanted to hear his chosen instrument played by a master.

If we avoid undue pedantry in respect of the finer points of proportion, it can be said that the *saxhorn contralto* in B-flat and the flugel horn are one and the same instrument. Sax made his instruments in both upright and in trumpet shapes. The "improved bugle in B-flat (old form, new proportions)" as illustrated in Kastner (1848) follows closely the characteristic modern shape. The flugel horn, rather than the cornet-à-pistons, was the direct valved successor to the key-bugle. It was first made in Vienna about 1830 and quickly found its way, often in large numbers, into German and Austrian military bands. Although Sax's version, apparently much superior in construction to many existing instruments, was an important member of the original saxhorn group, the older name was never superseded. In ensuing years, flugel horns crossed the North Sea and became established in the bands of the British Army. In America, too, they found a home; Patrick Gilmore's band of 1878 had two.

Although this popularity continued on the Continent, bands in English-speaking countries did not keep to them for long so that, although not quite to the same extent as the E-flat horn and the B-flat baritone, the British brass band offers a sanctuary where the flugel horn can find regular employment. With its thick tone and rich lower register, the flugel horn is a welcome voice in the all-brass combination. In earlier days it was often well represented in the alto harmonies with the lower cornets and alto saxhorns. As a standard instrumentation became established under the discipline of contest regulations, flugel horns tended to disappear until, with occasional exceptions, only a solitary instrument remained in the full complement. Even this lost its independent line in the score, being reduced to sharing a stave with a supporting ("repiano") cornet. Except in some major works and in Salvation Army senior band journals, this deplorable practice obtains even today. It gives rise to the instrument often being badly sited among the cornets and played not by specialists but by seconded cornet players who tend to retain much of their original tone on the wider-bore instrument. Evoking its saxhorn connections, its logical place is with the E-flat horns with which it has a close affinity of tone.

With its generous proportions, the flugel horn can quite easily sound its fundamental so that the addition of a fourth valve, as appeared in Sax's first constructions, is of some practical use. Nevertheless, in band work it is never required to descend below its 3-valve compass; it is effective from its lowest note to about the top of the treble stave. Higher notes are possible but more difficult than on the cornet or trumpet. In the hands of a sensitive player, the flugel horn is a mellow soloist; its possibilities have been recognised in recent years by leading composers in the medium.

Until recent years, the flugel horn was rarely found outside of the band. It has on a few occasions been used in the orchestra, the most notable instance being by Vaughan Williams. In his later years, this composer had a predelection for using strange (orchestrally speaking) instruments and gave the flugel horn an important solo part in the second movement of his Ninth Symphony. Vaughan Williams' own assessment of its tone is revealed by the directions printed on the score. He charges the conductor to ensure that a proper flugel horn mouthpiece is used but, appreciating that an instrument might not always be available, he gives an explicit command that a cornet must *never* be substituted. The part is cued in for the first horn.

Of late, the flugel horn has been brought to popular attention since it was "discovered" by jazz and dance-band players. Trumpeter Miles Davis was probably the first to use it in this sphere. Unlike saxophonists, the trumpet player has seldom been expected to play any kindred instrument as a "double". He has relied, for tonal variety, on a collection of mutes and perhaps a bowler hat to muffle the sound. Use of the flugel horn for this purpose is a considerable additional expense hardly warranted in some instances where players fail to exploit sufficiently the contrast in tone between the "edgy" trumpet and the "blunt" bugle. Happily there are many examples of a true flugel horn tone being cultivated and, as has happened so often in this medium with conventional instruments, players are happy to demonstrate the instrument's aptitude for florid, high-register work. Away from jazz, there are a few exclusive solos but in the main the flugel horn looks for suitable adaptions from the trumpet and cornet repertoire.

Although in Continental bands, the flugel horn is frequently used on parts which elsewhere would be taken by cornets, the instrument is not really incisive enough to lead an ensemble, especially out of doors. It would seem that Sax appreciated this since he gave the leading part in his group to the soprano saxhorn in E-flat, the instrument on which John Distin led his family quintet. Sax was among the first to make a valved instrument at this pitch but, because its rather large bore made the higher notes more difficult, it was soon replaced in general use by the more gently-tapering soprano cornet. With regard to tone, the ordinary listener may find it difficult to differentiate at this altitude between soprano saxhorns, cornets or trumpets, so that ease of playing and the instrumentalist's preference must be the chief consideration in the choice of instrument.

There were two soprano cornets in the Royal Artillery Band of 1857 but the Band of the *Garde Républicaine* was still using a soprano saxhorn in 1912. In ones and twos, they found a place for a time in the bands, particularly the mounted bands, of many nations. Since the part is covered with less effort by the piccolo and the small E-flat clarinet, it was eventually dispensed with. The soprano cornet in E-flat is, however, an important member of the brass band. The tone is thin but it occasionally gets a solo. Its normal function is to support the solo cornets in the higher register, to ride above the melody at the octave or to add harmony notes or decorations above melody. Those who wish to extend the possibilities of the brass band sometimes wish for two or more soprano cornets to be included in the instrumentation. This interesting suggestion is slow in being followed, possibly because most bands have difficulty enough in recruiting even one first-grade player for this taxing part. The soprano cornet has no solo repertoire of note.

Sax produced sopranino saxhorns in high B-flat and C. The latter had the briefest of lives; the other was occasionally to be found in Continental bands and were still being made by the French house of Sudre as late as 1905. No surviving specimen is at present traceable. Its compass would appear to have been restricted to little more than an octave since the lower notes were of poor quality and, in any case, rather pointless, whilst its comfortable upper limit was no more than written d''. Three higher semitones were possible but Berlioz, who originally used the instrument in *The Trojans* and the *Te Deum*, warns that these should be used sparingly and with great skill.[3] The soprano saxhorn has a modern counterpart in the B-flat piccolo trumpet. Modern manufacturing, design and executant techniques have overcome the limitations of the old instrument.

Whatever case is advanced in claiming saxhorn parentage for the middle and higher bugles, the lower instruments are on even less sure ground. The *saxhorn basse* in C and B-flat, a construction of more generous proportions but of the same pitch as the baritone was little different from the three-valved *tenorbass horn* which Wieprecht had brought into Prussian bands before 1830. That much castigated instrument, the ophicleide had nevertheless been the most successful member of the key-bugle family. When played properly, it combined a sonorous bass with an acceptable baritone voice; the epithets cast in its direction for no other reason than that it was sometimes played badly were as the stigma attached to the cornet and the saxophone for the same reason. Dissatisfaction lay, paradoxically, in its rather gentle nature and its delicate key mechanism which was easily disturbed in the rough usage of military life.

When the comparitively robust valve began to be attached to instruments of similar pitch, the days of the ophicleide were shortened even though the time of its final passing occupied many years. The first valved instruments in B-flat and the lower E-flat were usually made in close physical resemblance to the ophicleide and indeed retained that name for some time. When Sax adopted the broad, squat, upright tuba shape for his *saxhorn basse* he was more or less duplicating a design already well on the way to becoming established. In fact, the lower saxhorns depart from the proportions first envisaged by their designer and this disturbs, to a subtle degree, a perfect homogeneity of tone. This had no practical significance in performance; the point is that the valved ophicleide in C or B-flat made under various names and in numerous shapes, received yet another addition when Sax launched his model.

Under the name "euphonium", or less usually "euphonion", the instrument met with widespread popularity and acceptance, although not usually beyond the confines of the brass and military band. By 1855 it had established itself in British Army bands. According to H. G. Farmer, the Continental euphonium as first used in Britain was of only medium bore; it was Bandsman Phasey of the Coldstream Guards, later, in 1859, a professor at Kneller Hall, who designed the present wide bore version which quickly displaced the ophicleide.[4]

Although three-valved euphoniums are not uncommon, a fourth valve to complete the octave to the easily-produced fundamental is usual and desirable. Compensating devices are incorporated in the best instruments and shapes vary in different parts of the world from the big out-turned bell in the U.S.A. to the elliptical form in Germany. The standard military band carries one euphonium which is an important soloist. The brass band has two which, incongruously, play from one part marked "solo euphonium". Only occasionally do they play *divisi;* the part is often a demanding one and the presence of two players is largely a matter of playing safe as well as an endeavour to balance out a large section of cornets.

The standard American instrument, known as the "baritone horn", has a slightly more ample bore than the British baritone but not as great as the euphonium. This mid-way version is the instrument too often used by dance-band and theatre trombonists when required to double. It has the worst of both worlds with a tone which one critic describes as an "amorphous hoot". Again, when used under the name of "tenor tuba" in the orchestra, there are occasions when a tone is forthcoming which does not do justice to the instrument. For once, brass and military bands can point the way since their euphoniumists cultivate a full tone from the rich pedal register to the penetrating, silky upper reaches.

The euphonium has an extensive repertoire but little of it is of high quality. There is no reason why it should not play the solo part in such major works as the Vaughan Williams concerto where the composer does not particularly specify the pitch of tuba required. However, it would appear from the character of the music that the lower F or E-flat tuba is more suited to such performances. Whilst not having the expressive range of the French horn, the euphonium does offer the serious composer a highly-versatile, rich-toned, large-ranged vehicle for his inspiration. It has often been called the cello of the band. It now needs a modern Dvořák or Elgar to give it deserved concerto status.[5]

The *saxhorn-contrabass*, the lowest of the original group, was the Sax version in E-flat of the five-valved Wieprecht-Moritz bombardon in F of 1835. Stölzel apparently has a similar instrument as early as 1828. These useful acquisitions furthered the end of the ophicleide in all countries. Again they were established in Germany some years before Sax got them accepted in France. Some of the first to reach Britain were probably made by Sax and imported through the agency of Henry Distin about the middle of the century. They were enthusiastically absorbed into brass and military bands with 155 being used at the first Crystal Palace contest of 1860.

Under the colourless description "E-flat bass", the standard British military band has one and the brass band two. Its usual role is to supply a firm bass although it can and is sometimes required to, execute passages of considerable dexterity. In seeking to exploit the resources of the band to the full, composers have found the E-flat bass to possess a fine singing voice. Episodal passages are now met within advanced works; once in a while it is a featured soloist, having opportunity to show off its sonorous pedals and its lyrical, horn-like, top notes.

The instrument generally in use in Britain is in tuba shape, with four valves, often being incorrectly designated "EE-flat bass" — the double letter referring not to its pitch but to its ample proportions. This shape is now not so common in America where the helicon form retains popularity. Because of its orchestral associations as "tuba in F" or "E-flat", this instrument has possibly the most distinguished repertoire of all the saxhorn-types. Among the most celebrated from established composers is a sonata by Hindemith and a full-scale concerto with orchestra by Vaughan Williams. It has attained recital status where a demonstration of its capabilities in the hands of a virtuoso performer seems to indicate that, particularly in wind-bands, the instrument's full potentials have not yet been fully realised.

Lowest of the saxhorns — leaving aside the impractical monster in EE-flat, was the contrabass in BB-flat brought out after 1850. The first such instruments in CC and BB-flat appeared about 1845 being a natural extension downwards of the existing bombardon. They were soon to be seen in Prussian bands and two were to be found in Sax's revised instrumentation for the Imperial Guard of 1854. In many of the instrumental lists of the period, all basses are covered by the all-embracing term "bombardons" but it is likely that many British bands had BB-flat basses before the end of the fifties. Two were at the Crystal Palace contest of 1860.

Bombardons in BB-flat have been made in a variety of shapes, the helicon being popular on the Continent and in America. In the latter country upright and out-turned bells are to be found; in Britain the upright tuba shape generally obtains. Compact instruments of comparatively narrow bore known as "medium" basses were once to be seen but nowadays the wide-bore BB-flat bass is almost universal. Standard military and brass bands in Britain have one and two respectively.

Although capable of considerable agility, the instrument is most usually required to act as a sonorous sub-bass in unison or at the octave with the E-flat bass. Solos are more in the nature of

The British Brass Band — a home for the modern saxhorn

An illustrated price-list showing some of Sax's brass instruments
Note the prominent inscriptions on the bell of each instrument

a novelty than any musical value.

It will by now readily be realised that valved bugles in one form or another would have been absorbed into bands the world over without the aid of Sax. Even his great influence on the British brass-band movement was fortuitous rather than contrived. All the same, it *was* his saxhorns which gave the necessary stimulus and his capability of supplying finely-wrought, evenly-tuned instruments should not be overlooked.

It is more than likely that the saxhorn was first introduced into America by the Distin family in 1848; many bands incorporated the word "Saxhorn" into their titles and the instruments were widely used before the Civil War. In many cases they were supplied through natural channels established between France and the French-speaking American communities. The Bethlehem Concert Band of Pennsylvania, when founded in 1848, had eight saxhorns — 3 E-flat altos, 2 B-flat baritones, 3 E-flat contrabasses. The university band of Notre Dame, started in the same year as the saxhorn patent and claiming to be the first college band in the U.S.A., had, by 1869, become fully equipped with 24 saxhorns all with upright bells. Twenty-five years later, most of the saxhorns were being retained being by then joined by cornets and a few woodwind instruments. But perhaps the first band to be equipped with the instruments of Sax manufacture was the Stonewall Brigade Band of Staunton, Virginia, which carried them on service during the Civil War.

Official Union bands of the Civil War were mainly supplied with Austrian "cornets" of many sizes designed so that the bell section rested on the players shoulder and pointed backwards, towards the marching troops.

These instruments had been designed and patented in 1838 by Allen Dodworth manufactured in Austria and for many years imported into the U.S.A. by the Dodworth family. However, he was not enamoured with their use in the concert hall. In his *Dodworth's Brass Band School* of 1853 he recommends: "For general purposes, those (instruments) with the bell upwards, like the Sax Horn, are most convenient and should be adopted by all whose business is not exclusively military; care should be taken to have all the bells one way".

A bandmaster who pioneered saxhorns in America appears later to have regretted his initiative. William R. Bayley, writing in 1893 in the "Philadelphia Evening Star" reminisces on earlier days and regrets the disappearance of many instruments: *The sweet, mellow tone of the bugle is lost; the ringing clarion-like trumpet is silent; the alto horn has entirely superseded the French horn in bands, and this was perhaps my fault, for I had the first three altos used in this country made to order in Paris and used in my band. I would not have done this had it been possible at that time to get the French horn with valves.* Unfortunately, the date of the importation is not given. The saxhorn, although extensively used in America, did not make quite the lasting impact that it did in France and Britain and gave way more quickly to the more extrovert brass.[6] Its ultimate demise is reflected in a report issued by the National Band Association of America in 1972. This concluded that current band instrumentation makes it probably unnecessary to provide E-flat horn parts.

Today, the British brass band offers perhaps the most comprehensive display of saxhorn-types to be seen anywhere in one ensemble. Its instrumentation has been stabilised from about the beginning of the century; a contesting band of 24 players rarely differs from 1 E-flat soprano cornet, 8 B-flat cornets (subdivided solo, repiano, 2nd and 3rd), 1 B-flat flugel horn, 3 E-flat tenor (alto) horns (Solo, 1st and 2nd), 2 B-flat baritones (tenors) (1st and 2nd). 2 B-flat tenor trombones (1st and 2nd), 1 bass trombone, 2 B-flat euphoniums, 2 E-flat basses, 2 BB-flat basses.

What should be a balanced contrast between the brilliant cornet-trombone tone and the mellow saxhorn is, in realisation, not such a happy prospect. The duplicated euphoniums and quadruplicated basses can hold their own in a *tutti* but the middle saxhorns are obliterated if they are not overblown and their tone ruined. Bands not restricted in size by contesting requirements (these are almost exclusively those of the Salvation Army) sometimes duplicate horn and baritone parts with beneficial effect. Too often, however, any augmentation for concert purposes is applied to the popular cornets and trombones, so accentuating the lack of balance.

A perennial argument in band circles concerns the question of whether or not to include French horns and trumpets. The difference between the modern trumpet and the cornet is now so slight as to be of less consequence than hitherto but the entirely "foreign" *timbre* of the French horn is another matter. At a time when interest in the brass band was waning in the face of the ready-made electronic entertainment, it received an unexpected stimulant. Music teachers in schools discovered a truth fully appreciated by 19th-century bandsmen and promulgated by Sax in his Saxhorn Method: that, with a technique and notation common to all the valved instruments, a group of keen novices could be moulded into an acceptable musical entity in an amazingly short time. Many school brass bands have reached high standards, the best of the players having the opportunity to play in the National Youth Brass Band of Great Britain. Such is the personal satisfaction to be gained from this kind of music-making that many wish to continue playing after leaving school. Thus old bands are revitalised and new bands initiated.

There are, however, a large number of schools where the orchestral concept holds sway and only orchestral brass is taught. These sections of trumpets, trombones, French horns and tubas can give a good account of music read directly from conventional brass band parts. One argument often propounded against the inclusion of French horns has always been the expected difficulty of recruiting players for a different instrument which differs in principle from the established uniform system. Transposition at sight is part of the normal stock-in-trade of the hornist; these young instrumentalists are able to read E-flat horn, B-flat baritone and other parts at sight on their F French horns. At the end of their school days many will wish to continue playing, yet there are not enough amateur orchestras and symphonic wind-bands to absorb them. In many cases there must surely be a gravitation towards the brass band. Will they, then, be prepared to give up their hard-won technique on a "prestige" instrument in favour of the mundane saxhorn? If they will not, and yet insist on being heard, it is not beyond projected imagination to see a time when saxhorns of, at least, the middle register, will take their place alongside serpents, ophicleides, cornopeans and bass horns as museum curiosities.

Despite this, a stay of execution — if not a full reprieve — may well obtain. A number of prestigious younger conductors and composers have taken a hand so that the musical establishment is fast becoming aware of the brass band's potential as an instrument of the highest artistic worth. The finest of the bands, amateur in everything but musical aptitude, are heard regularly on radio, television and in the leading concert halls. The famous bands of Black Dyke Mills and Grimethorpe Colliery have appeared at the celebrated Promenade Concerts playing music of the modern and *avant garde* conception.

Competitions are still a major part of banding activities. The traditional national contests continue with undiminished support as new ones come into being. Typical of the latter, and indicative of the support given to the Movement by commercial companies, the noted engineering company, Lansing Bagnall Limited, has had spectacular success in sponsoring a two-day Brass Band Festival at their headquarters in Basingstoke, Hampshire. Meticulous organising together with a number of generous awards attracts some of the finest bands in the country.

This resurgence is happening without the traditional instrumentation being seriously called into question. There appears to be no shortage of youthful players to fill the "unglamorous" desks when a band is well constituted. The flugel horn, the E-flat tenor horn and the E-flat bass in particular now attract a higher calibre of solo player to meet the demands of the modern composer.

Whether this apparent satisfaction with the old instrumentation will endure remains to be seen. Ensembles of orchestral brass instruments have sprung up and appear to be establishing themselves as chamber groups quite distinct from the traditional brass band. An erudite quarterly magazine, "Sounding Brass", keeps each side informed of the other's activities without seeking to amalgamate them.

The conservative spirit which still largely permeates the band fraternity, and the all-levelling regulations of the contest platform, may in themselves delay any radical change for the time being, despite the wishes expressed by composers.

So, for the present at least, we still have with us the lively offspring of Sax's controversial horns and a direct link with their doubtful inventor.

Notes on Chapter XIII

1. Schwartz, H. W.: *Bands of America*, p.51.
2. Horwood, W.: *A Horn by any other Name*, British Bandsman, 16th November 1968.
3. Berlioz, H.: A Treatise on Modern Instrumentation and Orchestration, *vide* Saxhorns
4. Farmer, H. G.: *Rise and Development of Military Music*, p.112.
5. A *Concerto for Euphonium and Brass Band* by Joseph Horovitz received a first performance at the Royal Albert Hall, London, on 14th October 1972.
6. During his European tour of 1900-1905, J. P. Sousa criticised French bands for their use of the alto horn, calling it a concession to laziness and a poor substitute for the French horn. *Vide* Schwartz, p.142.

The Brown Brothers Saxophone Sextet did much to make the instrument familiar and popular in the second decade of the century.

XIV
The Saxophone Phenomenon

Posterity will never forgive you, Adolphe Sax! ran a caption beneath a cartoon in the *Saturday Review of Literature* depicting Sax in his workshop surrounded by saxophones. A paragraph in the London "Daily News" *circa* 1926 amplifies this astonishing statement:

The saxophone is a long metal instrument bent at both ends. It is alleged to be musical. As regards markings, the creature has a series of tiny taps stuck upon it, apparently at random. These taps are very sensitive; when touched they cause the instrument to utter miserable sounds suggesting untold agony. Sometimes it bursts into tears. At either end there is a hole. People, sometimes for no reason at all, blow down the small end of the saxophone which then shrieks and moans as if attacked by a million imps of torture. The shrieks issue from the large end. So do the moans. The saxophone comes from where the black-eyed Susans grow and coal-black mammies flourish. The concensus of opinion is that it should have stayed there.[1]

From about 1920 onwards, the writings of the world of legitimate music are full of snide, often uninformed and inaccurate remarks about the saxophone. On reading them one might wonder: Is this the same instrument over which eminent composers went into raptures? Is this the achievement on which we base our subject's claim to immortality?

The fact is that the impact on public awareness of hordes of inept, plangent electric-guitarists in the 'sixties was but a pale shadow besides the furore created by the saxophone in the 'twenties. Something happened to change this obscure, little-known but well-regarded instrument almost overnight into what many saw as a hideous monster created to corrupt the morals of youth. Before we seek to understand the reason for this drastic transubstantiation, let us take a brief look at the seventy-five or so years which followed its birth.

After, and in some cases before, the twenty-year patent had expired, many other makers began to manufacture saxophones. Despite the closure of the Conservatoire class, which deprived the instrument of the best in tuition, its quiet success in French military bands assured it of a place in manufacturers' catalogues. In Germany too, in spite of a deep-rooted resentment at Sax's extravagant claims, it was made and used, although not nearly so widely as in France. Because of antipathy to and a general dislike of Boehm-principle fingering, the firm of Heckel, world-renowned as bassoon makers, patented in 1890 a variation of the saxophone under the name *Heckel-Clarina* which incorporated the old method of fingering for the right hand. This instrument persisted with scant success for some years until completely ousted by its older rival. Its main claim to fame lay in its automatic-octave mechanism in place of the two separate speaker keys essential to early saxophones. This device simplifies fingering considerably and indeed was a major advance. However, the Heckel claim to have been the first with this innovation is open to dispute.

Although on the face of it the saxophone has not undergone any radical change since its invention, a great deal of thought and effort by Sax and other early makers had gone into improvements in the fingering. The original keywork with its placing and covering of the tone-holes was advanced for its time, but these were the days of rapid technical progress in the sphere. The Paris house of P. Goumas et Cie and their successors Paul Evette and Ernest Schaeffer were notable in effecting refinements. Fontaine Besson pioneered the mounting of keys on axles. It was Arzène-Zoé Lecomte who, apart from the introducing alternative keys for the little fingers in the manner of the Boehm clarinet (an idea which did not endure) has the prior claim to having initiated the automatic octave mechanism. This is evidenced from the tone of Pierre's writings which suggest that the mechanism had already been in existence some time before 1890.[2] It would appear from the 1846 patent specification that the first saxophones were designed to descend two semitones below the key-note — to written b-flat. The lowest semitone was soon discarded. Although it was restored as early as 1887, saxophones with the smaller compass and the two-key octave control continued to be made for many years until, by the arrival of the "jazz age", the improvements were widely accepted.

Before the last decade of the 19th-century, the saxophone's progress as a serious instrument of music was not impressive. French composers took some pains to include it in their scores. Sax's friends and contemporaries, including Adam, Arban, Cressonnois, Klosé and Mohr, wrote solos with piano, and small chamber works which included it. Kastner had used it first in a major but undistinguished composition; Ambrois Thomas included an important part for an E-flat alto saxophone in his opera *Hamlet*: Meyerbeer and Massenet wrote cantilenas for alto, as did Bizet whose use of the instrument in *L'Arlésienne* became, perhaps, the most celebrated of the early solos. Saint-Saëns included a part for the soprano saxophone in his symphonic poem *La Jeunesse*, but even if a number of pieces by long-forgotten minor composers are included the whole adds up to a painfully sparse repertoire for a new and exciting instrument. To quote Cecil Forsyth: "French composers do not as a rule get much beyond the idea of writing little tunes for the instrument".[3]

There is little doubt that Sax's invention would have been put to better use had there been a greater supply of proficient players. The saxophone was caught in the vicious circle which has so often ensnared new musical instruments: composers are loth to write a part for an instrument which might not get played; players will not take it up because nobody writes for it!

In Britain the position, if anything, regressed. The quartet, once the pride of the Royal Artillery Band, had disappeared after some years to be replaced by less effective alto clarinets and not to re-appear until the turn of the century. The Grenadier Guards took one saxophone on the strength in 1858 but this had gone by 1864. Several line regiments continued to use saxophones, notably the Oxfordshire Light Infantry, the 4th Dragoons, the Border Regiment, the 16th Lancers, the Lancashire Fusiliers, the 2nd Royal Kent Regiment, and the 2nd Norfolk Regiment but in 1888, at a time when the Belgian Guides had four saxophones (a soprano, two altos and a tenor) and the *Garde Républicaine* twice that number, the premier bands of the British Army had none at all.

Towards the end of the century, Edward Elgar was about to establish himself as a composer of international stature with *Caractacus*, a cantata for four solo voices and orchestra, first performed at the Leeds Festival of 1898. He had heard the saxophone and had been entranced, declaring it to be "beautiful and expressive and, if you wish, subdued". He wanted to include four saxophones in the cantata but was dissuaded from doing so because of the problems attaching to the finding of suitable players and the expense of rehearsing them.[4] Another British composer, but one whose considerable output failed to appeal, was Joseph Holbrooke. His *Apollo and the Seaman*, already mentioned in connection with the sarrusophone, included parts for soprano and tenor saxophones. Other small works using saxophones came from his pen and, in 1928, a full-scale *Concerto in B-flat* for alto saxophone and orchestra which characteristically failed to find acclaim.

If Elgar was thwarted in his saxophones, Richard Strauss was successful. Unfortunately, his scoring for soprano and bass in C, and alto and baritone in F, as part of an enormous orchestra for *Sinfonia Domestica* (1902/3) is largely ineffectual. The parts, which are marked *ad lib.*, are carefully duplicated by other instruments pointing to Strauss's lack of confidence that they might not be available in performance. This policy of insurance reduces the quartet to mere harmonic support. Such forebodings were apparently justified. At the first London performance, four saxophonists were, with difficulty, procured. They were not present at the second performance and their absence made little difference. Richard Strauss is the first composer of international repute to use a quartet of saxophones in a major work. He can hardly claim credit for having advanced by much the cause of the saxophone.[16]

There was, however, a notable instance of a reversal of this position: an enthusiastic available saxophonist and a reluctant composer. In 1895, Claude Debussy was busy on his opera, *Pelléas et Mélisande* when a letter reached him from Boston, Massachusetts. The writer was a Mrs. Elise Hall who explained that she had taken up the saxophone for health reasons (the ailment was not specified) and, since the instrument's repertoire was so limited, requested the composer to write a little original something especially for her. Being a lady of some means, she backed up her application with a substantial cheque. The remittance was of greater appeal than the commission; Debussy prompty thanked the *femme saxophone*, as he called her, banked the cheque and got on with his opera.

Eight years passed. "That aquatic instrument" — Debussy's mysterious description of the saxophone — could not have been further from his thoughts. Without warning one day, there appeared on the doorstep of his Rue Cardinet apartment the redoubtable Mrs. Hall come to enquire what had become of her solo. Forced to admit that he had not even tried to give value for money, Debussy was in a quandary. What did he know of the saxophone? Technical details were easily come by, but what of its character? — Where could one hear it played? "Does it indulge in romantic tenderness like the clarinet?" he enquired rather desperately of his friend the writer Pierre Louÿs.

By way of enlightenment he attended a recital in Paris given by Mrs. Hall in the following year. She was there to be seen, resplendent in a pink evening gown, giving fair execution to a commission from Vincent D'Indy. At least D'Indy was familiar with the saxophone, having used a quartet in his opera *Fervaal* and a sextet in *La Legende de Saint-Christophe*. He had no difficulty in writing a *Choral varié* for Mrs. Hall to play.

Not to be outdone, Debussy got to work. But weightier matters distracted and another year passed before a rough draft was ready. By 1911 he had made several attempts to orchestrate the piece before, finally exasperated, he sent it to his patron incomplete. The lady, now President of the Boston Orchestral Club, had continued her saxophonic career having received better service in response to her requests from Charles Loeffler, Florent Schmitt, Georges Sporck and no doubt others. It was left to Roger Ducasse, after Debussy's death in 1918, to complete the orchestration. Even the title was the subject of indecision, the composer having toyed in turn with *Fantasie, Rapsodie orientale* and *Rapsodie mauresque*. From its first performance at the *Société Nationale* in 1919 it has been known simply as *Rhapsody for saxophone and orchestra*.[5]

One cannot help but admire the lady from Boston. Even today, a concert in Paris, London or New York by a serious saxophoniste would probably cause a little stir. In those pre-emancipated days, it must have been the height of eccentricity. The pieces written for her demand an accomplished if not a virtuoso technique. We might presume that she was equal to them; we can surely credit her with having enriched early saxophone literature.

In the hands of the "serious" musician, the saxophone would surely have wilted through neglect. The general public knew little of it other than seeing it occasionally in military bands playing in street and park. The brass band at one time thought highly of the instrument and some non-contesting bands had sections of them. In 1908, Dr. Charles Vincent strongly urged their inclusion describing their tone as "beautiful but weird". He goes on: *the combination of a quartet or of the entire family of saxophones is simply marvellous; they make beautiful and smooth that which before was harsh and rough, and they blend most perfectly with the brass. They bring to a band a tone quality which, when once introduced, can never be dispensed with.*[6] Brave words which, although having much validity, have, at least in the last part, been disproved in fact.

The myth still persists that it was jazz which made the saxophone popular. Long before this new wild sound hit the world of conventional music, the ordinary person was beginning to notice the saxophone and to like what he heard. The instrument was strange, not difficult to play up to an elementary standard, with a pleasant sound solo or in concert and with a great novelty value. Variety artists in the Music Halls welcomed it; over the years there has been more than one "act" which got through a career by marching around stages blowing a set of saxophones. There were too, more refined acts like "The Five Symphony Girls" who can be seen gazing with alluring modesty from a sheet-music cover of 1916 which implies that, besides singing beautifully, they played between them a piano, a harp, a violin — and a saxophone! Troops on leave in London from the trenches might have been intrigued by a new solo instrument supplying interval music at West-End theatres. If value in musical terms was little above zero, it did bring the saxophone to a wider and more appreciative audience. It is surprising how long the novelty appeal persisted. It can be recalled that, well into the 1930's, audiences were quite happy to hear that gargantuan vaudevillian, Teddy Brown, play a simple, unadorned ballad on his tenor saxophone between rounds of xylophonic gymnastics.

In the early years of the twentieth century, a lot of antipathy towards the saxophone came from the musicians in light, theatre and dance orchestras. To these hard-bitten professionals, the soldier-musician was beneath contempt and, since the saxophone was associated with the military band, the two were lumped together. Vic Filmer, a legitimately trained pianist who was leading a dance band in England before the First World War was not aware that there was a dance saxophonist in the country in 1910; the instrument was considered "not respectable". He tells of a Musical Director of the old school who, even after the War when many string players had taken up the saxophone in response to the popular vogue, would scathingly remind his players, "Don't forget to bring your MACHINES along!" It is interesting to note this idea of the day that the saxophone was something mechanical; accomplished players of that era were often known as "saxophone technicians".

As to who was the very first dance band saxophonist could be the subject of painstaking and probably inconclusive research. In England, a possible contender for the distinction might be Adolphe Voorsanger who studied at the Amsterdam Conservatoire and played the double-bass in the Concertgebouw Orchestra under Wilhelm Mengelberg. From details supplied by his grandson it transpires that he came to England early in the 1890's and played saxophone solos with his own orchestra. He led a Ladies Orchestra before the War; the second edition of *Melody Maker* in February 1926 credits him with having led a dance-band in Maida Vale on saxophone in 1908!

For those born after 1918 who have never been unaware of the saxophone's extrovert presence, it is difficult to imagine how rare it was to find one but a few years before. The pioneer recording engineer Joe Batten tells how, in 1920, he had to comb London for an alto saxophone for the Edison Bell house dance-band. Having eventually located an ancient piece, he was just as hard put to, to find someone to play it.[7]

The saxophone was early to be found in the recording studio. Jean Moeremans made records as early as 1907, with variations of *Carnival of Venice, Old Folks at Home*, and similar light pieces. S. Popora, Wheeler Wadsworth (later, from 1918, to lead the celebrated "All Star Trio" — saxophone, piano and xylophone — an extensively recorded cabaret act and dance-band) and H. Bennie Henton are names which appear on early record issues, the last named with his own adaption of *Scenes that are brightest* on a four-minute cylinder.[8] Henton first rose to fame as saxophone soloist with Bohumir Kryl's band in the early years of the century. About 1910 he began a long association with the band of Patrick Conway. In one of his featured solos, entitled *Eleven O'Clock*, there was a staggeringly difficult *cadenza* covering more than three octaves from (written) b-flat to c.'''' He was rated as one of the most competent and artistic saxophonists of the day.

Here we are aware that we have crossed the Atlantic prematurely. The saxophone may have been a European invention; it was the New World which first realised its possibilities, a process which, as we shall see later, currently continues.

It is Harvey Dodworth, conductor of the 13th Regiment Band from 1839, and, in succession to his brother Allen, of the famous Dodworth Band from 1860, who is credited with having introduced saxophones, as well as the bass clarinet and the BB-flat bass tuba, into American band instrumentation.

The first saxophonist of distinction to appear in the Western Hemisphere arrived from France with the orchestra of Antoine Jullien in 1853. Not yet 20, Eduard A. Lefèbre was already a virtuoso clarinettist. He had met Sax personally in Paris and had become entranced with the saxophone. He had promised the inventor to devote himself to the study of the instrument and to promote its use.

Lefèbre stayed in America, joining Patrick Gilmore's 22nd Regiment of New York Band in 1873 and enjoying enormous popularity with audiences for the novelty of the instrument and his impressive technique. After Gilmore's death in 1892, Lefèbre joined Sousa and was still appearing as a concert soloist until his own demise at the age of 77 in 1911. He is still regarded today as one of the greatest saxophonists of all time.

Sections of saxophones were soon to be a normal feature of American wind bands; Gilmore's band, organised for their European tour of 1878 had three — an alto, a soprano and a baritone. In a series of winter concerts given at the Grand Opera House, New York, in the same year, the band featured a quartet composed of Messrs. Lefèbre, Walrabe, Steckelberg and Schultz.

Barnum and Bailey's Circus Band, led by James L. Robinson, had three saxophones which London audiences at Olympia in 1889 may have noticed. This team was retained for the circus's European tour of 1897-1902. Sousa's Marine Band of 1891 had a quartet of saxophones. The oldest civilian band in America, founded in Allentown, Pennsylvania in 1828 and conducted since 1926 by Dr. Albertus L. Meyers, included an alto soon after 1890 and a tenor a year or two later.

In 1887, the band of Frederick N. Innes had a quintet of saxophones played by Messrs. Fagotti, Conway, Williams, Klosé and Trout; a few years later he formed what was to become a celebrated trio of H. Morrin (alto), E. Shaap (tenor) and Vincent Ragone (baritone). Other notable saxophonists before the turn of the century were J. Paul Waite (Thomas Preston Brooke's band), F. A. Maginel (Liberati's Band), R. E. Trognitz (City Guards Band of San Diego) and baritone saxophonist Rudolph Becker (Sousa's Band). It was mainly due to these and to the many excellent bands then playing — not to forget vaudeville acts such as "The Five Nosses" — that the saxophone began to become both familiar and popular with American audiences.

The "American Saxophone Band" whose 1907 recording of *The Bullfrog and the Coon* enjoyed wide popularity, was typical of several saxophone groups which emerged to play light novelty pieces. Saxophones began to be seen in minstrel troupes, ragtime bands and groups which actually seem to have been called "jazz orchestras". James Weldon Johnson tells of a concert given in New York in 1905 by Memphis students. There was a "playing — singing — dancing — orchestra" which introduced a dancing conductor; the instrumentation included a violin, a couple of brass instruments and a double-bass and made use of banjos, mandolins, guitars, drums and saxophones.[9]

A saxophone group led by Tom Brown toured vaudeville halls with conspicuous success before 1914, the year in which they caused something of a sensation in the Broadway revue *Chin Chin*. The much-recorded Brown Brothers Saxophone Sextet (in fact, the members were not related) had a repertoire ranging from the quartet from *Rigoletto* to *Saxophone Sobs* and *The Moaning Saxophone Rag*, revealing that already the instrument was manufacturing for itself some of the epithets which would shortly be flung back at it. Other ensembles, designated "Wiedoeft's Saxophone Ensemble", "Wiedoeft's Symphonic Saxophones" and "The Palace Trio" were led by a man who, probably more than any other individual, helped to change the saxophone from quiet obscurity to the phenomenon it became in America and, by inference, in Britain in the 1920's.

Rudy Wiedoeft, born in Detroit in 1893, was the youngest of a large family of musicians. At the age of ten he was playing the clarinet in the family orchestra then resident at the Imperial Hotel, Los Angeles. As a young man, he discovered the saxophone with such enthusiasm that he often devoted ten hours a day to its mastery. In 1916, a year before joining the Marines Band in Washington, he recorded his first solo for the Edison Company, going on over the years to become the most recorded saxophonist of the age.

No doubt because he found a paucity of suitable material for the instrument, Wiedoeft became a prolific composer, penning literally scores of novelty solos, many of which, if we eschew musical snobbery, are of a high standard and have become classics of their type. Equipped with a beautiful tone, a prodigious technique, a flair for showmanship and a fame spread by his fast-selling records, the style of Wiedoeft caught the mood of those post-war years exactly. He was not a jazz player; his idiom was linked to ragtime, echoing on the saxophone something akin to Zez Confrey's piano music.

In the early 'twenties, the saxophone became a craze such has been enjoyed (or endured!) by the concertina, the ukelele, the banjo, the harmonica, the piano-accordion and the electric guitar at different times. Wiedoeft was foremost in the vogue, setting a high standard for all young men who wished to imitate him. Inspiration was not confined to carefree youth. There is known to be one eminent officer of the Salvation Army who was led to learn to play the C-melody saxophone for use in evangelical work after hearing Wiedoeft play in New York.

Rudy Wiedoeft exploited the saxophone's sense of humour to the full, using but never overdoing, all the tricks and effects which, in the hands of his imitators, became an anathema to conventional music circles. A typical novelty, *Sax-O-Phun*, first published in the "Sax-O-Phun Magazine", requires the use of the "laugh", slap-tonguing and false fingering. *Valse Vanité* is the soul of the sentimental saxophone and for decades has been the mainstay of section players if called upon for a "stand-up" solo.

To Wiedoeft may go to the distinction of mounting the first "classical" concert in America devoted to the saxophone. On 17th April 1926, a concert sponsored by the Associated Musical Instrument Dealers of New York filled the Aeolian Hall and was heard by an estimated million people by radio.

Wiedoeft, billed as the "World's Premier Saxophonist", played groups of solos, mainly of his own composition, on the C-melody saxophone. In other groups he was joined by Arnold Brilhart, Alford Evans and Harold Sturr, all saxophonists with the Roger Wolfe Kahn Orchestra. The quartet — three altos and a tenor, with Wiedoeft and Evans occasionally doubling on soprano — played arrangements of Bach and Tschaikowsky together with such salon pieces as Nevin's *Narcissus*. The principal work of the evening was *Four Futuristic Themes* by Willard Robinson, played by the four saxophones with the composer at the piano.

The music critic of *The Metronome* wrote:

To the music lover it marked the first complete and satisfying appearance of the saxophone ensemble in the legitimate concert field — an offering untinged by any of the so-called "jazz" effects of the present day dance combination, yet a refreshing diversion from other offerings in the concert field ... the saxophone is not only eminently suitable as a solo instrument but presents a family of instruments whose rendition of true classics not only requires no apology but permits a completeness of tone pictures and tone colouring of pleasing uniqueness.

Rudy Wiedoeft, who was only 46 when he died in 1940, was truly a pioneer in making the saxophone "respectable".

The "saxophone craze" which swept America was remarkable even by the standards of that country. It would seem that few young men did not see something attractive, not to say heroic, in being seen to hold this swan-shaped tube. The tenor saxophone in C — re-christened "C-melody" — was popular with amateurs who could read directly from the voice line of cheap popular-song piano copies. Many who possessed instruments in E-flat or B-flat learned to finger them as non-transposing instruments for the same purpose. For such who might wish for the prestige of being a saxophone player without the hard work of learning about all those apparently complicated keys, there was the "Swanee Saxophone" — fitted with an ordinary mouthpiece but activated in pitch by a slide device in the manner of the slide whistle.

The new saxophone-dominated music had an effect on the concert bands who for so long had been the main purveyors of popular music. Broadcasting and the gramophone were bringing music to large audiences and were helping substantially in making the new style familiar. As a concession to popular taste, Sousa's band of 1924 carried no less than eight saxophones — 4 altos, 2 tenors, and baritone and a bass — and included in all its programmes a half-hour session of "syncopated music". But, as Schwartz points out, "This concert band, unquestionably an excellent one, could no more play authentic jazz than the Sousa band of

Isham Jones — an early saxophone "technician"
He is a claimant to the distinction of being the first dance-band leader to have used a section of saxophones playing in close harmony.

A pioneer versatile saxophone 'section'
This three-man team appear to be able to manage no less than nineteen instruments between them

1904 could play true ragtime".[10]

With the saxophone forcing itself into popularity with the paying public, the jazz band could afford to ignore it no longer. Without yet again delving into the origins of jazz it can be taken that the polyphonic New Orleans style was well established in the streets, bars and pleasure-halls by the time the United States entered the Great War. In these bands the alto and baritone horns, as well as the bass tuba, had played an important part in the polyphony, but had gradually dropped out in favour of what became the classic front-line of this style; cornet, clarinet and trombone. The band that was playing at Tom Anderson's cafe at the corner of Basin Street in 1915 had an alto, a tenor and a soprano, probably all played by Albert Nicholas. No doubt there were others, but the instrument was comparatively rare and had no part in the standard New Orleans-style instrumentation. On the whole it was regarded as something of a freak. Its thick voice was not happy in this context and its intrusion was resented by many. In the words of cornettist Bunk Johnson, "It just runs up and down with nowhere to go."[11]

When, on November 12th 1917, the Storyville red-light district was closed by Government order, the hub of the jazz world shifted to Chicago and the Middle West. Here the saxophone was already entrenched in public esteem and, when it had to be grafted on to New Orleans-style bands, in the minds of many it served only to adulterate the pure, open sound. Jazz really didn't want the saxophone; the public did. Being both philosophers and showmen, band-leaders fell back on the old dictum of giving the public what it wants and allowing the payer to call the tune. To the purist the effect of the "fashionable foghorn", as Rudi Blesh called it,[12] was disastrous. When the traditionally-instrumented *New Orleans Rhythm Kings* recorded in 1921, they included a saxophone as a sop to public taste with lamentable results to the ensemble, the interloper turning the open counterpoint into sheer cacophony.

Since the new instrument could not be beaten, it had to be joined with. Even the great King Oliver was forced to take two saxophones into his celebrated band to counter the effects of loss of custom to a rival band playing nearby which already had them. However much as some might regret it, a new "Chicago-style" emerged in which the alto and soprano saxophones tended to push out the clarinet, and the tenor the trombone.

It is not our place here to draw too fine a distinction between jazz and and dance-music; from the saxophone's point of view it was all the same. At first, saxophones were used in ones and twos but, as the music became less polyphonic, tending in the case of dance-music to mere harmonized melody, the idea of the saxophone "section" was born. This functioned in a different way from the classical saxophone ensemble where each instrument would have an independent part flowing in smooth symmetry. The early saxophone sections — generally two altos and a tenor — played straightforward triads with the first alto taking the melody note and the second alto and the tenor having the harmony notes directly below it, the parts proceding without any regard for angularity of line. Their constant use of a wide vibrato was another element which infuriated legitimate musicians.

Just when or who was the first band leader to introduce a third saxophone to make this practice possible cannot be accurately pin-pointed. Many leaders have laid claim to having been the first to use what has become traditional dance-band instrumentation — sections of brass, saxophones and rhythm instruments. Art Hickman had a dance-band without saxophones in 1913 but had two by 1919. When in the next year his band was featured on Broadway in the *Ziegfield Follies of 1920,* it is probable that a third saxophone was then added. Isham Jones, who was playing the saxophone before 1915 and who pioneered in Chicago the smooth, relaxed style of dance-music is another contender for the distinction. But whatever the truth, saxophone sections generally of three players became an accepted part of dance-bands as the 1920's began.

The violin, mainstay of the dance orchestra for so long, had to struggle to maintain its place. Wind instruments, until then comparatively rare in the dance hall, were becoming prominent, and the most conspicuous of the intruders was the saxophone. For many years after this change in dance-band instrumentation, it was surprising to note the number of saxophone players who doubled on violin. To reach even modest professional standards on that instrument requires some years of close study; strange that a musician would take so much trouble over a secondary instrument which he might play only occasionally in a whole evening. The fact was, of course, that such a player had started his career as a string instrumentalist but was astute enough to take up the comparatively easy saxophone in line with changing demand.

It was often the case of learn the saxophone or starve! Sidney Bechet had no desire to foresake his clarinet but, like the rest, he was by 1921 forced to take up the saxophone to keep in work. He was one of the few to choose the soprano which, he felt, was nearest to his beloved clarinet and which could easily be discarded when the fad had passed. Paradoxically, well-regarded clarinettist as he was, he is now mostly remembered as a soprano saxophonist.

Jazz is generally reckoned to have arrived in Britain with the visit of the Original Dixieland Jazz Band to the London Hippodrome in 1919. The group had, of course, the traditional instrumentation of the New Orleans style. The two saxophones which graced the stage of the Hammersmith *Palais de Danse*, together with mascots and other bric-a-brac when the band appeared there later in the same year, were no doubt just part of the décor. It is interesting that they should have been thought desirable even in their silent state, suggesting that there was already a subtle connection in the public mind between this new raucous music and the saxophone. When the band met to record in New York on November 24th 1920, the directors of the Victor Company insisted that the group keep up-to-date by including a saxophone. The musicians strongly protested; the demand was enforced but, even in the accomplished hands of Benny Krueger, the dominant tenor saxophone was far from a happy addition. However by 1923, the saxophone had so far established itself as a symbol of the age that the band's leader, Nick La Rocca, then insisted on its inclusion since they could hardly expect to survive in popularity without it.[13]

In the year before the Original Dixieland Jazz Band's visit, the American-born drummer, Murray Pilcer and his Jazz Band, were making records with a nine piece combination which included an alto saxophone played by Arthur Coombes and a tenor in the hands of Sam de Jong. Great Britain's extended involvement in the Great War delayed the changes in dance-band instrumentation such as had already occured in America. Nevertheless, Pilcer, who had first come to London in 1916 with the "American Sherbo Sextet", playing at Maison Lyons, Oxford Street; the Trocadero and the Old Oxford Theatre, had a banjoist, Phil Goodman, who also played the alto saxophone.

The British public at large particularly made aware of the saxophone by the activities of the Savoy Havana and Orpheans Bands, inspired by the American saxophonist, Bert Ralton. Ralton, with Clyde Doerr — another early "saxophone technician" later to become a notable bandleader — had been a member of Art Hickman's band. To demonstrate his flair for showmanship, he possessed the doubtful accomplishment of being able to blow a saxophone and smoke a cigarette at the same time. All the same, he was a fine instrumentalist on both saxophone and oboe. In 1921 he was offered, by the Savoy Hotel management, leadership of their new full-sized band patterned on the already-famous American band of Paul Whiteman. Ralton's Savoy Havana Band, together with the Savoy Orpheans led by Debroy Somers and formed two years later, diffused the strange sound of the saxophone into thousands of appreciative earphones by courtesy of the newly-founded British Broadcasting Company.

The legitimate world of music was, in varying degrees, shocked, disgusted and outraged by this commercial cacophony. With what, in hindsight, seems to have been a queer lack of perception, most of its wrath and sarcasm was directed at the saxophone as though the instrument itself, and not the way it was played, was responsible for the offence. The other instruments of the dance band — trumpet, trombone, clarinet and others — did not come in for anything like the same criticism although their treatment in the hands of jazz and dance musicians was every bit as unorthodox as was the saxophone's. Perhaps this was because those instruments had a "respectable" existence in the symphony orchestra and elsewhere; the saxophone had no such noble connections and was thus the obvious scapegoat.

To its credit, the sober *Musical Times*, in 1926, invited the popular bandleader, Jack Hylton, to comment on *Dance Music of Today*.[14] In his article, Hylton describes the dance-

An early British broadcasting dance band. Popular broadcasts from the Savoy Hotel and other London nightspots made the sound of the saxophone familiar in the early 'twenties. It aroused adulation or fury according to the age and background of the listener.

Rudy Wiedeoft (1893-1940) — a pioneer of the 1920's saxophone craze

band as a functional unit, correctly stating that the syncopated music it plays is not jazz, but curiously implying that jazz had been a purely transient excess which had, by then, disappeared. He shows that the average dance-band consists of three saxophones, three brass instruments and four rhythm instruments, and credits the saxophones with providing the volume which makes further augmentation superfluous.

The three-man saxophone team persisted for many years with players almost always being required to double on other sizes of saxophones as well as clarinet and other woodwind. In fact, the amount of doubling required, particularly in the early days, was prodigious; photographs of the period show saxophonists almost engulfed in a forest of tubing of all shapes and sizes, likely and unlikely. Edward O. Pogson, whose long and distinguished career in dance bands began about this time, actually "doubled" on all saxophones — sopranino to bass — as well as clarinet, bass clarinet, contrabass clarinet, flute, piccolo, oboe, oboe d'amore, cor anglais, bass oboe, bassoon, heckelphone, tarogato, octavin and various novelties including the ocarina and "hot fountain pen". In his case, a high standard of musicianship was brought to each instrument but he points out that, although the vast miscellany of pieces to be found on the bandstands were played from time to time, *how* they were played is another question!

As bands became larger, a fourth saxophone was added to the established trio. This was usually a baritone which became more of a specialist study than a mere double, although in some cases it was not so emancipated and the fourth saxophone was an alto or tenor. At first the additional instrument did no more than enable the melody to be doubled at the octave, thus retaining the triad formula. More ambitious harmony with "added notes", which was a development of the mid-1930's gave each saxophone an independent line and eventually led to a five-man team becoming standard. Many permutations of pitches are possible within this quintet but the most common voicings are for two altos, two tenors and a baritone. The sound of early bands was dominated by the shrill tones of altos and sopranos; reaction against this "top-heavy" complexion came in the form of the tenor saxophone trios of "Society" bands of the 1930's and the "Four Brothers" sonorities of three tenors and a baritone devised by Jimmy Guiffre in the next decade.

Currently, the saxophone in its gregarious state is suffering something of an eclipse. From being the main force in the jazz orchestra and any ensemble playing music to any degree jazz-influenced, there are many instances where the role of the instrument is now seriously diminished or even discarded altogether. Brass sections have grown enormously from the once standard two-trumpets-and-trombone. Trombones have long since been a section in their own right. Five trumpets and five trombones, sometimes with a bass tuba, are not uncommon. When in full stride, the free-blowing brass can quite easily obliterate the five softer-toned saxophones. To make a more equitable balance, the tendency has been neither to reduce the brass nor to increase the saxophones. From its once held position of being an intermediate and blending force between woodwind and brass, it is now sometimes found desirable to have a similar agent between brass and saxophones. Sections of French horns have been tried but since these usually have to be imported *en bloc* from symphony orchestras their use is an unusually expensive way of providing mere harmonic support. The brilliant arranger and band leader Stan Kenton was probably the most successful in this type of experiment; his band of the 1960's included four "mellophoniums", another variation on the E-flat tenor saxhorn. In the hands of jazz-trained players, they added a new tonal tint as well as redressing the balance between the edgy brass and the mellow reeds. It is a pity that hard economics caused their abandonment.

Away from the "Palais" dance band and the large jazz orchestra, the saxophone specialist is at the present time, in a more difficult position than hitherto. In the light orchestras and studio ensembles gathered together for film, radio, television and recording sessions, although saxophone sections can be mustered and are often required, the players are expected between them to be *experts*, and not mere doublers, on the whole range of orchestral woodwind in its many pitches. The flute has replaced the clarinet in being the saxophonist's main double except that nowadays it is more often a case of the flautist doubling saxophone.

As an instrument for the jazz soloist, the saxophone is unsurpassed. Our concern here is for the instrument rather than the player; yet, in this realm, it is difficult to divorce one from the other. In the hands of a supreme exponent, the instrument becomes an extension of the player. So individual is a sound and style that it is open to a knowledgeable listener to name a particular player without hesitation after hearing but a few bars of his playing. As Coleman Hawkins once said: "The only thing nobody can steal from you is your sound; sound alone is important".[15]

Literally hundreds of saxophone players have reached supreme heights in this art form such as to warrant at least mentions wherever the annals of jazz are recorded. The work of an élite few has, in certain instances, been the subject of such close scrutiny as to make it appear that every note, every nuance and indeed every intake of breath is the subject of minute analytical study. Here we must limit ourselves to but brief mentions of a few pioneers who perhaps did as much for the saxophone as the saxophone did for them, stifling any feeling of injustice in the knowledge that the great number thus passed over are honoured at great length in so many excellent specialist works.

Of all the saxophone family, it is the alto which has been the most constantly favoured. With its vocal quality of tone and a range lying comfortably across the normal vocal span it was, for a long time, the sound most obviously associated in general awareness with the saxophone. The second most popular, the tenor, was first used mainly for support work, often in place of the trombone, with the occasional sentimental solo. Yet it was a tenor which first demonstrated what a saxophone could become in the hands of an imaginitive jazz artist. Coleman Hawkins, after joining the Fletcher Henderson orchestra in 1924, sought to imitate the inventive phrasing of his trumpeter colleague Louis Armstrong and, in so doing, shed an influence on practically every jazz saxophonist who followed. Due to this, the driving, masculine tenor, from about 1929 onwards, took premier place as the favourite instrument of the family for the jazz soloist. The gentler, ladylike, alto had its notable pioneers in such as Benny Carter and Johnny Hodges but it was not until the advent of the legendary Charlie Parker in 1941 that a real challenge was given to the tenor. Parker was from Kansas City which, together with Texas and other places in the South West, produced a disproportionate number of top-flight jazz saxophonists, both alto and tenor. Here the latter instrument made its appearance some years after the alto was well established but dedicated musicians, who only doubled other instruments on sufferance, brought the tenor to a pitch of popularity.

Although the alto has attracted and continues to attract many fine exponents, the larger instrument has never been dethroned. It must not be overlooked that the musicians whose names are here and elsewhere mentioned, were and are, apart from their impromptu inventiveness in performance, masters of saxophone technique. To hear Charlie Parker playing with a non-jazz orchestra with a large string section is to reveal an artist who, had his leanings been otherwise, could have been a notable concert artist.

Early in his lifetime's association with the Duke Ellington band, Harry Carney demonstrated that the baritone saxophone is more than just a sonorous bass but a fluent, richly-toned distinctive voice equal to the greatest demands of the jazz improvisor. The soprano saxophone is currently enjoying something of a revival, possibly due to the technical excellence of modern instruments over former versions and the fact that the public, probably hearing it played really well for the first time, likes it. Sopranos were widely used in the early 'twenties, their shrill tones characterising bands of the day and having much to do with the coining of the "wailing saxophone" epithet. Ten years later it had virtually disappeared. When the Anglo-Irish jazz composer, Spike Hughes, was recording in New York in 1933, he was anxious that a certain passage be played on a soprano. Due to exingencies of those hungry days, Benny Carter had pawned his soprano thinking that he would never need it again and had to persuade the local pawnbroker to release it for the afternoon session.

Rarely seen today, the "C-melody" saxophone — a relic of Sax's original orchestral group — was once almost the sole prerogative of Frankie Trumbauer. It is said that this was the pitch on which Charlie Parker first played; Rudy Wiedoeft used it extensively as did the popular bandleader, Rudy Vallee. Its peculiar light tone has appealed at times to jazz players, particularly to Lester Young — musician of a later generation whose name ranks with Hawkins as a trail blazer — who tried to capture this quality on the B-flat tenor.

The reedy lower notes of the magnificent bass saxophone are now no longer heard in this context. In the early hands of Adrian Rollini, it could provide a rhythmic bass better than the sousaphone if not so subtle as the string bass, switching to its higher register to become a flexible, lyrical soloist. Bands often kept it for its novelty value; for some years after the last War, British bandleader Oscar Rabin, who preferred playing to fronting the band, could be seen with a bass saxophone at the end of a large section. Sopraninos and other variants must, to judge from old photographs, have been used at times without lasting effect and are never seen today.

Stemming from the 1920's craze it would be intriguing to know just how many saxophones have been made to date. An estimate just ten years after its first impact put the figure at a million; its manufacture in terms of numbers must surely far exceed that of any other wind instrument. To the layman, it is the mostly easily recognisable of all wind instruments. Its swan-like curves will deceive him into identifying a bass clarinet as a saxophone and a straight soprano as a clarinet. Some sopranos have been made unnecessarily curved seemingly just to prove that they really are saxophones.

Had the saxophone's phenomenal popularity come during the time that Adolphe Sax's patents held good he would surely have become a millionaire many times over. Yet, thinking back on his story, who can doubt that somehow he would have let yet another chance slip through his fingers?

Notes on Chapter XIV

1. *The Golden Years,* Vol. II, No. 23, April 1972. p. 46. Newspaper clipping in the collection of dance-band trumpeter Alfie Noakes.
2. Bate, P., Grove, 1954, VII, p.432.
3. Forsyth, C., *Orchestration,* p. 169.
4. Kennedy, M., *Elgar Orchestral Music,* p. 12.
5. Debussy's *Rhapsody* has little sympathy with the saxophone. Whilst not a virtuoso piece, much of it is in the concert key of A-major, putting the alto saxophone into the inhospitable enharmonic key of G-flat.
6. Vincent, C., *The Brass Band,* pp. 55 — 6.
7. *Joe Batten's Book,* p. 93.
8. *Saxophone Recordings from the Past,* W.S.C. Newsletter, Vol. 2, No. 1, pp. 10—11, (Spring 1971).
9. Blesh R. and Janis H., *They All Played Ragtime,* p. 155.
10. Schwarts, H. W., *Bands of America,* pp. 287 — 289.
11. Blesh, R., *Shining Trumpets,* p. 190.
12. *ibid.,* p.233.
13. Brun, H.O.., *The Original Dixieland Jazz Band,* p. 177.
14. *Musical Times,* 1st September 1926, p. 799.
15. Berendt, J., *The New Jazz Book,* p. 59.
16. Strauss's specification of saxophones for *Sinfonia Domestica* is a "fact" asserted by a large number of authorities, distinguished and otherwise, and including Grove from the earliest editions. Since this paragraph was set in type, it has become apparent that, when marking his score, "1,2,3,4, Sax", Strauss meant not saxophones but *saxhorns!* Jack Brymer, *From Where I Sit,* p.177.

An early saxophone compared with a contemporary model.

The modern instrument has a greater compass, a more generous bore, automatic octave mechanism and other refinements, yet differs in no essential feature from its predecessor.

XV
The Classical Saxophone

It is idle, but not without interest, to speculate on what would have happened to the saxophone had jazz and the dance craze of the 1920's never occurred. By their patronage, the saxophone was brought to fame or notoriety depending on the point of view. On the mistaken premise that anything which is popular cannot be of any worth, did "serious" composers, who may otherwise have written for the instrument, demur? It is clear that it was sometimes used for its plebian overtones, as in William Walton's witty *Façade*; or its supposedly disreputable associations as, to quote a much overplayed piece, where the F-sopranino, soprano and tenor saxophones are used to heighten the wild barbarity of Ravel's *Bolero*. In this connection, Vaughan Williams' writing for solo alto saxophone in his Masque for Dancing, *Job*, is masterly. He uses the instrument's oily tone and capacity for *portamento* to depict the hypocritical Comforters. Most conductors exploit this to the full, insisting on a "sleazy" approach to characterise the wickedness of the charlatans and, by implication, the saxophone itself. So effectively was the instrument typecast in this role that, when the work was produced in Worcester Cathedral during the "Three Choirs" Festival of 1948, the ecclesiastical authorities insisted that the movement incorporating the saxophone be omitted rather than let the instrument's profane voice speak within the sacred edifice. To the credit of the assembled crowd of music-lovers, this fatuous piece of muddled thinking brought widespread criticism.

With few honourable exceptions, examples of saxophone writing by composers of international stature are, at least to mid-way into the twentieth century, so rare that we may be forgiven in assuming that many condemned the instrument because its reputation was so bound up with supposedly worthless music. This is probably too harsh a judgement and no composer worthy of his salt ought to be put off by so trivial a consideration. The most likely explanation could be that many had not heard the saxophone played within the context of their art, or, if they did sense the possibilities, felt correctly that there were all too few classically trained saxophonists available.

The position has not radically changed to this day; it is no exaggeration to suggest that the majority of music-lovers hardly believe that the saxophone can exist outside of jazz and popular music. When they are made aware, the verdict is quite often more than favourable. The writer remembers the feeling of pleasurable astonishment at the first broadcast performance of Eric Coates' *Saxo-rhapsody* in 1937 as the silky-toned alto emerged through the orchestral texture. Although this work makes no claims to profundity and, apart from two short passages and the final *altissimo* note, does not demand a virtuoso technique, it is engagingly melodic and shows that the composer had absorbed the spirit of the saxophone in a way that Debussy never did.

This modest piece, dedicated to and first performed by Sigurd Rascher, has remained a favourite in the saxophone repertoire, but it is to France, birthplace of the instrument, that we must look for signs of a revival in the classical saxophone. There have, over the years, been a few — precious few — musicians of great virtuosity who have chosen the saxophone as a vehicle for their talents. One of the first was Dupaquier, featured soloist with the *Garde Républicaine* band, in the early years of this century. On a saxophone made to his own design by Couesnon et Cie, he could play over a chromatic compass of three octaves from g. As the "jazz age" began, a little known but even more remarkable virtuoso emerged from the Argentine. Texiero de Ladario commanded the staggering compass of four full octaves!

Eminent orchestral clarinettist, Brian Manton-Myatt, recalls a personal meeting with this amazing man:

I did meet Ladario on two occasions at the shop and residence of my dear friend, the late M. Henri Selmer, around two or three years after the first War. I could not be more exact regarding the year as I was a fairly frequent visitor to chez Selmer *during the decade.*

M. Selmer introduced me to Ladario one morning in the room behind the showroom at No. 4 Place Dancourt, and told me that he had a blind virtuoso, an Argentinian, there, who was a saxophonist the like of whom he had never heard before in his life. As Henri was not a man given to superlatives (except when referring justifiably to the merits of the products of his superb factory!) I was greatly intrigued to meet, and especially hear, the artist who aroused him to such exceptional opinions.

Ladario, who was a sturdily built man, somewhat below average height, and showing not the least sign of awareness of his undoubted genius, spoke with the greatest modesty regarding his abilities, but with every readiness to play his instrument which embodied several features that were exclusively of his own conceiving, chiefly consisting of extra keys for extending the compass down to a low a-flat and by means — I think — of an extra octave key, as well as some extra mechanism that I did not have the opportunity of inspecting, the compass was extended upwards to a considerable degree above the normal limit, though this may possibly have been accomplished to some extent by his extraordinary flexible and highly developed embouchure.

His tongue articulation was amazing, and he gave proof of this when he played for me a transcription of the Scherzo tarantelle *for violin and piano by Wieniawski that served to demonstrate his finger technique that was wonderful in its complete command over the most formidable demands that could be contemplated.*

Ladario, despite his extraordinary ability, was the most modest of men and of charming personality.

No tribute can be greater than that due to Marcel Mule for his work in keeping alive the idea of the classical saxophone. Born in the first years of the new century at Aube, Mule was a saxophonist at eight years of age in the band conducted by his father at Beaumont-le-Roger. In this town he eventually became a teacher, the War having interrupted his musical studies. On being called for military service, he joined the band of the 6th Infantry Regiment in Paris, later transferring to the *Garde Républicaine.* Here he succeeded François Combelle as saxophone soloist and in this capacity built a worldwide reputation. As a soloist he attracted the attention of several French composers who provided him with the basis of an original repertoire.

In 1928, Marcel Mule organised what was to become the celebrated saxophone quartet of the *Garde Républicaine.* Using transcriptions entirely, the quartet was launched at La Rochelle on December 2nd. It was an immediate success and it was not long before transcriptions could be discarded for the exclusive use of original works. Of the many pieces written for the group especially, perhaps the most famous are Glazunov's *Quartet for Saxophones* and the *Introduction and Variations on a Popular Rondo* by Gabriel Pierné. Over the years, there were a number of changes in personnel but, under Mule's dedicated leadership, standards were superlatively maintained. After 1936, the group became known as the Paris Saxophone Quartet and attracted considerable attention to the classical saxophone through their broadcasting, recording and tours in many lands.

The saxophone class at the Paris Conservatoire had been closed at the outbreak of the Franco-Prussian war in 1870. Despite this, the instrument had survived in France and was in such demand that, in 1939, saxophone makers in Britain were granted exemption from military service because of a severe shortage of saxophones in French bands. The following year, France had fallen to the invader and it was during the dark days of 1942 that the saxophone class was re-opened. Claude Delvincourt, then Director of the Conservatoire, invited Marcel Mule to become the new director of the class ensuring that his unique experience and conception of the French classical style was passed on to a select and dedicated small group of students. A number of these eventually became noted orchestral and recital saxophonists.

Mule held the post for 26 years after which he was succeeded by Daniel Deffayet. The class now caters for twelve French and five foreign students who must be, at the time of commencement of their studies, under 23 years of age, undertaking to study for a period of from two to five years. Mule's scales, arpeggios and studies are an integral part of the curriculum. So the work started by Adolphe Sax, who taught more than 150 pupils between 1858 and 1870, went forward again after a gap of 72 years, piloted by a master of the saxophone whose influence as a soloist, quartet leader and teacher was felt throughout the world.[1]

A saxophonist of like stature who rose to eminence in pre-War days and thus brought the idea of the classical saxophone to many who had never previously considered it in this context came, paradoxically, from the saxophobe Germany. Sigurd Rascher holds a unique place among players of the instrument, his work having inspired so many composers to write for the saxophone, many of the works being dedicated to him personally.

Taking to the saxophone early in life, it was his playing of Bach in 1931 which led to him being invited to sit in with the Berlin Philharmonic Orchestra for a work composed and conducted by Edmund von Borck. This led directly to a concerto from Borck which Rascher played twice in the following year to enthusiastic audiences; the ripples from these performances were felt in music centres throughout Europe. In 1933, the Nazis made it clear that the "foreign" saxophone had no place in their schemes; Rascher left Germany and became a professor at the Royal Academy of Music in Copenhagen for the next five years. During this time he played throughout Europe, Australia and the United States, attracting many compositions for saxophone and orchestra including now-celebrated works by Glazunov, Coates, Larssen and Ibert.

It was 34 years before he again appeared with the Berlin Philharmonic when he played for the 92nd and 93rd time the Ibert *Concertino da Camera*. The intervening years were spent in America, playing with all the leading and most of the lesser orchestras besides teaching the art of the classical saxophone to an ever-increasing circle of interest. In later years his daughter Karen appeared with him on the concert platform, she being a concert soloist in her own right, specialising in the comparatively rare soprano saxophone.

Despite the existence of these supreme exponents of the saxophone, the instrument, even to the present time, has never succeeded in establishing itself as a permanent member of the symphony orchestra. This is more surprising when one considers the lavish praise showered on the instrument by composers from the mid-19th-century onwards but, apart from a shortage of players, the reason for its non-acceptance could lie in the fact that the symphony orchestra had reached a degree of standardisation when the saxophone arrived, with a large number of masterpieces already in existence. However, the cause of the instrument in this connection has often been advanced but perhaps never so strongly as by Victor Ullman. Writing in *Auftakt* in March 1929 he suggests firstly that a contrabass saxophone would be an asset to the orchestra and then he goes on to examine the possibility of replacing nearly all of the woodwind with a septet of saxophones from sopranino to contrabass. Acknowledging that some problems would arise, he is inclined to retain the flute and seems genuinely regretful that the tones of the oboe and clarinet would no longer be heard. However, on the credit side it is pointed out that saxophone players do not have to hold in their lungs quantities of oxidised air as do oboe and bassoon players with the consequent hazard to health![2]

Another reason sometimes advanced for not giving the saxophone a permanent place in the orchestra is that the instrument is by nature an individualist and does not blend well with other instruments. This is clearly nonsense for whilst it is a fact that where a body of saxophones are included in an ensemble they are immediately missed the moment they stop playing they are an excellent "binding" agent especially to the divergent *timbres* of the traditional orchestral woodwind. What more individual instrument less able to blend with its colleagues than the oboe? Yet an orchestra without oboes is unthinkable. It may be noted that, in the two instances where Vaughan Williams has employed saxophones symphonically, where the instruments are not required to be prominent they support the general harmonic *tutti* without any untoward effects.

The old excuse of not being able to find conservatoire-trained players for the saxophone no longer holds good. Not only is there an ample number of specialist players either retained by or on call to leading orchestras; musicians trained in different schools and styles are becoming more and more immersed in the various types of musical form as they intermingle in film, television and recording studios. The idea of what is a desirable saxophone tone may differ widely between classical and jazz; yet such are the standards now prevalent that it is quite common for a musician to be equally at home in both fields. When, in 1971, the Sadlers Wells Opera staged the Broadway musical, *Kiss Me, Kate*, the orchestra was able to muster a team of five saxophones, only two of which were imported.

Although they have contributed practically nothing to the saxophone's solo literature, British composers of the first rank have provided a few noteworthy instances of its effectiveness as an orchestral instrument. William Walton uses an alto to telling effect in *Belshazzar's Feast;* Vaughan Williams, whose *Job* has already been mentioned has a splendidly effective part for the tenor saxophone in his Sixth Symphony and, in the Ninth, uses a "section" of two altos and a tenor to indulge in bouts of acid humour.

The saxophone is a gregarious animal blending and getting along generally well with its fellows. Next to the string quartet, a quartet of saxophones provides what is perhaps the most satisfying blend of kindred instruments. The French instrumentation — soprano, alto, tenor and baritone — is the most common and by now a lot of music has been written for it. There is a considerable amount of published material for the American quartet — two altos, tenor and baritone. The soprano saxophone in particular demands a high standard of technique and control. Because of its wide, straight, open tube and certain oboe-like characteristics, it can, in the hands of an undiscerning player, dominate the ensemble to an unacceptable degree. Although the substitution of an alto can give a more matched sound, the distinctive voice of the soprano is then lost and the first alto player is forced to utilise extensively the higher part of the compass with frequent excursions into the *altissimo* register if the range of the music is not to be severely curtailed. This, of course, requires exceptional technique and is probably why, as a compromise, an attempt was made about 1930 to popularise a "mezzo-soprano" saxophone in F — a counterpart of Sax's original orchestral alto. The tone of this version commended itself to composers, in particular, Percy Grainger, but any success it enjoyed was short-lived.[3]

It is in the form of the quartet that the classical saxophone is most often heard, at least in Europe. There are signs that this idea is catching on among amateur and semi-professional players who find in quartet playing a satisfying and refreshing relaxation from dance-band work. Although there is a shortage of quality original works, there are plenty of published transcriptions of all grades for the medium. Here there is scope for even the novice arranger; vocal music in the form of part-songs and madrigals transcribes easily and is most effective in this form.

At the other end of the scale, there exist a few professional saxophone quartets whose standards are at least the equal of the world's finest chamber ensembles. One has only to hear the work of such groups as François Daneels Belgian Quartet, the Paris Quartet led by Daniel Deffayet and the superb New York Quartet — leader, Ray Beckenstein — to realise that these are no man's poor relations. Of the last-named ensemble, the leader of a rival quartet was moved to write: "They are the ultimate professionals . . . their playing has everything from an attack like a knee in the crutch to pianissimo chords like a summer breeze too gentle to ruffle a butterfly's wings".[4]

Without disdaining the pleasure afforded in somewhat lighter vein by the late Michael Krein's Quartet, now carried on by Jack Brymer, Great Britain had no tradition of serious saxophone quartet playing until the advent of the London Saxophone Quartet. Led by Paul Harvey (soprano), with Hale Hambleton (alto),[5] Christopher Gradwell (tenor) and David Lawrence (baritone), they made their London *début* at the Queen Elizabeth Hall in April 1971 to critical acclaim. The quartet has quickly established for itself an international reputation laying claim to be ranked among the world's best. Since all four members are professional orchestral clarinettists and saxophonists, it is part of their avowed policy to persuade contemporary composers that the saxophone is worthy of a place in the instrumentation of new

A modern saxophone chamber group

The London Saxophone Quartet (The fifth member is an EE-flat contrabass saxophone)
(Photograph by Michael Farnham — Reproduced by permission)

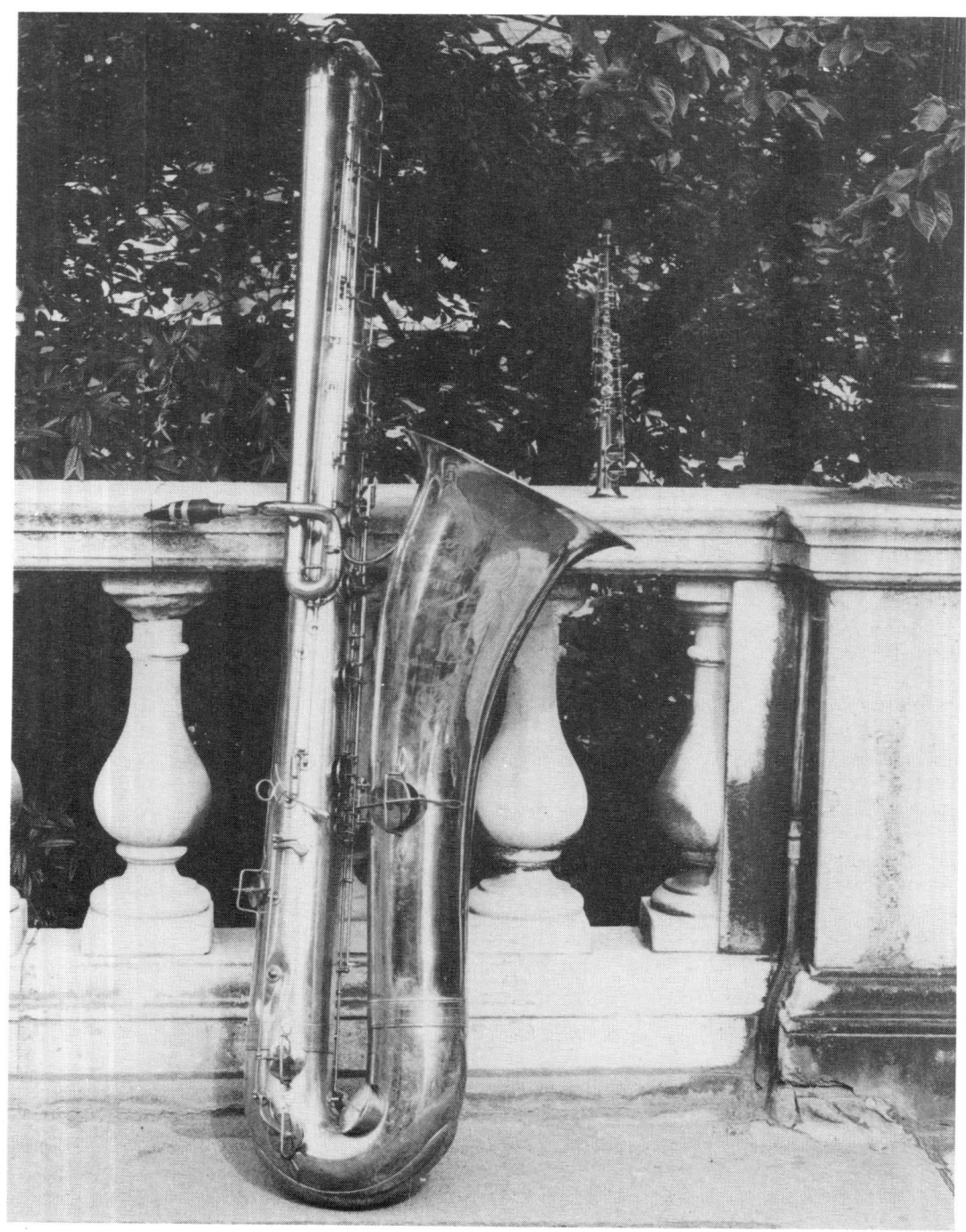

E-flat contrabass and E-flat sopranino saxophones
These modern extremes of the family demonstrate a practical compass of some five-and-a-half octaves

large-scale works.

The L.S.Q. quickly appreciated that programmes containing a preponderance of transcriptions and long-established works would not advance either their cause or their instruments'. From their existence they attracted original works from British composers but, to throw the net wider, they organised in 1972 a competition for new works for saxophone quartet. Independently judged, there was an encouraging response which yielded a variety of pieces from the ultra-*avant-garde* to the witty trifle, thus enriching their repertoire with a score of worthy numbers.

As of yet, the saxophone has had little chance of taking part in international music competitions. A rare exception was the "International Competition for Musical Performers" held in Geneva in 1970. Of the thirty works chosen for the contest list, only one was a transcription. French composers were responsible for 19 of the pieces, American 4, Swiss and German two each, and one each from Norwegian, Russian and Czechoslovakian writers. Only the alto saxophone was admitted and, because the general standard of playing and musicianship was not high, only a second prize and two silver medals were awarded. Nevertheless, the fact that the saxophone was allowed in at all was a minor triumph and it is hoped that the interest generated will lead to higher future standards.

In extending the saxophone ensemble, there appears to be little interest in sopranino instruments but there is opportunity to bring back the fine B-flat bass saxophone. Although there is little enough published music for the saxophone sextet, its instrumentation appears to have become standardised as soprano, two altos, tenor, baritone and bass. No doubt larger groups have been and will be tried, giving opportunity for the use of the EE-flat contrabass. In recent times there were two of these in England owned and available for hire from George Howarth and Company of London. They have existed in the U.S.A. for some years; a paragraph in *The School Musician* of February 1933 proclaimed: *The large saxophone* (in an accompanying photograph) *is absolutely the grandaddy of them all. It is the largest in the World and was made especially for the Shriner band. After the first try-out of this EE-flat Contra Bass, it was unanimously proclaimed a success. By the way, you don't have to be a grandaddy to play the EE-flat Contra Bass.*

There is no doubt that this giant contrabass could find a valued place in large saxophone groups. There are mentions by Lavoix and Sachs that a BB-flat contrabass once existed; if interest in the classical saxophone is maintained it is conceivable that one might again appear.[6]

In 1971, the noted French saxophonist, Jean-Marie Londeix published a catalogue of all traceable compositions for the saxophone in its 125 years of existence. This covers some 3,000 titles by 1,000 composers and, allowing that many arrangements of music originally written for other media are included, the amount of original material remaining is enlightening to any who feel that the instrument has been neglected by composers. By far the bulk of the solo material is for the alto which has long been regarded as the principal soloist of the family. This is to do less than justice to other members of this closely homogeneous but highly individual family and specialists are now appearing particularly for the soprano and tenor saxophones. Solo works for these instruments are still in short supply but there are signs that contemporary composers are becoming attracted by the fine musicianship shown by these specialists and are prepared to write for their instruments.

Although many jazz players, like John Coltrane, have made good use of the saxophone's *altissimo* register, the rank-and-file dance musician has generally been content to play within the accepted compass. The normal range of some altos and tenors has been extended upwards by a semitone to f"-sharp and the very useful low A is now common on the baritone. Advanced classical saxophonists are expected to be fluent in the upper harmonics and the high register which Adolphe Sax once claimed and then had to abandon, is now an accepted part of the instrument's compass.

No other wind instrument has changed so little between its inception and the present day. Changes that have been made have been more in the nature of refinements than radical alterations. Perhaps the most important innovation in recent years has been Charles

Houvenaghel's *Saxophone le Rationnel* which looks and fingers like a normal instrument but which, by a simple expedient, has the faculty of lowering many notes by a semitone thus opening up considerable possibilities in the easier fingering of difficult passages.[7]

The most encouraging signs of an upsurge of interest in the classical saxophone are to be noted currently in the North American continent. At the same time when Sigurd Rascher arrived as an immigrant in the United States, the "Swing" era of jazz was in vogue and the concert saxophonist was very much a rarity. There was, however, a small circle of players dedicated to the non-jazz saxophone. Chief among these was Dr. Cecil Leeson who had begun a serious study of the instrument in 1925. It has been said that most of the serious compositions for the saxophone before 1950 were written especially for either Mule, Rascher or Leeson.

The work of this pioneer triumvirate has happily borne fruit. Despite some entrenched opposition from university and college administrators, the saxophone is now accepted as a principal study for doctorial degrees in many major universities. For instance, the North Texas State University had, in 1971, an enrolment of seventy students of the instrument on the Bachelor, Master and Doctorial levels. Their tuition is in the hands of a full-time professor with four assistants. In this way, there is something of an historical repeat, opposition from the establishment being overcome by popular interest and demand which, in this case, has been supported by the ever-growing repertoire for the instrument. There is still a shortage of specialist teachers, instruction being, in many cases the sideline of a general woodwind teacher who may not be particularly interested in this facet of his duties. However, led by Larry Teal, Professor of Saxophone at the University of Michigan, the way is pointed to such posts being attractive to the specialised saxophone teacher.

The idea of a World Saxophone Congress sprang from a realisation that the wide interest in the classical saxophone needed a focal rallying point. Paul Brodie, Canadian saxophone virtuoso and teacher of the instrument at the University of Toronto, had been impressed by the interest and enthusiasm shown by both players and listeners at a world accordion convention held in that city. In an article in "The Instrumentalist" in October 1968, he put forward proposals for a similar worldwide gathering of those interested in the development of the classical saxophone. Due to the dedicated efforts of Paul Brodie and Dr. Eugene Rousseau of the University of Indiana, the first meeting of the World Saxophone Congress was a reality in little more than a year. This was held in Chicago in December 1969 with five hundred enthusiasts attending.

Brodie's original proposals had encompassed six points, but after the first Congress, the prime movers issued a succinct statement of purpose which could secure universal acceptance, leaving details as to how objectives could be achieved to the elected officers:

The World Saxophone Congress has as its purpose the firm establishment of the Saxophone as a medium of serious musical expression. This includes the performance of solo and chamber works, the use of the Saxophone in the orchestra and band, the establishment of a substantial body of literature that includes the Saxophone, and — above all — the dissemination of all pertinent information about the Saxophone to performers, students, teachers and composers, the general musical public and to any and all other appropriate persons.[8]

The second Congress was held exactly a year later, again in Chicago, by which time considerable progress had been made towards the objectives, particularly in the publication of a periodic newsletter. From a modest first issue, "The W.S.C. Newsletter" has grown into a well-produced vehicle for disseminating news, views, reports on classes and seminars, reviews of new music and of matters technical.

Membership of the Congress is predominately American but, by the time the third congress was staged in August 1972, this time in Toronto, it had been able to take on a more international aspect with contributions from the Belgian and London Quartets, and soloists from France and Japan.

To underline the international concept of the Movement, the next Congress was held in France. In 1976, an impressive array of saxophone talent from many parts of the world assembled in London for the Fifth World Saxophone Congress. This year also saw the founding of the Clarinet and Saxophone Society of Great Britain, reflecting the upsurge of interest in the "classical" saxophone in the United Kingdom.

Whether Congresses and Societies will achieve their aims of getting the saxophone accepted as a serious orchestral and chamber instrument, or whether they will remain, like accordion rallies and brass band contests, platforms for preaching to the converted remains to be seen. It may well be that the more effective means lies in the activities of such as the four members of the London Saxophone Quartet. As well as pursuing their careers as professional saxophonists they each, as multi-instrumentalists chiefly on the several members of the clarinet family, are actively engaged in the British music scene from recording television commercial jingles, through theatre and dance orchestra work to appearing as required with the leading symphony orchestras. Impressive as the title "Professor of Saxophone" sounds, it has been suggested that many American holders of this office are completely isolated from the music profession, leading cloistered lives in small-town universities, producing potential virtuosi who are seldom heard of again, and essaying, from time to time, brilliant recitals on the alto saxophone to fellow-professors and students. Against this it must be said that other teachers, like James Houlick — one of the few virtuosi to specialise in the tenor saxophone — link with their professional activities extensive recital tours both in the United States and abroad.

In the early days of the saxophone's burst into popularity in popular music, the world of "art" music was greatly incensed at the unrefined sounds and effects the new style extracted from the instrument. It is now clear that these were quite innocuous compared with what is now being demanded by the successors to these critics under the banner of *avant-garde.* When such a work was actually commissioned for the 1972 World Saxophone Congress, it moved one English hearer to suggest a new slogan:

Vive le saxophone but don't stand idly by while, under the guise of emancipation, it merely exchanges one form of musical exploitation for another.[9]

Yet, in spite of any shortcomings, these meetings and the regular international intercourse which now takes place between lovers of the saxophone are a considerable step in the right direction. As yet, the symphony orchestra does not realise that it needs the saxophone. But there was a time when it seemed to get along quite well without the trombone, the clarinet, the cor anglais and other instruments until composers saw their possibilities and demanded them, often after hearing particular fine players. In this world of rapid change there is no reason for the symphony orchestra to feel that its present form must for ever be sacrosanct. Indeed, such ultra-conservative attitudes usually lead to stagnation, perhaps in this case to the orchestra indeed becoming, as has been often prophesied, a mere museum piece for the performance of outmoded music.

Few would wish to see any established orchestral instrument displaced; but, after hearing what the saxophone has to offer in the hands of such brilliant players as there are around, it is to be hoped that modern composers will see that the modern symphony orchestra has still much to offer as a vehicle for their inspirations, especially when augmented with one or more of Adolphe Sax's inventions.

Notes on Chapter XV

1. Deffayet, D., *Saxophone Study at the Paris Conservatory,* W.S.C. Newsletter, Vol. 1, No. 3, p.3. (Winter 1971).
2. *Musical Times*, 1st June, 1929, p.512.
3. Conn Corporation catalogue, c.1930, pp.56-7.
4. Harvey, P., *Cresendo*, October, 1972, p.17.
5. Succeeded in 1978 by Peter Ripper.
6. *Vide* Notes on Chapter IX, No. 11.
7. Macgillivray, J. A., *Recent Advances in Woodwind Fingering Systems*, Galpin Society Journal, XII, June, 1959, pp.68-9.
8. *W.S.C. Newsletter,* Vol. 1, No. 2, p.1. (September 1970).
9. Harvey, P., *ibid.*

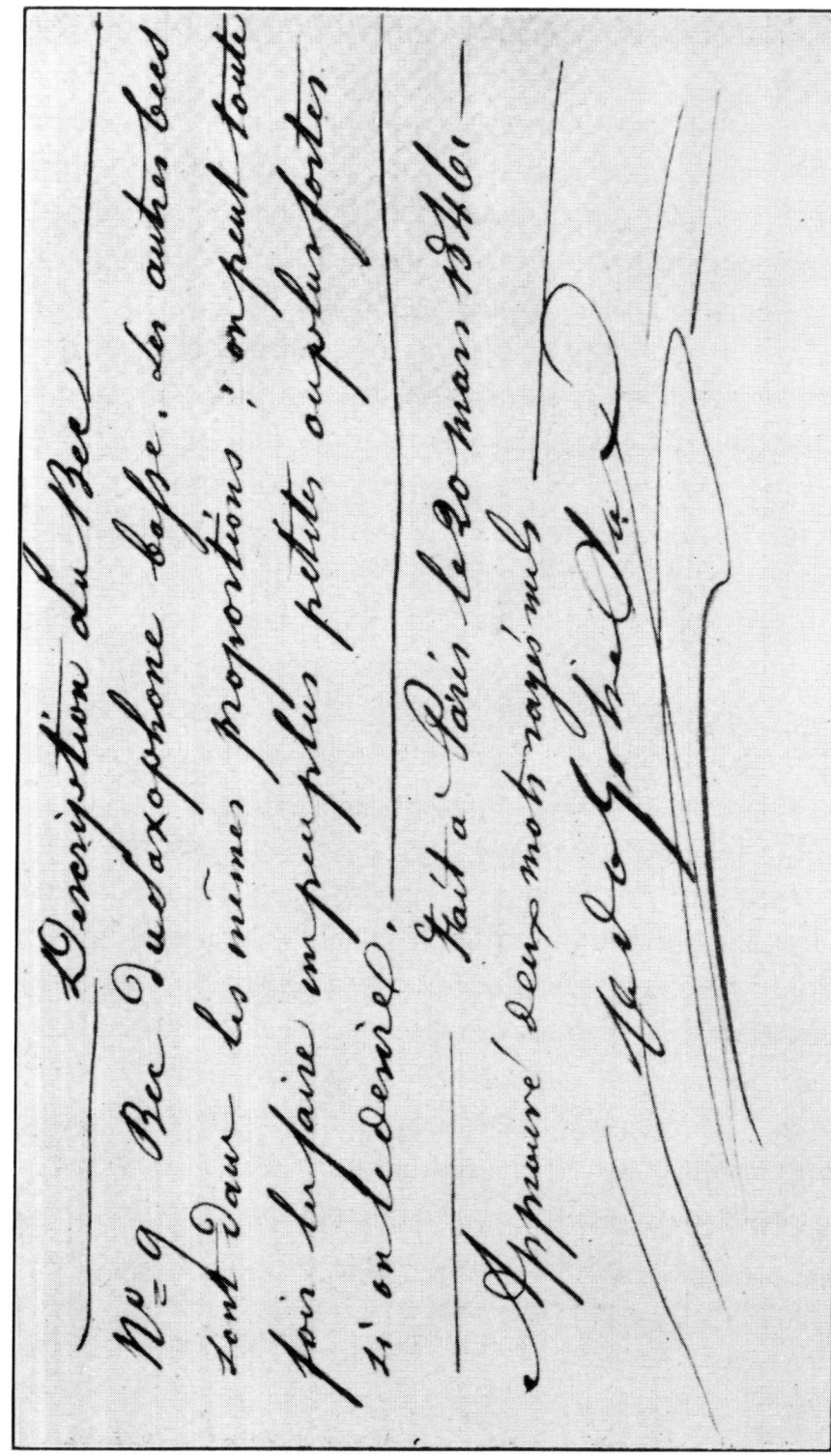

Description of a saxophone mouthpiece, written and signed by Adolphe Sax.

Postscript

The *St. James's Gazette* of February 12th 1894 carried an obscure paragraph which told English readers that:

The death is announced of M. Adolphe Sax, to whom the modern orchestra is indebted for a whole family of improved wind instruments. A Belgian by birth, M. Sax settled more than half a century ago in Paris, where his newly invented keyed horns were first introduced on a large scale and by important composers. A quartet of saxhorns, besides saxophones and saxtubas, figured in the score of Halévy's "Wandering Jew" and were particularly effective in the scene of the Day of Judgement at the very conclusion of the opera. Meyerbeer too — always on the look-out for new kinds of sonority — hastened to adopt them in "The Prophet" where they added greatly to the brilliancy of the march, and in several of his magnificently orchestrated Irish dances. Rossini, the first composer to adopt the cornet (in the ballet music of "William Tell"), would certainly have found a place in his orchestra for M. Sax's system of horns had he not already given up writing for the stage.

Today, there is unreality in these words. The orchestra owes hardly anything to Sax; the instruments mentioned in the obituary, and others not enumerated, have been used so little over the years in symphony orchestras that an occasional inclusion in a score is a matter for comment.

Some would say that Sax's greatest contribution to the musical art was his set of matched valved bugles which enabled the wind band, and particularly the British brass band, to take a big leap forward and to settle on an instrumental form. This is a matter of history. Nowadays, such instruments as the flugel horn, the euphonium and the bass tuba, which have something of the saxhorn strain in them, do not much acknowledge this thread of their ancestry. Those which might be more positively identified are now comparatively little used and, it would seem, may steadily fade into greater obscurity. In any case, these products of Sax's skill were improvements only. There can be no doubt that the patentee of the saxhorn was not the inventor of the valved bugle.

It would seem, therefore, that Sax's entire posthumous reputation must rest on one instrument, the neglected saxophone. Neglected? The most familiar, widely-made, mass-produced wind instrument of all time? Yet the word is apt. The instrument's use and popularity has been restricted almost entirely to the realms of popular music and jazz. Without seeming to denigrate in any way the contributions made to musical experience by these more transient forms, their near-exclusive hold on the saxophone has resulted in its almost total neglect in the main stream of music. Despite all the bunkum written and said over many years as to the saxophone's place in music, there remains a strong feeling that, in ignoring the possibilities of the instrument in its several forms and as a group, art music denies itself a valuable asset.

With acknowledgements to the influence of Charles Sax, Adolphe Sax invented the last successful acoustical musical wind instrument. Of the many which once bore the names of their inventors, it alone survives. It was a remarkable thing to have done and gives the inventor a unique place in the history of musical-instrument making.

The question is: was it worth inventing? — or, since it had been invented, is it worth preserving?

There are some who will profess a dislike for the saxophone. Epithets like "vulgar" and "coarse-grained" are flung. Since likes and dislikes are such personal things, they are above question by others. But sometimes there remains suspicion that the expressed dislike is more due to prejudice than objectivity. Could it be that the half-recalled hoot of some extrovert jazz exponent with a searing tone directed solely at the initiated gives the impression that this is the instrument's true or only nature?

It is here contended that the saxophone has a pleasingly distinctive tone, an expressive and dynamic range, and is in no way inferior within its personality to any orchestral instrument. Marcel Mule once commented that the saxophone "can play a role of the first level in the symphony orchestra with the same importance as all wind instruments habitually employed in the orchestration". Anyone who, for instance, has heard Vaughan William's masterly use of the orchestral saxophone must find it difficult to deny its effectiveness. As a virtuoso instrument for the concerto, it is second to no other wind instrument, as is clearly illustrated in the works of Glazunov, Villa-Lobos, Ibert, Dubois and others.

The reasons for the saxophone's orchestral neglect are complex; some of them have been touched on in this book. It might be fair to say that, had the saxophone been invented before the orchestra had more-or-less settled on its form; had it been evolved rather than suddenly produced; had it been public property rather than a patented personal asset, it could well be that a group of saxophones would be as familiar on the orchestral platform as horns or flutes.

While orchestras are, in the main, tied to the standard repertoire, the appearance of a saxophone in the ranks must remain a rarity. It is to modern composers and new works that the saxophone must look for emancipation. We say "the saxophone" when meaning — if the extreme instruments are excluded — three and perhaps four distinctive solo instruments. The alto saxophone continues to hold pride of place as the prime soloist of the group. Composers, however, are beginning to discover the separate individualities, of the tenor, the soprano, and even the baritone saxophones.

A recent (1972) check of one major American catalogue of contemporary music reveals that 18 per cent of the works listed included parts for saxophones. Further, a questionaire sent to thirty leading symphony orchestras in North America shows that 62 per cent had full-time players among their numbers who played the saxophone when necessary, whilst most of the rest claimed no difficulty in getting the services of orchestrally-trained saxophonists when they required them. A far cry from the days when Sir Henry Wood's players denied all knowledge of the instrument for fear that it would taint their reputations.

The standard of saxophone playing has now reached a level where a composer or conductor can be assured of a competent performance of the highest artistic standards.

In the hands of the dedicated instrumentalist and the discerning composer, Adolphe Sax's brain-child may yet secure its inheritance.

A modern memorial to Adolphe Sax on the site of his birthplace at Dinant.

Motif by Daoust
for the Committee of the Sax Festival, Dinant.

Appendix A

The Concert at the Salle Herz, 3rd February 1844.

There are two main unsolved questions concerning the events of that night: what was the exact instrumentation of the sextet which demonstrated Sax's new instruments, and what piece did they play?

The concert was an important one for Berlioz. On January 28th 1844 he wrote to his old friend of student days, Louis Schloesser, then *Kapellmeister* at Darmstadt:

"I gave my first concert at the Conservatoire and I am organising another for next week in a hall you do not know (Herz's), I have written for it a new overture (this was "Roman Carnival"), *a scene with chorus and two other pieces. I have my usual orchestra but even so I am worried: we have to prepare the programme at one rehearsal ..."*

There is little doubt that Berlioz saw this occasion to be an ideal one by which to assist his friend Sax in a practical way and, at the same time, introduce an additional crowd-pulling novelty into the programme. In an undated letter, placed by both Barzum and Searle as "late 1843" the composer wrote to Sax in somewhat enigmatic terms:

I went to your house a little while ago to ask you to bring Arban with you to my house one of these days with a B-flat cornet and your little trumpet or soprano Sax-horn in B-flat. I want to study the extreme notes of their compass and show you both a table I have just drawn up, a comparative table of the compass of the four instruments based on the harmonics of the tube we were discussing this morning. There must be no uncertainty as to the manner of writing for your little trumpet ...

There are a number of mysteries created by these few words. He mentions *four* instruments but enumerates only *three* with an "or" between trumpet and saxhorn as if either would do. Thus, in his laudable attempt to obviate uncertainty from his scoring, he introduces a good deal of it for the researcher.

At first reading, he appears to be referring to the tiny saxhorn *(saxhorn suraigu)* in high B flat, but there is nothing to suppose that this sopranino instrument existed until some time after 1850. No specimen was included in Sax's large prize-winning display at the Great Exhibition of 1851. If he was using the word "trumpet" in a vague (and rather unprofessional) sense when he really meant the *contralto* saxhorn in B-flat, then surely no comparative table of harmonics was necessary since these are the same for both the cornet and the contralto saxhorn; and, for that matter, the B-flat trumpet. It is possible that the reference is indeed to a B-flat trumpet of a size corresponding to the modern orchestral instrument which might appear "little" when compared with the F or E-flat trumpet then commonly in use.

As far as the *Salle Herz* instrumentation is concerned, we can be reasonably sure of two things; (i) there were three brass valved instruments and a saxophone of unspecified pitch but almost certainly of the bass register, and (ii) on the Distin's testimony, only three saxhorns then existed; E-flat soprano, B-flat contralto and E-flat alto (or tenor). A mystery lies with the three brass instruments. Comettant (p.51) whose views as a contemporary observer ought to be respected, gives these as:

trompette suraigu in si bémol.
nouveau cornet
bugle perfectionné

which Adam Carse ("The Music Review", Nov. 1945, p.194) interprets as:

B-flat trumpet
cornet
"improved bugle" (otherwise a saxhorn)

A lot depends as to what is meant by "suraigu". The term is relative but, since it could not possibly apply to a larger B-flat instrument like the baritone saxhorn and the very tiny B-flat saxhorn did not at this time exist, it can only apply in this context to an instrument of the same pitch as the modern B-flat trumpet or cornet. However, it is a rather misplaced term when used in connection with this pitch and is much more appropriate to an instrument pitched a fifth or an octave higher.

The only other writer to give detailed consideration to the *Salle Herz* episode some time after the event is Julien Tiersot. Writing in *Le Ménestrel* in 1906 (pp.75-6), he quotes accurately the instrumentation given in a contemporary account of the concert by Maurice Bourges in the *Revue et Gazette Musicale* of 11th February 1844:

Petite Trompette dixième à cylindres, en mi bémol aigu.
                                                          (Small cylinder trumpet in high E-flat (tenth))
Petite Bugle à cylindres en mi bémol.   (Small cylinder bugle in E-flat)
Grand Bugle à cylindres en si bémol.   (Large cylinder bugle in B-flat)

Here is a "band of a curious tone" with a vengeance! — a shrill treble, a stentorian bass and very little in the middle!

First the trumpet: the "dixième" indicates the high E-flat pitch most specifically. Could it be that Berlioz really meant, "your little trumpet or saxhorn in *E-flat*? If so, some of the pieces fall into position more readily. The comparative table might then have some utility, and, at this high range, tone is so thin that it matters little whether a soprano trumpet, a soprano cornet or a soprano saxhorn is used. This too could be why Berlioz was concerned with the extreme notes of the compass which are much more problematical with high-register instruments than with those of more intermediate pitch.

Having pursued this conjecture, if there is any substance in it, the contemporary Comettant must have been mistaken in noting the trumpet to be in B-flat. Then there is the question of Comettant's "new cornet" and Bourges' "small bugle in E-flat". A saxhorn would have a more generously tapered bore than a cornet and, at B-flat pitch, would have approximated more towards flugel horn dimensions. However, at the E-flat pitch, and allowing for variations of tone contributed by individual players, the aural difference between the two instruments would have been minimal. Nevertheless, to one of Sax's calling where bore dimensions were of paramount importance, the difference in nomenclature would have made the point of some consequence.

This now leaves the "improved bugle" to be equated with the "large saxhorn in B-flat" and we must assume that the alto saxhorn in E-flat, which would surely have helped in the securing of a better balance within the ensemble, was not used on this occasion.

Of course, music critics can be wrong and it is possible that Bourges, equally as much as Comettant, could have got his E-flats and B-flats confused. Comettant's line-up, as interpreted by Carse, would be the more satisfying, although in other contexts we have discounted the automatic acceptance of some of Sax's friends merely because Sax approved of what they had written.

To take all this inconclusiveness one step further, doubt has been cast as to the dating of the Berlioz letter to Sax. Dr. Hugh Macdonald, General Editor of the New Berlioz Edition, is of the opinion that it belongs to 1851-2 or thereabouts, so that the "little trumpet or soprano Sax-horn in B-flat" really does refer to the *saxhorn suraigu* in high B-flat for which the composer included a part in the original version of "The Trojans".

From these various permutations and possibilities, we might venture a guess at the instrumentation which at least bears with some of the information handed down, and which would, with careful scoring, fit the six voice parts of the *Hymne:*

      Saxhorn soprano in E-flat   (Soprano)
      Trumpet in B-flat   (Alto)
      Saxhorn contralto in B-flat   (Tenor I)
      Clarinet in B-flat   (Tenor II)

Bass Clarinet in B-flat   (Bass I)
Bass Saxophone in C or B-flat   (Bass II)

There is nothing to say, of course, that the instruments followed exactly the voice lines and Berlioz probably did a fair amount of switching, especially among the inner parts, to secure a good balance.

Yet one is left with a feeling that no one, least of all Berlioz, would really be happy given such a sextet, with some of the instruments playing out of their best registers and one, at least, in the very worst part of its compass. Why should a trumpet and a clarinet have been included when a far better ensemble was available from Sax's own instruments?

For a clue as to what instruments may have been available at the time of the *Salle Herz* concert we may look at a letter written to Sax by one Finck, a musical instrument maker of Strasbourg, and quoted by Pontecoulant (pp.234-5). This is ambiguously dated "December 1844" at the head of the letter and "14th October 1844" at the foot. The writer is loud in his praise of the instruments he had lately seen at Sax's house, which he lists as:

Contralto saxhorn in B-flat   Cornets — Trumpets.
Tenor saxhorn in E-flat.   Saxo — Tromba.
Baritone saxhorn in B-flat with 3 valves.   New Bass Clarinet.
Bass saxhorn in B-flat with 4 valves.   Saxophones, bass and tenor.
Contrabass saxhorn in B-flat (sic)

Of the saxhorns, there is evidence that only the first three listed, existed in February 1844. Finck makes no mention of Sax's clarinet; the bass saxophone, of course, was played by Sax himself. If we assume that there indeed were three brass and three reed instruments, the three existing saxhorns would appear to be the most logical choice, together with the near-certainty of the bass clarinet since this was an instrument Sax would be anxious to demonstrate before a large gathering. This, then, leaves either the clarinet or the "tenor" saxophone in E-flat as candidates for the remaining position. If both were available, the choice would surely fall on the saxophone as not only demonstrating a new sound but in helping the more to give a better balance. The clarinet, after all, would sound and, from any distance, look the same as any other without having any opportunity to show off alleged advantages and being required to play in its least effective register.

Sax demonstrated his tenor saxophone to the jury of the 1844 Exhibition when they mistook it for a bass clarinet. Such confusion may have happened in February. This instrument is listed as No. 1 in the 1846 patent specification which might imply that he built the E-flat "tenor" and the bass (listed as No. 2) concurrently and that both existed in February 1846.

Conjecturing thus, we tentatively arrive at an instrumentation for the sextet which would not only demonstrate five of Sax's claimed inventions and one radical improvement, but which would provide an infinitely better balance than any hitherto suggested:

Soprano saxhorn in E-flat   (Soprano)
Contralto saxhorn in B-flat   (Alto)
Tenor saxhorn in E-flat   (Tenor I)
Bass clarinet   (Tenor II)
"Tenor" (baritone) Saxophone in E-flat   (Bass I)
Bass saxophone in C or B-flat   (Bass II)

Bourges's 1844 report has something to say on both of the questions we are considering:

The Hymne *transcribed for M. Adolphe Sax's wind instruments was not originally written for the type of presentation given by M. Berlioz in this concert. Set to words, it was sung in Marseilles with great success. By changing it to the form of an instrumental sextet, the composer merely wanted to give M. Adolphe Sax the chance of displaying in public the inventions and improvements, the merit of which has been appreciated by almost all the leading composers and critics of the time. This was the general impression of the audience. The small cylinder trumpet in E-flat, the small cylinder bugle also in E-flat, the large cylinder bugle in B-flat, the soprano clarinet, the bass clarinet and the saxophone seemed to have fine tone and full satisfying resonance. If the players alone have the right to comment on the difficulties of the mechanism of* which they are the natural judges, every well-tuned ear, however unused to the task, is able to appreciate the quality of the sound of an instrument. Public opinion has ratified by its claim the endeavours of M. Adolphe Sax, while recognising, despite their incontestable talent, the players had not had the time to become familiar with these new instruments; but this is only of secondary importance. More stringent and more lengthily prepared tests will succeed in establishing this conviction in all completely impartial minds.

Commenting on the above sixty-two years later, Tiersot poses the question we are still asking:

Is it possible to identify with some known work this hymn, setting words, and sung in Marseilles before 1844? First we have no knowledge of Berlioz hearing any performance in Marseilles before the concert which the composer conducted after this date in this town, an account of which he has given in his Grotesques de la musique. *It is up to our Marseilles brethren to elucidate this small historical point. Let us look through Berlioz's work to see whether we can find any passages of which the form corresponds with the pattern outlined above. We can find two. First there is a* Sacred Song (Chant Sacré) *which he composed for his collection of* Irish Melodies, Opus 2, *which appeared in 1830 and which he later orchestrated; then the* Méditation religieuse *dated Rome 4th August 1831 and which was the first piece of his* Tristia; *both were for six voices, the same number as the instruments given: the orchestra was there, the performance could have been given. We do not think we are venturing too far into the realms of hypothesis in acknowledging that the* Hymne *of 1844 is one of these two pieces, and we prefer to choose the first which offers more varied resources and which in places allows one to hear solo instruments.*

Chant Sacré had begun life as the *Prayer* from Berlioz's second-prize cantata *Herminie* written in 1828 to words by P. A. Vieillard after Tasso's *Gerusalemme Liberata*. This item was, two years later, reworked as part of the *Irlande* song-cycle, with words by Gounet after Thomas Moore. Both this and the *Méditation religieuse* from Opus 18, No. 1, again with words after Thomas Moore, are slow-moving and with comparatively simple voice parts divided as sopranos, altos, tenor I and II, and basses I and II which could be transcribed for easy performance by the six instruments mentioned. On the face of it, either piece would constitute a curious choice by which to show off the exciting possibilities of new instrumental constructions.

It would perhaps have been more fitting had Berlioz written something completely original for his motley collection of instruments. However, the demands on his time can be appreciated and, in seeking something almost ready-made, he may have been attracted by this very simplicity for musicians grappling with the complexities of unfamiliar instruments, and again by the compositions having already six individual parts and a ready-scored orchestral accompaniment.

Most writers have agreed with Tiersot that the *Chant Sacré* is the most likely contender, but really there is no reason to think that this was more suitable that the *Méditation religieuse*. Of course, it could have been some other *Hymne* entirely.

Such pieces would have served to demonstrate the effect of the six instruments playing in concert but, despite Tiersot's comments, it is difficult to see where, in either piece, there could have been much room for solo performance without a good deal of re-arrangement and extension. The episode where Sax was forced to hold an interminably long note whilst he grappled with the saxophone's teething troubles could hardly have taken place as the music was moving forward to the orchestral accompaniment. It would therefore seem likely that the performance of the *Hymne* was part of an interlude during which each player demonstrated the possibilities of his instrument, possibly in an unaccompanied *cadenza*.

There is no record that the *Hymne* was ever again performed in this way, but the same instrumental combination, having enjoyed some technical improvements, did turn out to serenade Berlioz later in the same year.

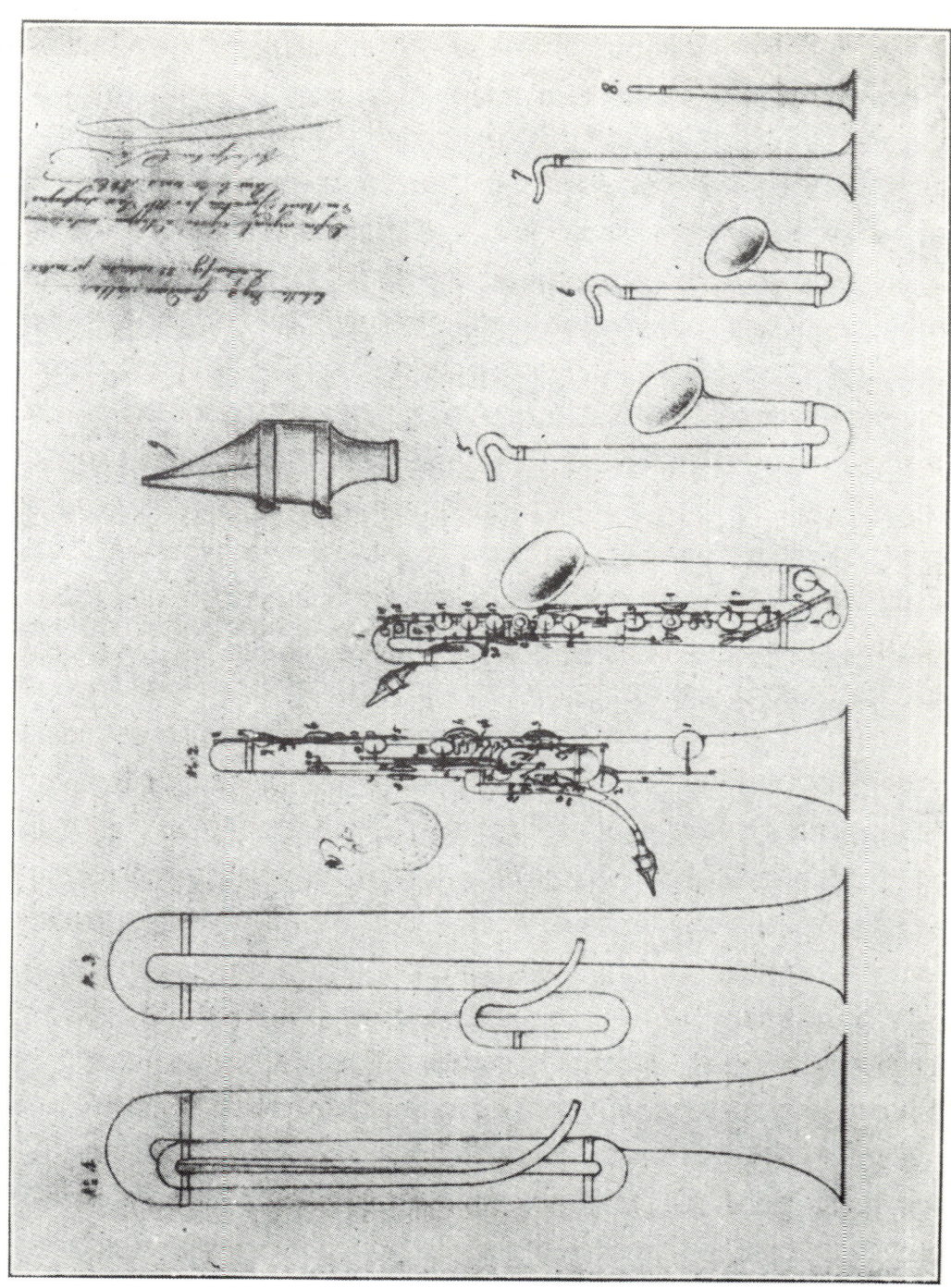

Drawing for the original saxophone patent, 20th March, 1846

Sax's original description of his saxophone attached to the Patent of 20th March 1846

Appendix B

Advertisement in "Musical World" — June 1853.

SAX'S CORNETS, SAXOPHONES, SAXHORNS & c.

Rudall, Rose & Carte, patentees of the only prize flutes, and manufacturers of Military Musical Instruments beg to announce to the commanding officers of Her Majesty's Army & Navy; the masters of bands and the musical public that they have been appointed the SOLE AGENTS IN GREAT BRITAIN for the sale of Sax's celebrated instruments — THE SAX CORNETS, SAX TROMBAS, SAX HORNS, SAX TROMBONES, BOMBARDONS, and his arrangements with M. Sax (to whom was awarded the only Council Medal for military instruments at the Great Exhibition) as will enable them to supply his instruments direct from his own manufactory at prices not higher than those charged for numerous imitations of them. The security and advantages thus afforded will be obvious.

M. Sax's Instruments, among which are several new models, may be seen at Rudall, Rose & Carte's 100 New Bond Street.

Messrs. Rudall, Rose & Carte beg to subjoin the following letter which they have received from Mr. Sax:

Paris, 28th May 1853.

To Messrs. Rudall, Rose & Carte.

Gentlemen, — I accept your proposals relative to the sale of my instruments in England; and I am happy to think that owing to the arrangements entered into by us which constitute you my sole Agent in Great Britain, I shall be worthily represented, at the same time the Public will no longer be misled by those who appropriate the goods of others.

There have been issued, under cover of my name, a crowd of counterfeit Sax Horns and other instruments invented by me which the purchasers necessarily thought came from my factory, but to which I never put a hand. My reputation must have been very firmly established in your country, to have withstood the effects of so much tending to injure it. But now there need be no further mistakes of this kind. Everyone who purchases my instruments from you, will know of a certainty that they are manufactured by me.

I do not doubt, Gentlemen, but that with your activity and commercial habits, you will soon realise a large amount of business, by promoting the sale of many instruments which are at present but little known among you; but which, I may be allowed to say, cannot fail to obtain a brilliant success, not only with Musicians and Connoisseurs, but with Amateurs. We shall thus be rendering a great service to the Musical Art and to ourselves at the same time.

Accept, Gentlemen, my warm salutations,
Adolphe Sax

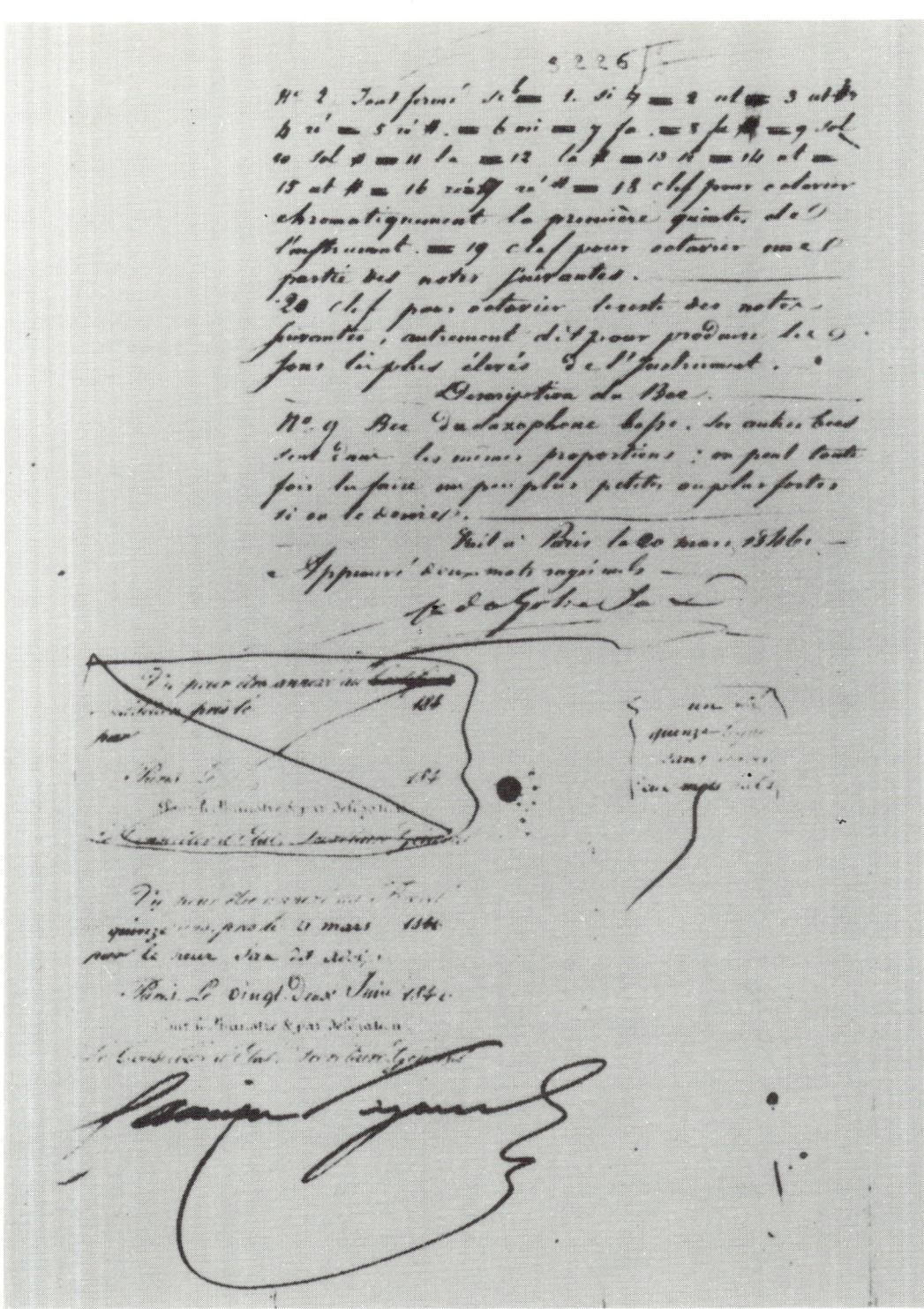

Final page of the saxophone patent of 20th March 1846

Appendix C

Patent of Adolphe Sax. No. 3226, of 21st March 1846 for systems of wind instruments called Saxophone.

Descriptive memorandum filed in support of the application for a patent of fifteen years by M. Antoine Joseph (called Adolphe) Sax, manufacturer of musical instruments, living in Paris at Rue Neuve St. Georges No. 10 and domiciled at present at the house of M. Perpigna, lawyer, at 10 Rue Neuve St. Augustin, for a new type of wind instrument called saxophones.

Statement

One knows that in general wind instruments are too harsh or too soft in sonority; it is particularly in the basses that one or other of these faults is most obvious. The Ophicleide for example, which reinforces the trombones, produces such an unpleasant sound that it cannot be used indoors because one cannot modify the tone. On the contrary, the bassoon makes such a feeble sound that it can only be used for filling in and for accompaniment; for *forte* passages it is completely useless. You will notice this latter instrument is the only one that I combine with the strings.

Only brass wind instruments are satisfactory in the open air; consequently an orchestra containing these instruments is the only one that can be used in these circumstances.

As for stringed instruments, everyone knows that in the open air they are of no use because of their lack of power. This renders their use almost impossible in like circumstances.

Noticing these different problems, I have been looking for a way of rectifying the matter by making an instrument which, by its tone, could combine with strings, but which was stronger and more full than they were. This instrument is the Saxophone. Better than any other the Saxophone's tone can be varied to give it the qualities which I have just mentioned and to preserve a perfect smoothness over its whole range. I have made it of brass in the shape of a parabolic cone. The saxophone has a simple reed mouthpiece in which the interior is much flared, narrowing to the part which adapts to the body of the instrument.

Description and names of the various individual members of the saxophone family.

No. 1. Saxophone in E-flat tenor all closed; B to E-flat sounding D-natural to C.
No. 2. Saxophone in C descending to B-flat in sound pitch. The same instrument made also in B-flat descends in consequence to A-flat which makes B-flat in the same pitch.
No. 3. Saxophone in G contrabass; which may also be made in A-flat.
No. 4. Saxophone in C Bourdon, which may also be made in B-flat (a tone lower).
Saxophones Nos. 5, 6, 7 and 8 are of the same pitch as the preceding at an octave above.

Fingerings

No. 1. The fingering of this model has some of the characteristics of the flute and of the clarinet, one may apply to the rest all the possible fingerings and uses.
All closed D-natural to C.
1. Key of C open; 2. C-sharp; 3. D; 4. D-sharp; 5. E; 6. F; 7. F-sharp; 8. G; 9. G-sharp; 10. A; 11. A-sharp; 12. B; 13. C; 14. C-sharp; 15. D; 16. Octave key for the first part of the instrument; 17 D-sharp; 18. E; 19. F; 20. Octave key for the second part of the instrument.
No. 2. All closed B-flat — 1. B-natural; 2. C; 3. C-sharp; 4. D; 5. D-sharp; 6. E; 7. F; 8. F-sharp; 9. G; 10. G-sharp; 11. A; 12. A-sharp; 13. B; 14. C; 15. C-sharp; 16. D; 17.

D-sharp; 18. chromatic octave key for the first fifth of the instrument; 19. Octave key for the notes of the next part; 20. Octave key for the rest of the next notes, otherwise for producing the high notes of the instrument.

Description of Mouthpiece

No. 9. Bass saxophone mouthpiece. The other mouthpieces are in the same proportion; they may at all times be made a little smaller or larger as desired.

Given in Paris on the 20th March 1846.
Approved with two words deleted.
(signed) Adolphe Sax.

Seen to be attached to the Patent for fifteen years from 21st March 1846. Paris, 22nd June 1846.
For the Minister and by delegation.
The Councellor of State. Secretary General.
(signature).....

Bibliography

Adkins, H. E. *A Treatise on the Military Band* — London, 1945

Baines, Anthony. *European & American Musical Instruments* — London, 1966
Baines, Anthony. (Ed.) *Musical Instruments Through the Ages* — London, 1966
Baines, Anthony. *Woodwind Instruments and Their History* — London, 1957
Barzun, Jacques. *New Letters of Berlioz* — New York, 1954
Barzun, Jacques. *Berlioz and His Century* — New York, 1956
Bate, Philip. *The Oboe* — London, 1962
Bate, Philip. *The Trumpet and Trombone* — London, 1966
Batten, Joe. *Joe Batten's Book* — London, 1956
Bechet, Sidney. *Treat it Gentle* — London, 1960
Beecham, Sir Thomas. *A Mingled Chime* — London, 1944
Berendt, Joachim. *The New Jazz Book* — London, 1964
Berlioz, Hector. *A treatise on Modern Instrumentation and Orchestration* — Paris, 1848. London, 1958
Berlioz, Hector. *Memoirs* — Paris, 1870. London, 1969. (trans. David Cairns)
Bassaraboff, Nicholas. *Ancient European Musical Instruments* — New York, 1941
Binns, P. L. *A Hundred Years of Military Music* — Gillingham, Dorset. (Eng.) 1959
Blesh, Rudi. *Shining Trumpets* — London, 1949, 1958
Blesh, Rudi and Jannis, Harriet. *They All Played Ragtime* — New York 1950
Brenta, Gaston. *Adolphe Sax et le facture instrumentalé (Bulletin de la Classe des Beaux-Arts — Académie Royale de Belgique, Tome XLIX)* — Brussels, 1967
Brook, Donald. *Five Great French Composers* — London, 1946
Brymer, Jack. *From Where I Sit* — London, 1979
Carse, Adam. *Musical Wind Instruments* — London, 1939
Carse, Adam. *The Orchestra from Beethoven to Berlioz* — Cambridge, 1948
Clappé, Arthur A. *The Wind Band and its Instruments* — London, 1912
Comettant, Oscar. *Histoire d'un inventeur au Dix-Neuvième Siècle* — Paris, 1860
Cook, Kenneth (Ed.) *The Bandsman's Everything Within* — London, 1950
Crouch, Rebekah Ellen. *The Contribution of Adolphe Sax to the Wind Band* — Florida State University, 1969
Day, James. *Vaughan Williams* — London, 1961

Ehrlich, Blake. *Paris on the Seine* — London, 1962
Ella, John. *Musical Sketches at Home and Abroad* — London, 1869, 1878

Farmer, H. G. *Handel's Kettledrums and other papers on Military Music* — London, 1950
Farmer, H. G. *History of the Royal Artillery Band* — London, 1954
Farmer, H. G. *Military Music* — London, 1950
Farmer, H. G. *Rise and Development of Military Music* — London, 1950
Fétis, Francois J. *Biographie universelle des musiciens et bibliographie général de la musique* — Paris, 1864
Forsyth, Cecil. *Orchestration* — London, 1914, 1944

Galpin, F. W. *Textbook of European Musical Instruments* — London, 1937, 1946
Gammon, Peter and Clayton, Paul. *A Guide to Popular Music* — London, 1960
Gevaert, F. H. *Traité général d'Instrumentation* — Ghent, 1863

Gevaert, F. H. *Nouveau Traité* — Ghent, 1885
Gilson, Paul. *Les Geniales Inventions d'Adolphe Sax* — Brussels, 1939
Giraud, J. Fr. *Nouveau Traité Théoretique et Pratique de Musique Instrumentale* — Brussels, 1891
Grove, G. (Ed. Eric Blom) *Dictionary of Music and Musicians* — London, 1954
Giffiths, S. C. *The Military Band* — London, 1896
Gorgorat, Gerald. *Encyclopédie de la Musique pour instruments à* vent — Lausanne, 1955

Hind, Harold C. *The Brass Band* — London, 1934, 1952
Hoby, Charles. *Military Band Instrumentation* — London, 1936

Kappey, J. A. *Military Music* — London, 1894
Kastner, Georges. *Manuel général de musique militaire* — Paris, 1848
Kastner, Georges. *Traité général d'instrumentation* — Paris 1837, supp. 1844
Kennedy, Michael. *Elgar Orchestral Music* — London, 1970
Kochnitzky, Leon. *Adolphe Sax and his Saxophone* — New York, 1964
Kool, Jaap. *Das Saxophon* — Leipzig, 1931
Krager. *Wilhelm Wieprecht 1802 — 1872* — Berlin, 1882
Kroll, Oskar. *The Clarinet* — London, 1968

Lang, Philip J. *Scoring for the Band* — New York, 1950
Langwill, Lyndesay G. *An Index of Musical Wind Instrument Makers* — Edinburgh, 1972
Langwill, Lyndesay G. *The Bassoon and Contrabassoon* — London, 1965, 1971
Lajarte, Theodore de. *Instruments Sax et fanfares civiles* — Paris, 1876
Lavignac, A. *Encyclopédie de la Musique* — Paris, 1927
Lavoix, H. *Histoire de l'instrumentation* — Paris, 1878
Lee. Edward. *Music of the People* — London. 1970
Londeix. J. M. *125 Ans de Musique pour Saxophone* — Paris 1971
Lord, Francis A. and Wise, Arthur. *Bands and Drummer Boys of the Civil War* — South Brunswick (USA)

McCarthy, Albert. *The Dance Band Era* — London, 1971
Mackenzie-Rogan, J. *Fifty Years of Army Music* — London, 1926
Mackerness, E. D. *A Social History of English Music* — London, 1964
Mahillon, Victor C. *Catalogue du Musée du Conservatoire de Musique de Bruxelles* — Ghent, 1909
Miller, George. *The Military Band* — London, 1912
Morley-Pegge, R. *The French Horn* — London, 1960
Newton, Francis. *The Jazz Scene* — London, 1959

Panassie, Hughes and Gautier, Madeline. *A Dictionary of Jazz* — London, 1959
Perrin, Marcel. *Le Saxophone* — Paris, 1953
Pontécoulant, A. de. *Organographie* — Paris, 1861

Remy, Albert. *La Vie tourmentée d'Adolphe Sax* — Brussels, 1939
Rendall F. Geoffrey. *The Clarinet* — London, 1954 (Revised P. Bate 1971)
Rose, Algernon *Talks with Bandsmen* — London, 1895
Russell, J. F. and Elliott, J. H. *The Brass Band Movement* — London, 1936
Rust, Brian. *The Dance Bands* — London, 1972

Sachs, Curt. *Handbuch der Musikinstrumentenkunde* — Leipzig, 1920
Sachs, Curt. *The History of Musical Instruments* — London, 1947
Sax, Alphonse. *La Musique Instrumentale au point de vue de l'hygiène et la création des Orchestres Féminins* — Paris, 1865
Searle, Humphrey. *Hector Berlioz — A Selection from his Letters* — London, 1966
Schuller, Gunther. *Early Jazz* — New York, 1968
Schwartz, H. W. *Bands of America* — New York, 1957

Sousa, John Philip. *Marching Along* — New York, 1928
Stearns, Marshall. *The Story of Jazz* — New York, 1956
Stoeckl, Agnes de. *King of the French* — London, 1957

Toye, Francis. *Rossini — A Study in Tragi-Comedy* — London, 1934

Vincent, Charles. *The Brass Band and How to Write for it* — London, 1908

Wagner, Richard. *My Life* — London, 1911
Walker, E. S. and S. *English Ragtime — A Discography* — Chesterfield (Eng.) 1972
Weinstock, Herbet. *Rossini — A Biography* — London, 1968
White, William Carter. *A History of Military Music in America* — New York, 1944
Wood, Sir Henry J. *My Life of Music* — London, 1938
Wright, Denis. *Scoring for Brass Band* — Colne (Eng.) 1935

Zealley, A. E. and Hume, J. Ord. *Famous Bands of the British Empire* — London, 1925

Index

Adam, Adolphe, 73, 166.
Adelaide Gallery, 60.
Aeolian Hall, 170.
Albert, Eugene, 150.
Albert, Prince Consort, 60, 63, 82.
Allentown Band, 169.
Althorn, 153, 154.
Alto-fagotto, 34, 40, 81, 148.
Alto horn, 153, 154, 161, 163, 173.
American Saxophone Band, 169.
American Sherbo Sextet, 174.
Anderson, Tom, 173.
Apollo and the Seaman, 148, 166.
Arban, Jean-Baptise, 52, 60, 80, 83, 166, 195.
Arlésienne, L', 166.
Armstrong, Louis, 178.
Associated Musical Instrument Dealers of New York, 170.
Association of Instrument Makers (United), 80-82, 90, 95-105, 126, 129.
Auber, Daniel, 44, 50, 70, 73, 130.
Auftakt, 183.
Aumale, Duke d', 70.

Bach, J. S., 170, 183.
Bachman (clarinettist), 23.
Ballad Horn, 65.
Baritone (baritone horn), 32, 33, 154, 157, 161, 173.
Barlès (saxophonist), 125.
Barnum & Bailey's Circus Band, 169.
Barzun, Jaques, 195.
Bass Clarinet (Sax), 20-24, 34-38, 43, 48, 49, 76, 83, 84, 90, 115, 147, 150, 197.
Bassoon (Sax), 87, 130, 133.
Bate, Philip, 37.
Bathyphone, 81, 82, 115.
Batten, Joe, 168.
Baugniet, C., 59.
Baumenn, Frederick, 130.
Bayley, William, R., 161.
BB-flat bass, 115, 161, 168.
Bechet, Sidney, 174.
Beckenstein, Ray, 184.
Becker, Rudolph, 169.
Beecham, Sir Thomas, 148.
Beethoven, 59, 51, 82, 83.
Behread, Blumberg & Co., 63.
Belgian Guides, 19, 166.
Belle Vue, Manchester, 64, 65.

Bellini, Vincento, 57.
Belshazzar's Feast, 184.
Bender, Valentine, 19.
Benvenuto, 47.
Berlin Musical Gazette, The, 84.
Berlin Philharmonic Orchestra, 183.
Berlioz, Hector, 20, 23, 39, 43, 47, 49, 51, 52, 55, 59, 69, 71, 72, 81, 82, 88-90, 109, 110, 115, 125, 130, 134, 139, 140, 143, 157, 195-198.
Berr (musical director), 88.
Bertin, Louise, 47.
Besses o' the Barn Band, 64.
Besson, G. A., 99, 121.
Besson, Fontaine, 165.
Bethlehem Concert Band, 161.
Bizet, Georges, 166.
Black Dyke Mills Band, 64, 162.
Blaikley, D. J., 113.
Blaina Ironworks Band, 64.
Blanc, Étienne (lawyer), 99, 100.
Blandford, W. F. H., 133.
Blesh, Rudi, 173.
Blühmel, Frederich, 29, 83.
Boehm, Theobald, 24, 130, 133, 148-150, 165.
Bolero, 181.
Bombardon, 32, 71, 83, 161.
Boosey & Company, 65.
Boquillon, 104, 106.
Borck, Edmund von, 183.
Border Regiment, 166.
Boston Orchestral Club, 167.
Bourgeois Gentilhomme, Le, 105.
Bourges, Maurice, 196, 197.
Brandus (music publisher), 92.
Brass Band, 63, 65, 66, 74, 134, 153-155, 157-163, 167, 189, 191.
Breadalbane, Marquis of, 57.
Brenta, Gaston, 38, 50.
Brilhart, Arnold, 170.
British Braodcasting Company, 174.
Brodie, Paul, 188.
Brooke, Thomas Preston, 169.
Brown Brothers Saxophone Sextet, 169.
Brown, Teddy, 168.
Brown, Tom, 169.
Brymer, Jack, 184, 179.
Buccina, 110.
Buffet, Auguste, 20, 148, 150.
Buffet, Louis Auguste (Jr.), 95, 96.
Bullfrog and the Coon, The, 169.

Burghersh, Lord, 83.
Buteux (clarinettist), 48.

Caledonica, 40.
Caractacus, 166.
Carafa, Michael, 70-74, 77.
Carnaval Romain, 110, 195.
Carney, Harry, 178.
Carnival of Venice, 63, 168.
Carpenter, J. E., 66.
Carse, Adam, 65, 66, 196.
Carter, Benny, 178.
Castlemary (singer), 125.
Cello (Sax), 140.
Cerveny, V. F., 141.
Chabrier, Emmanuel, 144.
Chaix d'Est-Ange (lawyer), 99, 100, 104.
Champ-de-Mars, 71, 72, 74, 90, 96, 113.
Chant Sacré, 198.
Charivari, La, 74.
Chin Chin — revue, 169.
Choral-varié, 167.
City Guards Band of San Diego, 169.
Clagget, Charles, 29.
Clarinet (Sax), 19, 24, 34, 37, 43, 47, 72, 74, 83, 147-150, 196, 197.
Clarinet and Saxophone Society of Great Britain, 189.
Clarion-Sax, 139.
Clavicors, 32, 126, 153, 155.
Clegg's Reed Band, 64.
Coates, Eric, 181, 183.
Coeffet, J. B., 77.
Coldstream Guards, 157.
Coltrane, John, 187.
Combelle, François, 182.
Comettant, Oscar, 49, 51, 52, 58, 59, 65, 109, 113, 139, 142, 195, 196.
Compagnie du Nord, 80.
Concert hall (Sax), 140.
Concertino da Camera, 183.
Confrey, Zez, 170.
Constantine, Grand Duke, 57.
Constitutionnel (Paris), 84.
Contrabass clarinet (Sax), 115, 147.
Contrabassoon, 125, 204.
Conway, Patrick, 168.
Conway (saxophonist), 169.
Coombes, Arthur, 174.
Cornet (Sax), 29, 32, 72, 83, 133, 139, 195-197, 201.
Cornet-à-pistons (cornopean), 32, 64, 134, 139, 155, 162.
Corno-musa, 135.
Cor Omnitique, 18, 32.
Corona d'Italia, La, 51.
Covent Garden, 60.
Cressonnois, Jules, 166.
Crimean War, 129, 141.

Cromwell, Oliver, 63.
Crystal Palace, 63, 154, 158.
Cyfarthfa Band, 154.

Dacosta, Isaac Franco, 23, 113.
Daily News, 165.
Dalmatie, Duke de, 70, 96.
Damnation of Faust, The, 52, 89.
Danays (inventor), 32.
Daneels, Francois, 184.
Dauverne (trumpeter), 52.
David, Louis, 121.
Davis, Miles, 156.
Davison (critic), 92.
Debussy, Claude, 167, 179, 181.
Deffayet, Daniel, 183, 184.
Delvincourt, Claude, 182.
Demange (saxophonist), 135.
Denner, Johann Christian, 148.
Dernier Roi de Juda, Le, 51.
Desfontenelles (watchmaker), 20, 81, 82.
Dettingen Te Deum, 57.
Diable à Quatre, Le, 72.
Distin and Sons, 63.
Distin family, 57-63, 65, 66, 84, 133, 135, 154, 161, 195.
Distin, George, 59, 63.
Distin-guished Galop, The, 66.
Distin, Henry, 58, 59, 63, 65, 66, 135, 139, 154, 158.
Distin, Henry and Company, 65.
Distin, John, 33, 57-63, 66, 156.
Distin, Theodore, 59, 63, 66.
Distin, William, 59, 63.
Dodworth, Allen, 161, 168.
Dodworth, Harvey, 168.
Doerr, Clyde, 174.
Don Sebastian, 48.
Donizetti, Gaefano, 44, 48, 69.
'Double Cylinder', 60.
Double-bass (Sax), 140.
Drury Lane Theatre, 57, 139.
Dubois (instrumentalist), 60.
Dubois, Pierre Max, 192.
Ducasse, Rodger, 167.
Dufaure (lawyer), 105, 129.
Dufresne (cornettist), 52.
Dumas (inventor), 115.
Dupaquier (saxophonist), 181.
Duplex instruments, 140.
Duprez, E. (clarinettist), 50, 52.
Dvořák, Anton, 158.

E-flat bass, 115, 158-162.
E-flat horn, 153-155, 161, 162.
Eiffel, A. G., 71.
Eleven O'Clock, 168.
Elgar, Edward, 158, 166.
Ella's Musical Union, 135.

Ellington, Duke, 178.
Emboliclave, 71, 77.
Erard, Sebastian, 24.
Euphonic horn, 64.
Euphonium, 37, 83, 154, 155, 157-161, 163, 191.
Evans, Alford, 170.
Evette, Paul, 165.
Exhibitions:
   Brussels 1820, 18.
   Haarlem 1825, 130.
   Brussels 1830, 20.
   Brussels 1835, 20.
   Brussels 1841, 24, 38.
   Paris 1844, 50, 58, 96, 197.
   Paris 1849, 91, 92, 135.
   London 1851, 65, 92, 130, 133, 195, 201.
   Paris 1855, 115.
   London 1862, 133, 139, 142.
   Bayonne 1864, 141.
   Oporto 1865, 141.
   Paris 1867, 140, 142.
   London 1869, 143.

Facade, 181.
Fagotti (saxophonist), 169.
Farmer, H. G., 135, 136, 157.
Farmer, J., 66.
Faust (musical director), 83.
Fervaal, 167.
Fessy (musical director), 73, 88.
Fétis, Francois Joseph, 20, 23, 33, 38, 44, 88, 115, 133, 135, 139, 140, 143.
Filmer, Vic., 168.
Finck, C., 95, 197.
Fiorentino (journalist), 84.
Fischer-Dieskau, Dietrich, 155.
'Five Nosses, The', 169.
'Five Symphony Girls, The', 167.
Flugel horn, 32, 59, 63, 71, 75, 81, 155, 156, 161, 162, 191, 196.
Flute (Sax), 20, 133.
'Foreign Visitor Resident in London', 60, 63.
Forysth, Cecil, 166.
'Four Brothers', 177.
Four Futuristic Themes, 170.
Fourth Dragoons, 166.
Franck-Carré (lawyer), 105.
Franconi, Victor, 88.
Francs-Juges, 83.
Freischutz, Der, 66.
French horn (Sax), 29, 32.

Gallay (hornist), 32.
Gambaro Snr. (inventor), 81, 96, 99.
Garde République, 114, 148, 156, 166, 181, 182.
Gaujal (lawyer), 100, 103.
Gautrot, P. L. (Snr.), 95, 96, 121, 122, 126, 129.
George IV, King, 57, 64.
Gerlicke, Baron de, 80.

Gerusalemme Liberata, 198.
Gevaert, Francois Auguste, 51.
Gevarte (musical director), 114.
Gilmore, Patrick, 66, 155, 169.
Girand (musical director), 92.
Glazunov, Alexander, 182, 183, 192.
Godefroy, Clair, 81.
Goodman, Phil, 174.
Goudronnière Sax, 142.
Goumas, P. & Cie, 165.
Gounet (writer), 198.
Gradwell, Christopher, 184.
Grainger, Percy, 184.
Grande Duchesse, La, 71.
Grand Opera House, New York, 168.
Grenadier Guards, 166.
Grenser, Heinrich, 20.
Grimethorpe Colliery Band, 162.
Grotesques de la musique, 198.
Gudin, Count (Colonel), 70.
Gudin, Jean, 51, 84.
Guichard, A. G., 32, 81, 99.
Guiffre, Jimmy, 177.
Gutteridge, William, 149.

Haberneck, F. A., 23, 44, 50.
Halary, Antoine, 95, 96, 121.
Halary-Asté, J., 57, 81.
Halévy, Jacques, 23-26, 38, 44, 70, 104, 110, 114, 130, 191.
Hall, Elsie, 167.
Halliday, John, 57.
Hambleton, Hale, 184.
Hamlet, 114, 166.
Hammersmith *Palais de Danse*, 174.
Handel, G. F., 57.
Harold, 140.
Harper, Thomas, 57.
Harvey, Paul, 184.
Hawkins, Coleman, 178.
Heckel-Clarina, 165.
Heckel, Wilhelm, 133, 147, 165.
Henderson, Fletcher, 178.
Henton, H. Bennie, 168.
Herminie, 198.
Herold, Louis, 110.
Hetzel (inventor), 103.
Hickman, Art, 173, 174.
Hindemith, Paul, 154, 158.
Hodges, Johnny, 178.
Holbrooke, Joseph, 148, 166.
Horniman Museum, 66.
Horovitz, Joseph, 163.
Houlick, James, 189.
Houvenaghel, Charles, 147, 188.
Howarth, George & Company, 187.
Huguenots, Les, 20, 23, 26, 49.
Hughes, Spike, 178.
Huller, G. H., 147.

Huntsman's Chorus, The, 66.
Hylton, Jack, 174.
Hymme, 196-198.

Ibert, Jacques, 183, 192.
Illustrated London News, The, 133, 135.
Indy, D', Vincent, 167
Innes, Frederick, N., 169.
Instrumentalist, The, 188.
International Competition for Musical Performers, 187.
Irish Melodies, 198.
Irlande, 198.

Jackson, Endersby, 64, 66.
Janin, Jules, 82.
Jeunesse, La, 166.
Job, 181, 184.
John, King of Saxony, 125.
Johnson, Bunk, 173.
Johnson, James Weldon, 169.
Joinville, Prince de, 70.
Jones, Isham, 173.
Jong, Sam de, 174.
Joubard (museum director), 99.
Jourdain, M., 105.
Journal Amusant, Le, 115.
Journal des Débats, Le, 26, 38, 43, 47, 72, 77, 82, 89, 125.
Juiferrant, Le, 105.
Julliene, Antoine, 60, 135, 168.

Kastner, Jean-Georges, 23, 33, 34-39, 44, 51, 70, 90, 100, 115, 133, 143, 155, 166.
Kazoo, 23, 26, 113.
Kenton, Stan, 177.
Key-bugle, 32, 57, 58, 64, 83, 139, 155, 157.
Kiss Me, Kate, 184.
Klosé, Hyacinth Eleanore, 33, 148, 150, 166.
Klosé (saxophonist), 159.
Kneller Hall, 130, 155, 157.
Knoche, Augustus, 133.
Kochnitzky, Leon, 38.
Kohl, Richard, 147.
Kool, Jaap, 81.
Krein, Michael, 184.
Krueger, Benny, 174.
Kruspe, Franz, 83.
Kryl, Bohumir, 168.
Küffner, Joseph, 19, 83.

Labbaye, Jacques, 121.
Labou (flautist), 19.
Lacome, Paul Jean Jacques, 144.
Ladario, Texiero de, 181, 182.
Lancashire Fusiliers, 166.
Lansing Bagnall Limited, 162.
La Rocca, Nick, 173.
Larsson, Lars Erik, 183,

Last Rose of Summer, The, 66.
Laurent (instrumentalist), 60.
Lavaux (lawyer), 95.
Lavoix, Henri, 34, 115, 133, 187.
Lawrence, David, 184.
Leblanc, Georges, 147.
Lècomte, A-Z, 133, 165.
Leeson, Cecil, 188.
Lefébre, Eduard, A., 168, 169.
Légende de Saint Christophe, La, 167.
Legion of Honour, 135, 143.
Leperd (clarinettist), 52.
Liberati, Alessandro, 169.
Lind, Jennie, 83.
Lioville (lawyer), 104.
Liszt, Franz, 83, 84.
Liverani (clarinettist), 51.
Loeffler, Charles, 167.
Londeix, Jean-Marie, 187.
London Hippodrome, The, 174.
London Saxophone Quartet, The, 184, 188, 189.
Louis XVI, King, 24.
Louis-Philippe, King, 24, 50, 58-60, 71, 84, 90, 91, 140.
Louÿs, Pierre, 167.

Macdonald, Dr. Hugh, 196.
Macfarlane, George, 139.
Maginel, F. A., 169.
Mahillon, Charles, 150.
Mahillon, Victor, 114.
Mahler, Gustav, 155.
Maison Lyons, 174.
Manton-Myatt, Brian, 182.
Marie-Amélie, Queen, 50.
Marie (lawyer), 82, 99, 100, 104, 105, 129.
Marseillaise, La, 88.
Marzoli (bassoonist), 133.
Massanet, Jules, 144, 166.
Massart, Joseph, 88.
Masson, Maria, 18.
Méditation réligieuse, 198.
Meersman, De (arranger), 119.
Meikle, William, 33, 81, 148.
Ménestrel, Le, 196.
Meifred (inventor), 33.
Melody Maker, 168.
Mellophone, 154.
Mellophonium, 177.
Melun Prison, 89.
Mengelberg, Wilheim, 168.
Metronome, The, 170.
Meyerbeer, Giacomo, 20, 23, 44, 49, 59, 69, 90, 110, 114, 130, 166.
Meyers, Albertus L., 169.
Miller, George, 125.
Moaning Saxophone Rag, The, 169.
Moermans, Joe, 168.
Mohr, Jean, 32, 110, 166.

Molière (playwright), 105.
Moline St. Yon, Lt.-General, 69, 70, 96.
Moniteur de l'Armee, Le, 77, 96.
Monnais (composer), 44.
Montpensier, Duke of, 69, 88.
Moore, Thomas, 198.
Moritz, J. G., 32, 83, 103, 153, 158.
Morley-Pegge, R., 147.
Morrin, H. (saxophonist), 169.
Mossley Temperance Band, 65.
Mozart, W. A., 149.
Muette de Portie, La, 73.
Mule, Marcel, 182, 183, 188, 192.
Müller, Ivan, 24, 148, 149.
Musard (impressario), 52.
Musical Times, The, 122, 174.
Musical World, The, 60, 66, 135, 201.
Music Review, The, 195.

Napoleon Bonaparte, 18, 73, 95.
Napoleon III, Emperor (Louis Napoleon), 91, 92, 113, 121, 122, 135, 143.
Narcissus (Nevin), 170.
National Band Association of America, 161.
National Youth Brass Band of Great Britain, 162.
Neithardt (musical director), 83.
Nemours, Duke de, 70.
Néo-alto, 32, 126, 153, 155.
Never Say Die, 66.
New Orleans Rhythm Kings, 173.
New York Saxophone Quartet, The, 184.
Ney, Marshal, 24.
Nicholas, Albert, 173.
Nolan, Frederick, 150.
Norma, 57.
North Texas State University, 188.
Notre Dame University Band, 161.

Oboe (Sax), 130, 133.
Oberon, 110.
Old Folks at Home, 168.
Oliver, King, 173.
Olympia (London), 161.
Omnitonic horn, 18, 32.
Onslow, George, 70.
Opéra Comique, 58-60.
Ophicleide, 32, 37-39, 47, 57, 64, 70, 73-75, 76, 99, 104, 157, 203.
Orchestra Organ, 116.
Original Dixiland Jazz Band, 174.
Oxfordshire Light Infantry, 166.
Oxford Theatre, 174.

Paganini, Niccolo, 17.
Palace Trio, The, 169.
Paladilhe, Émile, 140.
Pan pipes (Sax), 140.
Paris Saxophone Quartet, The, 182, 187.

Parker, Charlie, 178.
Pasteur, Louis, 142.
Patrie, La, 140.
'Peck horn', 154.
Pelitti, Guiseppe, 99.
Pelléas et Mélisande, 167.
Percussion instruments (Sax), 133, 140.
Périnet, Étienne Francois, 32.
Perpigna (lawyer), 203.
Petite Messe Solenelle, 51.
Phasey, Bandsman, 157.
Philadelphia Evening Star, The, 161.
Pianoforte (Sax), 140.
Pierné, Gabriel, 182.
Pierre, C., 29, 114, 133, 143.
Pilcer, Murray, 174.
Pogson, Edward O., 177.
Pontecoulant, A., 197.
Popora, S. (saxophonist), 168.
Poultier (lawyer), 105.
Prophète, Le, 49, 90, 110, 114, 191.
Punch, 74.

Queen Elizabeth Hall, 184.

Rabin, Oscar, 179.
Ragone, Vincent, 169.
Ralton, Bert, 174.
Raoux, M. A., 51, 77, 81, 91, 95, 96, 100, 105, 121.
Rascher, Karen, 183.
Rascher, Sigurd, 181, 183, 188.
Ravel, Maurice, 181.
Raynard, Captain C., 92.
Reidle, Joseph Felix, 32.
Revue des deux mondes, La, 81.
Revue et Gazette Musicale, La, 23, 116, 196.
Rigby, Henry, 135.
Rigoletto, 169.
Ripper, Peter, 189.
Ritter, Theodore, 109.
Rivet (instrument maker), 125-129.
Robert Bruce, 114.
Robert le Diable, 58.
Robinson, James L., 169.
Robinson, Willard, 170.
Roger Wolfe Kahn Orchestra, 170.
Rollini, Adrian, 179.
Rose, Algernon, 63.
Rossini, G. A., 51, 113, 130, 191.
Roth, C., 95.
Rothschild, Baron James de, 79, 80.
Roujon, Henri, 144.
Rouland (lawyer), 105.
Roussel (lawyer), 126.
Rousseau, Eugene, 188.
Royal Albert Hall, 163.
Royal Artillery Band, 156, 166.
Royal College of Music, 37.
Rudall Rose and Carte, 65, 201.

Rumigny, Lt.-General de, 24, 33, 44, 48, 50, 60, 69, 70, 81.

Sachs, Curt, 187.
Sadlers Wells Opera, 184.
Saint Andrea, Count de, 70.
St. James's Gazette, 191.
Saint-Saëns, Camille, 125, 166.
Salle Herz, 52, 58, 59, 195, 197.
Salvation Army, 156, 161, 170.
Sargeant, Paul, 37.
Sarrus (bandmaster), 122.
Sarrusophone, 122, 125, 148, 166.
Sass, Marie-Constance, 125.
Saturday Review of Literature, 165.
Sault, Marshal, 69, 70
Savart, Colonel, 70, 103, 116.
Savoy Havana and Orpheans Bands, 174.
Sax, Adolphe Jr., 144, 177.
Sax, Alphonse, 24, 80, 109, 143, 144.
Sax, Antoine Joseph (Adolphe), Main events: Birth 17; visit to Paris 23; meets Berlioz 43; opens factory 44; challenges Bateux 48; attempts on life 49; meets Rossini 51; concert at Salle Herz 51; meets Distin family 57; writes on military music 69; contest on Champ de Mars 71; meets Rothschild 80; saxophone patent 81; meets Wieprecht 83; Hippodrome concert 88; Melun Prison 89; Revolution of 1848 90; bankruptcy 92; lawsuits 95; cancer 109; ascending valves 113; steam organ 116; sarrusophones 122; Marie Sass 125; Rivet 125; reform of pitch 129; bassoon 130; Wagner 133; honours 135; sundry inventions 139; 'saxocannon' 141; last appeal 144; death 144.
Sax, Charles Joseph, 17-20, 24, 26, 29-33, 38, 109, 121, 130, 140, 143, 191.
Saxhorn, 20, 33, 38, 50, 52, 58, 66, 69, 72-74, 75-77, 81, 83, 87, 90, 95, 99, 114, 115, 122, 126, 133-135, 139-141, 143, 147, 153-162, 191, 195-197.
    Sopranino, B-flat and C, 157, 195, 196.
    Soprano, E-flat, 58, 72, 74, 76, 156, 195-197.
    Contralto, B-flat, 58, 59, 72, 74-76, 139, 155, 195-197.
    Alto/Tenor, E-flat, 59, 72, 74-76, 126, 153-155, 161, 195-197.
    Tenor/Baritone, B-flat, 59, 65, 66, 72, 74, 76, 126, 154, 155, 161, 177, 196, 197.
    Bass, B-flat, 59, 72, 74-76, 126, 154, 157, 196, 197.
    Contrabass, E-flat, 72-76, 115, 126, 158, 197.
    Contrabass, BB-flat, 115, 158.
    Subcontrabass, EE-flat, 115, 158.
    Subcontrabass, BBB-flat, 115.
'Saxocannon', 141.

'Saxomblatarique', 143.
Saxophone, 20, 24, 33, 37-40, 43, 47, 50-52, 59, 72-74, 77, 81-84, 87, 90, 95, 103, 114, 122-126, 134, 135, 139, 140, 143, 147, 148, 154-157, 165 et seq.
    Sopranino, 39, 177, 179, 182, 187.
    Soprano, 37, 39, 166, 169-174, 187, 192.
    Mezzo-soprano, 184.
    Alto, 34, 40, 51, 135, 142, 154, 166, 169-177, 179, 181, 184, 187.
    'C-melody', 170, 178.
    Tenor, 39, 50, 52, 135, 155, 165, 168-179, 183-187, 189, 192, 197.
    Baritone, 39, 169, 170, 177, 178, 184, 187, 197.
    Bass, 38, 39, 166, 170, 177, 179, 187, 197.
    Contrabass, 39, 115-119, 182, 187.
    Subcontrabass, 115, 119.
Saxophone Sobs, 169.
Saxophone le Rationnel, 188.
Sax-O-Phun, 169.
Saxo-Rhapsody, 181.
Saxothunder, 115.
Saxotromba, 69, 75-77, 95, 105, 139, 140, 141, 197, 201.
Saxtuba, 113, 141.
Scenes that are Brightest, 168.
Schaeffer, Ernest, 165.
Scherzo tarantelle, 182.
Schloesser, Louis, 195.
Schmitt, Florent, 167.
School for Inventors, 141.
School Musician, The, 187.
Schultz (saxophonist), 169.
Schwartz, H. W., 170.
Scudo (clarinettist and critic), 82.
Searle, Humphrey, 195.
Sébastini, Marshal, 69, 70.
Second Norfolk Regiment, 166.
Second Royal Kent Regiment, 165.
Séguier, Baron de, 70.
Séha, H., 113.
Selmer, Henri, 182.
Shaap, E. (saxophonist), 169.
Shaw, John, 32.
Shriner Band, 187.
Signal whistle (Sax), 140.
Simiot, Jacques, 149.
Sinfonia Domestica, 166.
Sixteenth Lancers, 166.
Sixth Infantry Regiment, 182.
Skorra, Ed., 83.
Slide-trumpet, 29, 57, 58.
Snoeck, César, 144.
'Society' bands, 177.
Society for the Rights of Man, 91.
Somers, Debroy, 174.
Souallé (saxophonist), 135.
Sounding Brass, 162.

Sousa, John Philip, 163, 169, 170.
Spohr, Louis, 82, 115.
Spontini, Gasparo, 44, 70, 73, 106.
Sporck, Georges, 167.
Stadler, Anton, 149.
Stalybridge Old Band, 64.
Steckelberg (saxophonist), 169.
Stölzle, Heinrich, 29, 83, 158.
Stonewall Brigade Band, 161.
Stradivari, Antonio, 17.
Strauss, Richard, 166.
Streitt, John, 64.
Streitwolf, Gottlieb, 20, 115.
Sturr, Harold, 170.
Sudre, Francoise, 157.
'Swanee saxophone', 170.
Symphonie Funèbre et Triomphale, 88

Tannhäuser, 125, 134.
Tasso, 198.
Teal, Larry, 188.
Te Deum (Berlioz), 157.
Tenor, 154.
Tenorbass horn, 157.
Tenor cor, 154.
Tenor horn, 82, 147, 153, 154, 161, 162.
Tenoroon, 33, 81.
Tenor tuba, 158.
Théâtre Francais, 82.
Thirteenth Regiment Band, 168.
Thomas, Ambrois, 114, 129, 166.
Three Choirs Festival, 181.
Tiersot, Julien, 196, 198.
Timbale-à-pistons, 133.
Times, The, 92.
Triebért (instrument maker), 133.
Tristia, 198.
Trocadero, 174.
Trognitz, R. E., 169.
Trojans, The, 52, 157, 196.
Trombone (Sax), 29, 72, 73, 76, 113, 133, 201.
Trout (saxophonist), 169.
Trumbauer, Frankie, 178.
Trumpet (Sax), 29, 47, 48, 72, 74-76, 135, 195-197.
Tschaikowsky, P. I., 170.
Tuba (Sax), 29, 47, 48.
Twenty Second Regiment of New York, 169.

Ugalda, Mme. (singer), 125.
Uhlmann, Leopold, 32.
Ullman, Viktor, 182.

Vallee, Rudy, 178.
Valse Vanité, 170.
Valves (Sax), 29-33, 47, 65, 75, 95, 113, 114, 139, 143, 147, 155.
Vatou, 84.
Vaughan Williams, Ralph, 156, 158, 181, 183, 192.
Velpeau, Dr., 110, 142.
Victor Emanuel II, King, 51.
Victoria, Queen, 57, 63, 82.
Viellard, P. A., 198.
Vieutemp, Henri, 24.
Villa-Lobos, Heitor, 192.
Vincent, Dr. Charles, 167.
Voorsanger, Adolphe, 168.
Vriès, Dr., 110.

Wadsworth, Wheeler, 168.
Wagner, Richard, 134.
Wait, J. Paul, 169.
Walrabe (saxophonist), 169.
Walton, Sir William, 181, 184.
Wandering Jew, The, 110, 191.
Weber, Carl, 66, 110.
Whiteman, Paul, 174.
Wiedoeft, Rudy, 169, 170, 178.
Wiedoeft's Saxophone Ensemble, 169.
Wiedoeft's Symphonic Saxophones, 169.
Wieniawski, Henri, 182.
Wieprecht, Wilheim, 24, 32, 83, 84, 103, 115, 153, 158.
Willent-Bordogni, J. B. J., 133.
William, Crown Prince of Prussia, 83.
William I, King of the Netherlands, 18, 121.
William II, King of the Netherlands, 80, 84.
Williams (saxophonist), 169.
William Tell, 191.
Windsor Castle, 60, 63.
Wood, Sir Henry, 192.
World Saxophone Congress, 37, 188, 189.
Wuille (saxophone), 135.

Zampa, 110.
Ziegfield Follies, 173.
'Zouave', 135.